WRITER

Volume 2

SURINAM TURTLE PRESS

1. The Master of Mysteries — Gelett Burgess
2. The White Cat — Gelett Burgess
3. Two Oclock Courage — Gelett Burgess
4. Ladies in Boxes — Gelett Burgess
5. Find the Woman — Gelett Burgess
6. The Picaroons — Gelett Burgess & Will Irwin
7. The Heart Line — Gelett Burgess
8. The Triune Man — Richard A. Lupoff
9. The Time Armada — Fox Holden
10. A Shot Rang Out — Jon Breen
11. The Smiling Corpse — Philip Wylie
12. Sacred Locomotive Flies — Richard A. Lupoff
13. Welsh Rarebit Tales — Harle Cummins
14. Sideslip — White & Van Arnam
15. Blondy's Boy Friend — Philip Wylie
16. The Technique of Mystery — Carolyn Wells
17. Marblehead — Richard A. Lupoff
18. Deep Space — Richard A. Lupoff
19. Lady Mechante — Gelett Burgess
20. Away From The Here and Now — Harris
21. Tracer of Lost Persons — Robert Chambers
22. Hairbreadth Escapes of Major Mendax — F. Blake Crofton
23. The Book of Time — H.G Wells and Richard A. Lupoff
24. The Case of the Little Green Men — Mack Reynolds
25. Star Griffin — Michael Kurland
26. J. Poindexter, Colored — Irvin S. Cobb
27. Pair o' Jacks — Jack Woodford
28. Evangelical Cockroack — Jack Woodford
29. Money Brawl — Jack Woodford and H. Bedford-Jones
30. The Basil Wells Omnibus — Basil Wells
31. The Disentanglers — Andrew Lang
32. Tarnished Bomb — Malcolm Jameson
33. Satans of Saturn — Otis Adelbert Kline
34. A Gellett Burgess Sampler — Alfred Jan
35. John Carstairs, Space Detective — Frank Belknap Long
36. The Illustrious Corpse — Tiffany Thayer
37. Astonishing! Astounding! — Malcolm Jameson
38. The Town from Planet Five — Richard Wilson
39. Win, Place and Die! — Milton K. Ozaki
40. Dead Men's Money — J.S. Fletcher
41. Prince Pax — Charles Sylvester Viereck and Paul Eldridge
42. Tree of Life, Book of Death — Grania Davis
43. Bogart '48 — John Stanley and Kenn Davis
44. The Case in the Clinic — E.C.R. Lorac
45. Two-Timers — Ray Cummings and Malcolm Jameson
46. What If? #3 — Edited by Richard A. Lupoff
47. Carol Carr: The Collected Writings — Carol Carr
48. What If? #1 — Edited by Richard A. Lupoff
49. What If? #2 — Edited by Richard A. Lupoff
50a. Writer 1
50b. Writer 2
50c. Writer 3

WRITER

Volume 2

Richard A. Lupoff

Introduced by

John Pelan

RAMBLE HOUSE
2014

Writer Volume 2 © 2014 by Richard A. Lupoff

Introduction © 2014 by John Pelan

Cover Art © 2014 by Gavin O'Keefe

Preparation: Fender Tucker

ISBN 13: 978-1-60543-736-1

"It isn't over 'til the fat lady sings."

— Dan Cook, sportswriter, San Antonio Express, 1976

"It isn't over 'til the fat player swings."

— Unidentified fan of Minnesota Twins star Kirby Puckett, during playoff game at Oakland Coliseum, 1980s

Surinam Turtle Press #50b

WRITER Volume 2

TABLE OF CONTENTS

RICHARD LUPOFF'S BOOK   9
    Introduction by John Pelan
AS I WAS SAYING   13

INTERVIEWS
JOHN D. MACDONALD   19
ALLEN GINSBERG   33
MICHAEL CHABON   37
RICHARD PRATHER   47
MARION ZIMMER BRADLEY   67
RICHARD A. LUPOFF   83

ESSAYS
NICE MURDERS   93
NOT EXACTLY A SHOE SALESMAN   99
EDGAR RICE BURROUGHS AND ME   109
THE LONG ROAD TO BARSOOM   125
IN ANOTHER GALAXY   139
A HANDFUL OF DARKNESS   145
FINDING CHASE AND DELACROIX   159
SCIENCE FICTION HAWKS AND DOVES   165

SPEECHES
VERY NEAR TO MY HEART   177
A STORY AND A MESSAGE   189

THEM DAZE
SHAMELESS SELF-PROMOTION   195
CUT TO THE FLAG   201
HAND ME DOWN MY CAPE & TIGHTS   209

BOOK REVIEWS

H. BEAM PIPER	213
DOUG DORST	221
DAVID HAJDU	225
EDGAR ALLAN POE	231
EDMOND HAMILTON	237
MORE EDMOND HAMILTON	247
PHILIP HARBOTTLE	255
MALCOLM JAMESON	259
ARTHUR CONAN DOYLE	265
KLINE AND PRICE	269
ROBERT A. HEINLEIN	277
RAY PALMER	283
MILT OZAKI	291
FORREST J. ACKERMAN	295
CLARK ASHTON SMITH	299
MANLY WADE WELLMAN	307
BASIL WELLS	311
CREDITS AND ACKNOWLEDGEMENTS	317

LUPOFF'S BOOK

How does one write an introduction discussing a living legend? A difficult task, more so when said living legend is a dear friend and someone I've been reading diligently since I was eleven years of age... If you've read *Writer Volume 1,* then you already know that Dick Lupoff is one of those people who can write engagingly on any subject, whether it be obscure baseball lore such as the history of the House of David or the more esoteric features appearing in *Whiz Comics* to the works of Howard Phillips Lovecraft. In my case, I read a number of items before I connected the name to what I was reading.

At age eleven, (yes, I know the "Golden Age" of SF is twelve, but excuse me for being a tad precocious), there were many things I enjoyed reading but uppermost on the list would be comic books and Edgar Rice Burroughs' tales of John Carter of Mars, Carson of Venus, and his wonderful series set at the Earth's core. For some reason I never got the appeal of Lord Greystoke as a kid, though that was remedied years later... In any event, after exhausting the Barsoom series, I was thrilled to find a book *about* Edgar Rice Burroughs' books! The volume in question was *Edgar Rice Burroughs: Master of Adventure,* and while the author's name meant nothing to me, the book carried what to my way of thinking then was the seal of quality, a cover by Frank Frazetta...

A couple of years later I stumbled on another book that dealt with a favorite subject, the "Golden Age" of comics. The book was *All in Color for a Dime,* a volume that should still be on the shelf of any serious comic collector over forty years after its publication. Readers today are spoiled by the ready availability of so much Golden Age material; for example, I need only reach across my desk in order to lay my hands on large hardcover volumes reprinting the likes of the Justice Society of America, Simon & Kirby's Sandman, the complete solo adventures of Dr. Fate and the Spectre from *More Fun comics,* the Green Lama, the original Daredevil, and what was for any kid growing up in the 1960s with an interest in the Golden Age, the holy grail, the original Captain Marvel!

Now when we're talking about the comic collecting world forty years ago, long before eBay and the Internet made it possible for readers to find pretty much anything they wanted in a matter of minutes, one had to deal with a high-priced mail-order dealer or be lucky enough to have a much older brother or uncle pass his comics on to you. For those of us reading about the early years of comics while living in the "Silver Age", it was difficult to imagine a time when instead of two major companies (Marvel & DC), with a handful of minor players, (Charlton, Mighty, Dell, ACG, etc.) there were well over a dozen major companies offering a bewildering selection of titles. However, then as now, cream rose to the top and the general consensus as shown by prices on the secondary market and the enthusiasm of the readership in the 1940s was that the best of all was a character named "Captain Marvel".

The character of Captain Marvel was beyond clever in its conception; prior to the good Captain, kids had to make the stretch to identify with the adult superhero or settle for identifying with the kid sidekick. Now here was a whole different scenario. Captain Marvel, despite his resemblance to a younger and more muscular Fred MacMurray, was really Billy Batson, a kid that anyone of the same general age could identify with. Dick's piece on Captain Marvel was sufficient to make me try and search out any affordable issues of *Whiz Comics* that I could find.

As of yet, I hadn't connected the author of the Barsoom book with the comics historian, nor did I have any notion that the remarkably entertaining pieces by "Ova Hamlet" in the pages of *Amazing Stories* were in any way connected to the author of stories such as "12:01 P.M.", "Musspelsheim", and "With the Evening News". I finally started connecting the dots when FAX Publishing came out with their edition of *The Return of Skull-Face* in 1977. I'll admit now that I approached the book with some skepticism . . . By this time I'd read every word of Robert E. Howard that was in print and a considerable amount of material from old issues of *Weird Tales* and his two Arkham House collections, *Skull-Face & Others* and *The Dark Man*. I had also come to realize that a goodly amount of the posthumous collaborations, particularly the de Camp/Carter material, was (to not put too fine a point on it), utter crap. While L. Sprague de Camp was a fine author on his own or with Fletcher Pratt, his wry sense of humor clashed badly with Howard's straightforward approach, and Carter's contributions to the Conan series were the worst sort of fanboy pastiche.

"Skull-Face", with its Rohmeresque Gothic atmosphere had always been one of my favorite Howard yarns, and while I had no idea how this Lupoff chap would handle Howard's material, I was at least encouraged by looking over the Lupoff tales that I had in *The Magazine of Fantasy & Science-Fiction* and various Roger Elwood anthologies. To say that *The Return of Skull-Face* wildly exceeded any possible expectations on my part would be a gross understatement. Dick Lupoff nailed the style and nuances of Howard doing Rohmer perfectly. To this day, I can't tell where the Howard manuscript leaves off and where Dick's work begins. It's just that seamless a transition. From that point forward, I didn't just read Richard Lupoff stories as I came across them, I made it a point to seek his work out ...

Since that day over thirty-five years ago, I've been enriched by making it a point to seek out Dick's work. At roughly the same time that *The Return of Skull-Face* saw print, his mythos tale "Discovery of the Ghooric Zone" appeared in Roy Torgeson's *Chrysalis*. Not only was it the best story in the anthology (no small feat in a book with work by Ellison, Grant, Sturgeon, Lynn & others), but it remains one of the best Mythos stories written by anyone ... Then of course, there were a variety of novels, from the remarkable *Sword of the Demon* to the duo of *Circumpolar* and *Countersolar*... And of course, many more stories, a large amount of which have been collected in volumes such as *Terrors, Dreams, Visions*, and *Claremont Tales*. Then there were the terrific (if a bit controversial) anthologies of *What If*, wherein Dick awards the Hugos that *should* have been doled out. Then there are the noteworthy mystery series, which began with *The Comic Book Killer* in 1988 and is still going strong with *The Emerald Cat Killer* in 2012.

However, all of the aforementioned work, while well worth your time seeking out, has little to do with the present volume ... You see, *another* arena in which Dick excels is that of the essayist and reviewer. Yes, sometimes the label of "critic" is applied, but it won't be used by me as I hold to the definitions as follows: A "critic" will tell you why you're supposed to appreciate a particular work, just as a dietician may sing the praises of a particularly loathsome vegetable as it is *good for you*. A reviewer, (and I harken back to the self-applied description furnished by the late, great A. J. Budrys), serves as sort of an investment counselor, letting you know whether or not in his or her opinion a book is worth your time and money ... To me, this is a far more valuable service than the one provided by the critic, so I hope that Dick doesn't take offense by being called a "reviewer".

The material in this book contains a generous amount of review material, ranging from the early days of Andrew Porter's *Algol/Starship* in the 1960s to much more recent material from the venerable newspaper of the science fiction field, *Locus*. That's not to imply that *Writer Volume II* is limited to book reviews, (though were that the case, you would certainly be getting your money's worth). I have also invoked the term "essayist", and as I stated much earlier, Dick Lupoff is that rare sort of author who can write compellingly on any subject and bring it to life. Whether he's discussing the first full-time female science fiction author, Clare Winger Harris, the history of the original Captain Marvel, or the batting averages of the baseball players who participated in the House of David; he's going to draw you in, entertain, educate, and enrich; regardless of the subject matter. The authors that can do this consistently can likely be counted on the fingers of one hand ... For my money, Dick Lupoff joins Harlan Ellison and Graham Greene in that very small, very illustrious company where I'll read anything they've written on any subject, even if it's something that has previously been of no interest to me whatsoever.

The great news for readers of this three-volume set is that you likely haven't found these books by accident. You're likely a Ramble House reader which presupposes an interest in science fiction, mystery, or the just plain unusual. That being the case, that's exactly the sort of thing that you'll see covered herein. Whether Dick's discussing contemporary SF, his time in the armed forces, his love of the Great American Game, or the works that *should* have won the Hugo Award and didn't, there's going to be something here to stimulate your thinking, and after all, isn't that what being a *Writer* is all about? Enjoy!

John Pelan
Gallup NM

AS I WAS SAYING...
2014

... before I so rudely interrupted myself by closing off Volume 1 of this collection, my two grandmothers were amazing women. Sad to say, there are not many members of my family, of my own generation, left on this planet. When my brother died some twenty years ago, one of his sons and one of mine sat me down and urged me to write a family history. Well, I'm afraid that project eluded me.

I tried to accomplish the same task by writing a formal, or at least semi-formal, autobiography. I got a chapter written. It dealt with my maternal grandmother, Clara Hirsch's, arrival in New York. But I got bogged down in research. What ship had she sailed in? When had it left the Old World, and from what port, and when had it docked in the United States?

When I was very young my grandmother had told me about arriving in New York and finding a city in turmoil. It took her a while to find out the cause. The President had been shot. That would have been William McKinley, shot September 6, 1901. Well, that wasn't too hard. And there's an Ellis Island Foundation that offers passenger records of arriving ships.

But somehow I was distracted, and whether I'll ever get back to that book remains to be seen. But in the meanwhile I've managed to jot down several dozen brief memoirs. Volume 1 of this series contains a lot of them. I guess they're better than nothing.

But come on with me to those days of yesteryear when I was a teenager. My Aunt Marion gave birth to her only child, my Cousin Eleanor. We weren't especially close, as cousins. That was more the result of geography than antipathy. At different times we lived in different parts of the country. But when my peregrinations brought me back to New York, as happened from time to time, I would see my Aunt Marion, my Grandma Clara, and my Cousin Eleanor.

The last time I saw Marion she told me that Eleanor, by now a young woman, had met a wonderful boy named Bernie and they were planning to be married. I wished the young couple well, via

Marion (I never did meet Bernie) and then I was off to far lands. Well, Indiana, in fact. But never mind that.

As the years passed I became an at least somewhat successful author. I wondered what had become of Eleanor. My aunt and my grandmother were deceased. I didn't know Bernie's last name. I couldn't figure out how to find Eleanor, but I figured that she would find me. If I was lucky.

My Uncle Morris, Mother Sylvia, Aunt Marion

See, here was the plan:

I'd keep writing books. Perceptive editors would keep buying them from me and publishing them and getting them into bookstores where industrious booksellers would shelve them with my byline leering out at browsers.

Someday my Cousin Eleanor would find herself browsing in such a store and her attention would be caught by a familiar name—mine! She would write to me in care of the publisher. The publisher would forward her letter to me. And—*voila!*—we would have found each other.

Years went by, and then one day I had a message from Gary Turner, my publisher at Golden Gryphon Books. He'd received a letter from a woman wanting to be put in touch with me. Did I think she was a wanna-be groupie, a stalker, a . . . well, you get the drift. I asked him her name and he told me and, *yes!*, she was indeed my Cousin Eleanor.

She lived and worked in New York. We exchanged letters. Then Pat and I made a trip to the East Coast where the great Ellen Datlow had booked me into the KGB Bar to do a reading of one of my stories. Eleanor turned up and the result was a joyous family reunion. She also provided me with wonderful copies of some family photos, including the wedding portrait of my own parents. She said that they would make me laugh and make me cry.

There was the bride, Sylvia, my mother, looking gorgeous, confident, and tall. And there was the groom, my father, looking, in a word, terrified.

My many-times-great grandfather. What had he seen?

Eleanor also gave me my mother's autograph book from Public School 43, Bronx, New York dated January 28, 1920. I'm not sure how the public schools were structured in those days, but from the inscriptions in this book, "P.S. 43" would have been an elementary school, ending at the eighth grade.

One autograph reads, "Sylvia, May you sail in the ship of ambition, and land on the shore of success." It's signed, "Your sister grad-u-8, Yetta Tashlitsky"

Here's another: "Sylvia, Deep within my heart / Never to depart / Reigns a love supreme / Forever there to love and dream." It's signed, "S. Chany." I wonder who he was. Apparently my mother's beau, aged 14.

And: "Sylvia, When you are in the kitchen drinking tea / Burn your tongue and think of me." Signed, "Samuel Berger." Apparently S. Chany had a rival. Intriguingly, the page preceding young Mr. Berger's has been torn from the book.

One young man, apparently a master of brevity, wrote, "To Sylvia, May your path be strewn with roses / May your children have pug noses. . .your classmate, Joseph Friedman."

I did laugh and cry, and put away my mother's schoolgirl autograph book and my parents' wedding portrait, which I had never seen before. This was all more than a decade ago, and just a few days ago I went through a rusting file cabinet and found my mother's autograph book and decided to look through it again.

To my surprise, there were some photographs tucked in the back of the book. There was a portrait of a very old man. His eyes looked as if they had seen all the grief in the world. He had a long beard and wore a small visorless cap and a battered coat. The photo was labeled "Great-great-grandfather."

If we were poor farm folk in Austria, why did my great-grandmother look so fancy?

There was a photo of a stern-looking, elegant woman, labeled, "Great-grandma." Was she my maternal grandmother's mother? But Clara had told me she was a poor farm girl, and this woman had the almost imperious look of a lady of substance. Another mystery!

There was a photo of three small children. No question that one of them was my Uncle Morris. Even as a toddler, his strong, cheerful face was unmistakable. And with him were my mother, Sylvia, and my Aunt Marion.

But of all these photographs, the one that chilled me to the core was a photograph of two small children. They both wore dresses, as was the fashion a hundred and fifty years ago, but one was a girl—you could tell by the ribbon in her hair—and the other was a boy.

My grandmother's sister and brother – she never told me about them.

The back of the photograph was labeled, "Grandma's brother and sister."

Grandma's brother and sister? But Clara had never mentioned a brother and sister. What were their names? What had become of them? Clara had told me about her Cousin Hy, the first member of her family to come to America. She'd mentioned a Cousin Mollie. And Cousin Aaron, who had fought and died in the Spanish Civil War. But Aaron was from my father's side of the family.

But—a brother and sister? They would then have been my great-uncle and great-aunt. Two more mysterious figures. I can only guess that when Hy Hirsch and Mollie Hirsh and my grandmother, Clara Hirsch, left Austria and came to America, Clara's sister and brother stayed behind.

I can only guess, but I'm pretty sure what happened to them. I'm pretty sure that the Nazis murdered them. I want to know and I don't want to know. If I even knew their names, I think it would give me a little closure. Not vengeance, not justice, just a little sense of remembrance of those two beautiful children whose names I will never know.

JOHN D. MACDONALD
1981

Although I met John D. MacDonald for the first and only time in April of 1981, I had been reading his works for some thirty years. He became a professional writer upon returning from service with the OSS in Asia during World War II. As an enthusiastic science fiction fan, I was aware of his stories in most of the magazines of the late 1940's and early '50s.

MacDonald wrote for *Astounding, Startling, Fantastic Adventures, F&SF, Galaxy, Planet Stories, Weird Tales,* and other magazines in the field. He was also the author of three science fiction novels: *Wine of the Dreamers* (1951), *Ballroom of the Skies* (1952), and *The Girl, the Gold Watch, and Everything* (1962). The first two of those were conventional science fiction novels. The third, by MacDonald's own judgment, was "a fantasy, wish-fulfillment of the Thorne Smith genre."

While MacDonald was known to science fiction fans for his stories in that genre, he was actually working throughout the pulp field. He wrote westerns, sports stories, and general or mainstream fiction. But his true *forte* lay in the mystery-suspense field. He sold to the old *Black Mask* magazine, *Manhunt, Ellery Queen, The Shadow, Doc Savage,* and others. Eventually he left the pulps for the higher pay rates of *Cosmopolitan, Playboy,* and *The Saturday Evening Post.*

His earliest books were private eye and suspense novels. They were published as paperback originals because, under the practice of the era, hardcover publishers usually kept half of the payment for paperback reprints. In fact, the science fiction novel *Wine of the Dreamers* was MacDonald's first hardcover publication.

MacDonald's greatest success came with his Travis McGee series concerning a very offbeat private eye whose home and base of operations are a houseboat anchored at a Florida yacht basin. For many years, MacDonald was himself a resident of Siesta Key near Sarasota on the Gulf Coast of Florida.

McGee's colorful milieu, his distinctive automobile (an electric blue customized Rolls), his hale-fellow macho friendship with his intellectual mentor Meyer, and his free-swinging, danger-courting style, all smack of the pulp tradition from which MacDonald sprang.

Was John D. MacDonald really this young – ever?

Interview With John D. MacDonald
April, 1981

Lupoff: For starters, of course, there is *Free Fall in Crimson,* the new Travis McGee novel, which is the 19th in the series, is that right?

MacDonald: It's the 19th and the publication date was the 29th of April.

Lupoff: I'd like to talk about that, but I'd like first to back up a little and ease up on it. First of all, you mentioned in your introduction to *Night Shift,* Stephen King's collection, a sort of prescription for writers: compulsive diligence, a taste for words and empathy totaling to some degree of objectivity. I wondered if you'd like to talk about that a little bit in the context of your own writing.

MacDonald: Well, in that introduction I was referring indirectly, I suppose, to the fact that I have never, never met a successful writer who hasn't been from the age of five or so an absolutely compulsive reader. We read everything. Only later do we simmer down to the point where we can become selective in our reading.

In order to write, I think one has to have an awareness of all the nuances of words, the little delicate differences.

You can't get that by saying, "By Gosh, I can write a letter to Aunt Nancy so I can write a book." I get galleys in all the time by new writers—the publishers send them to me hoping for a friendly comment on them—and they are wretched. They're by people who have no understanding of the meanings of words. They put in grotesqueries without even realizing it. Here's one of my favorites that I picked out of one a little while ago. "His eyes slid down the front of her dress." Isn't that nice?

Lupoff: It's wonderful. If you're writing horror fiction . . .

MacDonald: Sounds creepy.

Lupoff: I did check out a little bit of your autobiography and bibliography in standard reference works.

MacDonald: You may find a lot of contradictions because I lie a lot.

Lupoff: Well, that's the business, isn't it? I discovered that, for one thing, aside from John D. MacDonald you are a few other people, including Scott O'Hara, which I loved.

MacDonald: That is ironic.

Lupoff: John Lane, Peter Reed, John Wade Farrell, Henry Reecer, Robert Henry—are those all for real?

MacDonald: Yes, but they were never used except when I had more than one story in, for example, *Black Mask* magazine. I had one magazine, I don't know which—I've still got it around somewhere—where I wrote every story in it, so that I used about five of those names in addition to my own. They're what's called house names. The reader doesn't want to buy a magazine and think that somebody wrote every story in it.

I devised those names with a lady named Babette Rosner who was editing the Street & Smith magazines and she later—I think she's still over at *Seventeen* now—but when I was doing pulps for Popular Publications, they asked what names I would like so I said, "If you have to use house names can we use the same ones?" They said of course, so I gave them a list and that's why they pop up again. I don't believe in people writing under a name other than their own. It tends towards sloppy writing. As long as you're going to expose yourself in the marketplace, it had better be under your own name.

Lupoff: I'd like you, if you would, to talk a bit about the editors you dealt with in those days and how the relationships . . . It seems to me that this was the last hurrah of the pulp era. The late forties and early fifties and, again, just checking standard bibliographies, you wrote for most of the pulps. In fact, I dug up a couple the other day—real gems. You know, these have gotten pretty valuable of late. At least valuable compared to what they sold for. Do you have copies of these?

MacDonald: All my materials are at the University of Florida and I don't know whether they have those specific ones or not, but they probably do because they've been very diligent about getting them together. It's fantastic.

Lupoff: Marvelous things—*Planet Stories, FBI Detective Stories.*

MacDonald: Right now I'm working on a collection of those old pulp stories which Harper & Row is going to publish in one or two volumes, depending on how many we find that I would be willing to have done again.

Lupoff: I'll look forward to it. I did actually read a couple of these ancient . . .

MacDonald: How did they go?

Lupoff: You're much better now.

MacDonald: I would hope better than last year.

Lupoff: There are touches though that just jump right up. In this "A Coffin a Day" in *FBI Detective Stories,* the very first sentence, bed-sheets being described as "as gray as a tooth with a dead nerve." That's a little bit lurid, but it's a marvelous, evocative simile.

MacDonald: Well, thank you. I like it too. What I'm discovering—one of the things I had a typist do with these stories is turn them from photostats back into nice clean typescripts and I'm reading them with great interest because I forget how they come out. What is going to happen next? I guess that's why we read, isn't it?

Lupoff: Some of these obviously had formulas. As for instance in *FBI Detective Stores,* in "A Coffin a Day" we start with a hero who is an ex-FBI man who is sort of drummed out of the corps.

That sounds a little like the late work of Dashiell Hammett. You take a guy that had been fired as the private detective. I suppose in this magazine there had to be an FBI man in every story.

MacDonald: In that one, yes. I believe that in some instances it was kind of a collusion because *FBI Detective Stories* was somewhat of a salvage market, and so if he didn't sell under some other guise to someone else, then I would turn him into an FBI man or an ex-FBI man. It is very probable that in the original typescript he wasn't. I'm not saying it's sure, it's probable.

Lupoff: You've dealt with rejection slips then?

MacDonald: Oh, definitely. I've papered a whole office with them.

Lupoff: You still have them?

MacDonald: Oh, no. I've painted it over since then. They were depressing.

Lupoff: You did a good deal of science fiction and fantasy in those days. I found, again, that you wrote for *Weird Tales* and *Startling Stories* and the early issues of *Galaxy* when Horace Gold was the editor, in addition to many other magazines. Did you deal personally with the editors then?

MacDonald: No, the editors I dealt personally with for the most part—when I say personally, well, yes, I sent them the stories—but the people I had personal contact with were mostly the people at Popular Publications. Mike Tilden and Alden Norton and Harry Widmer were the three that I principally dealt with.

Lupoff: Did Harry Steeger ever get involved? He was the kingpin who sat up in the big office . . . .

MacDonald: No. The only dealings I had with Harry Steeger were long after the pulps were over, which was maybe ten years ago. We wanted to find out what the rights were and when the stories were sold according to their records. Max Wilkinson, my agent, working through some Irish attorney in New York and tried to find out this information. There weren't that many stories—maybe sixty, seventy, something like that. And the word came back that they would be willing to search their files for them if I would pay their expenses. What were their expenses? They estimated $5,000. I thought that was not the kind of people that I am used to. And that was Steeger's decision.

Lupoff: In the case of Horace Gold at *Galaxy* there was a famous Horace Gold poker game combined with editorial conferences.

MacDonald: No, nothing like that. About the most intimate basis I got on with any of them was with Mike Tilden. After he was dead, I was talking one time with Dick Wormser, now dead also, who had done a lot of love pulp stories. We had a couple of drinks in New York and we were talking about memories of Mike Tilden and Dick said that he had loaned Mike three or four hundred dollars to pay for the cost of Mike's having—the birth of Mike's son, who was an only child. Twenty-one years later, I'd loaned Mike

$500 to pay for the kid's funeral expenses when he killed himself. A tragic, ironic kind of situation.

Lupoff: When you worked for *Black Mask,* was Cap Shaw still the editor there? The legendary Cap Shaw?

MacDonald: No, he wasn't. At the time that I . . . . . . I think Cap Shaw, Joseph Thompson Shaw, began working for Sidney Sanders' agency in about 1947 or '48. He worked for them until Sid died and when Marty Sanders, who was Sid's wife, decided she'd run the agency on her own, Shaw, at age 78, decided he'd rather go in business for himself, so he opened his own agency at the age of 78 and I went over with him. He, by the way, was the only man in New York licensed by the police to carry a sword cane. He had been some kind of champion in the 1924 Olympics.

He was a tremendously courteous and pleasant old gentleman and a very good story doctor with a very good touch. There is a biography of Dashiell Hammett coming out, which I reviewed for the *Washington Post*—I don't know if they'll use it or not. In the book, the biographer, a Mr. Lehman, says of Hammett that Joe Shaw was a promoter and not an editor, constantly hustling Hammett to try to make him put in more violence, more murders, more everything. Either Cap Shaw mellowed in his declining years or Lehman's analysis is in error.

Lupoff: Were you a great admirer of Hammett?

MacDonald: Not awfully. I think that Hammett and Chandler and Kane and Horace McCoy, who wrote *They Shoot Horses, Don't They?* and *No Pockets in a Shroud,* they cleared the way for the well-written pulp story in that they did characters through action and dialogue rather than saying, "He was a very stubborn man," which is bad writing. They would show him being stubborn. The prose style of Hammett is certainly a more solid and a more artful style than that of Chandler. But he was an idiot as far as plots are concerned. If you want to drive some high school or college kid nuts, make him do an outline of the plot of *The Maltese Falcon.* It's incredibly mixed up and nothing ever happens the way it's supposed to. But the flow of the narrative is such that you're caught up in it and you believe it. But you can't believe it if you try to dissect it.

Lupoff: Would you talk a little bit about other writers that you read when you were starting off? Or that you read now for that matter, that you think are particularly noteworthy.

MacDonald: I don't do very much reading in my own area. Most of my reading is outside that. The guys in my own area that I like right now—I think Ross Thomas is a very good writer, I like his books very much. Aside from him, nobody comes immediately to mind. I understand Kenneth Millar has recently had a stroke and he probably will not be writing very much any more, if anything. I can't think of anyone else right now—I don't want to sound as if I'm being disparaging of the field; it's just that I can't remember.

Lupoff: In your earlier writings, then—I happen to be very interested in science fiction. For instance, in *The Girl, the Gold Watch and Everything,* which is an interesting hybrid of genres . . .

MacDonald: A fantasy, wish-fulfillment sort of thing.

Lupoff: There are echoes that go all the way back to H.G. Wells.

MacDonald: Or all the way back to . . . the guy that wrote *The Stray Lamb?*

Lupoff: Thorne Smith.

MacDonald: Yes, *Rain in The Doorway.* It's more, I think, of the Thorne Smith genre than of anything else.

Lupoff: Thorne Smith seems to be making a little comeback as of late. Several of his books have been reissued.

MacDonald: *The Bishop's Jaegers.*

Lupoff: I've been trying to track down some of his more scarce titles. Of course, the ones that you can't find old copies of are the ones that they don't reissue either.

MacDonald: That's right. Get one of those book-finder places and sure, they'll dig it up for you. They'll only charge you $48-$50 for a two-dollar book.

Lupoff: In the introduction to your science fiction collection which come out about a year ago . . .

MacDonald: *Other Times, Other Worlds.* They've reissued that with a cover where you can read my name on it, and they've discovered: My Goodness, it's selling now.

Lupoff: I'm delighted to hear it, because a lot of people don't know the book exists.

MacDonald: Yes, that's because some art director there—I think if you . . . no, there's no way you can turn that book so you can read my name. Somebody up there hates me.

Lupoff: In fact, a bookstore friend of mine said, "Hey, have you seen this new MacDonald collection?" I said, "What's that?" He told me what it was and I said, "Oh, I'd like to see that book" and he handed to me. But I would never have known.

MacDonald: They sent me a stat of it where one of those colors didn't print. It didn't look great, but it looked legible. Then when it came out—it looks like somebody spilled something on the cover.

Lupoff: It is a good book. I was happy to rediscover some of the stories that I had read as a teenage science fiction fan.

MacDonald: They stuck in some—or we stuck in some—that were more recent, like . . .

Lupoff: That very late story about the phantom roadster?

MacDonald: "The Annex" was quite recent. I like that one. I'd say that of the short stories, there's two or three that I like better than any of the novels, it's a more rigid discipline, of course.

Lupoff: Would you care to mention your favorites, then?

MacDonald: Well, I like "The Annex" and I like "The Bear Trap" and I like the one—they changed the title and I can't remember the title they used—there's about four that I like.

Lupoff: "The Big Blue"—the fishing story?

MacDonald: I like that one, yes. That was sort of based . . . You know how little things happen. Bud Schulberg was telling me about going fishing with his father in Acapulco and having another person aboard ship that so enjoyed clubbing the fish that he wouldn't let the guide do it. He wanted to do it himself. It's kind of the germ of it.

I think the effectiveness of the story comes at least in part from the fact that you see that character and you say, I know him, or, I've known someone like that.

When I did that novel, *Condominium,* I thought that I'd lose the friendship of quite a few of the local developers and, not so, because every one of them that I've talked to said, "Hey, John, I know who you meant."

Lupoff: "Not me!"

MacDonald: Yes, every one.

Lupoff: That is wonderful. One of your books has a little cover band that says, "I wish I had written this book—Mickey Spillane." Was that all set up by the publisher or were you and he chums?

MacDonald: I didn't know the Mick at that time. Ralph Daigh who was editorial director at Fawcett at that time, loaned Spillane a set of galleys on the book and Mickey brought them back in and he said casually, "That's a good book. I wish I'd written it." Ralph wrote it out on a card and said, "Here, Mick, sign it." Mick said, "Yes, I'll sign it." So he signed it and Ralph immediately tucked it in the safe.

When the book came out, Spillane's editors and lawyers and agents and everybody descended like a cloud of locusts on Ralph Daigh, saying, "You can't do this. Spillane never gives a . . ."

He said, "Gentlemen, I have it in writing and I have it signed by Mr. Spillane and I have it dated. Now, what do you want to do?" That was the way it came about. Mickey is a pleasant guy. I've got some fantastic stories about him but there's no room for him in here.

Lupoff: We have picked up some odd Mickey Spillane stories from old comic book colleagues of his—a fellow named Don Rico who worked on "Captain America" and "Sub-Mariner" with Mickey, circa 1942, I would say.

MacDonald: He came here once, when we were living on the other side of the key and he was pretty heavy. He was coming down to do an article for a magazine on the people that get shot out of cannons for the circus—not the Wallendas, they're the high wire—I forget the name of the family. So he said, "I've got to come back down here."

I said, "Why?"

He said, "Well, they're going to show me how and I'm going to get shot out of that cannon."

I said, "Why can't you do it now? They're in town."

He said, "I'm the wrong caliber."

Lupoff: That's wonderful! Do you think of yourself as a hard-boiled writer?

MacDonald: No.

Lupoff: Would you put any label on yourself or would you rather avoid them?

MacDonald: I don't put any label on myself. I know that it's the American compulsion to label people. A certain kind of painter—abstract impressionist; a certain kind of writer—a mystery writer, a paperback writer, a historical writer. I think it's a lot of nonsense. Writing is writing is writing. So is painting. I used to hate it when—in fact, I resigned from the local art institute here when a new group got control of it and decided that when they had a show it was going to divide it into abstract and realistic and give separate prizes. Good is good and bad is bad, whether it's writing or painting or sculpture or lawn-mowing.

If you know the tools of your . . . . . . Thank God lines are getting a little blurred with the mystery writing, sort of like—this *Gorky Park,* now, is treated as a very, very respectable straight novel, which it is. In essence, it's the story of a Russian cop and an

American cop trying to solve the mystery of a multiple murder in Gorky Park in Moscow. What could be more of a mystery story than that? Tracking down every slight clue, reconstructing the face of the dead—I'm happy to see this treated as a straight novel.

Lupoff: Who wrote that? I don't know the book. I'll have to look it up.

MacDonald: Martin Cruz Smith. It has been reviewed this past month in *Time* magazine, front page review in *The New York Times*. I got it in galley proofs several months ago, took it to Mexico, wrote back to his agent, Knox Burger, who is my friend and said, "This is a very, very good novel; he's a damn fine writer. I recommend it highly."

Lupoff: I'll get it. Well, now this has finally brought us around the barn and back to Travis McGee. I would like to hit you with a few notions or questions about McGee, and then if you just want to free associate or anything about them... One thing that immediately strikes me as a problem you must encounter, or maybe not, but certainly one that hit me in the face was, How do you keep a character fresh and a series going fresh through nineteen books?

MacDonald: It wasn't easy. It's very difficult because, in a sense, there are a lot of strictures on that kind of writing. I'm not trying to patronize it, because once you decide what the format's going to be, then you take your tongue out of your cheek and write just as well as you can. But he's got to be alive in the beginning, alive at the end.

It's a folk dance, really. In the normal kind of folk dance, what you have is the guys in the white hats winning and the guys in the black hats losing. The plan here is to have the guys in the white hats lose, but not too much, and the guys in the black hats win, but not too much. You can't really make it reality because in real life the guys in the black hats tend to win a great deal and a great deal of the time. But that would depress people to read about that, because in a series we're celebrating the Judeo-Christian virtues of don't steal, don't lie and don't hurt anybody.

Lupoff: Another point that intrigued me about Travis McGee—well, two things. For one, he seems to be a middle-aged guy with a real biography behind him; he's not just the tough guy with the gat in his pocket or anything of that sort. How old is Travis? And is he John D. MacDonald?

MacDonald: He's as old as you figure he is. Put it this way. The writer writes a code, C-A-T, whatever. C-A-T doesn't look like a cat, but as soon as you read that, a cat happens in your head. Now, visions that people make in their heads, the richness and the detail of those visions in their heads depend upon the richness of the life that they have led and are leading. One doesn't want to try to guide the reader too much. I don't want to say Travis is 38 or 48 or 52 or 31 or 70 years old. I want people to see him internally, right? That's why television is so unsatisfying, because you have other people making the pictures for you and those pictures are never as good as the ones you make yourself.

As far as any relationship between me and McGee, if I related to anybody, I'd relate, probably, to Meyer. McGee has a lot more positive, specific opinions about things than I have. He responds intellectually in a little more arbitrary fashion than I do—like he hates computers and I use one to write the books on.

Lupoff: There are hints, but again, they're subject to interpretation. In *Free Fall,* we see that Travis was a sergeant in a war and saved a lieutenant's life, who turns up again as a character in this book. You didn't tell us which war. I would guess World War II, but another reader might say Vietnam.

MacDonald: Actually, if I had any war in my mind, it was Korea.

Lupoff: Another aspect of *Free Fall* that struck me very strongly was the amount of background detail that's in there and I wonder about the research methods versus how much is just stuff that's already there.

Let me just give you a brief list—there's at least some expert data there on unarmed combat, motorcycle hardware and technology, the sociology of motorcycle gangs, filmmaking, drugs including specifically LSD, hashish, marijuana, downers, cocaine, of course codeine, hotel management—just an incredible stew of information is there behind the story as the story moves over it. Is that specific research or is that just stuff that . . . ?

MacDonald: I have what the British call—I like the expression—a dustbin mind that everything that I pick up from any source seems to stay available—not readily available in conversation, not readily available when I try to remember something specific and can't, but it seems to pop up when I'm working. Then I have two methods of dealing with the ugly facts when I get to them, if my memory has failed. I either go look them up or I drop it and write around it so I don't have to. Writing around it is a case of trying to do it deftly enough so that nobody will know I'm cheating.

Lupoff: You fooled me.

MacDonald: Well, a lot of that is—I did quite a bit of research on the whole balloon thing and I'm afraid I put a little bit too much in, but I'm not sure.

Lupoff: I loved it.

MacDonald: The current hot air balloon fad is one of the thousand adventures I've never taken because I'm basically a cowardly person. The strange thing is that at the time I started the book it wasn't a fad. All of a sudden, everywhere I look is balloons.

Lupoff: I thought that was very enjoyable. That does raise another question about *Free Fall* specifically but also, it seems to me, typical of many works, not just John D. MacDonald works but a great many present-day authors. There seems to be a certain sort of death ethic in the story. We start with Travis trying to unravel a relatively modest puzzle: Why was this elderly man, who was terminally ill anyway, beaten to death? But in the course of the next 200 pages, Travis has unraveled this incredible snarl of corruption and violence and, to coin a phrase, the landscape is strewn with corpses.

MacDonald: Well, you're asking—you called it a death ethic. Why is there so much violence?

Lupoff: Well, if you feel there's a particular . . . Maybe that's just the form you're working in.

MacDonald: I think that's probably the most intriguing thing for people. Understand I'm trying to entertain the folk, I'm not trying to change the mores of society. I think that everyone, not only specifically these days, but everyone in the western world since . . . well, the 18th, 19th, 20th centuries, we wonder how we would react faced with a sudden, bloody something. We tend to think about it in quiet times. You say to yourself, how would I react if a guy jumps out from behind a car as I'm going from the supermarket, right? You think about it, right?

What we want is to see how somebody else has reacted, in case that might in some way guide our own response and behavior. The male wants to be assured in his own mind that he's going to respond in a reasonably macho way—of course, that gets a lot of people killed. Violence, I don't think is a particular attribute of contemporary America. I think it's been an attribute of the Western World since recorded history. I think it's a proper province of the writer. I think there are a lot of areas where it's totally internal, like in the works of Cheever or Updike or Vance Bourjaily. They contain the elements of violence, even though a lot of it's interior monologue. And they are in the business of (telephone interruption)—you're wondering if this is ever going to amount to any kind of useful comment anyway—the phone took me off the hook.

Lupoff: Okay, I guess we can leave violence at that point.

MacDonald: I got an interesting thing on violence that I just— I've been reviewing some old clippings because I've got to do two lectures to sing for my supper in Lauderdale on Saturday. So I went over these clippings and I found Anthony Burgess, who as the creator of *A Clockwork Orange,* has a vested interest in violence.

He says, talking about Hemingway, a civilized man being replaced by natural man, a creature reverting to his impulses, discarding much of his humanistic inheritance, "There are no Shakespearian personalities in Hemingway, only tough but apparatuses of instinct. The way was open for American fictional man: touchy, uncerebral, capricious. We find him everywhere today, in movies as well as books. We don't have characters on the old model any more. There was in Hemingway's creations a residual Boy Scout honor, stoicism, grace under pressure. But those are not to be found in the curious automata that stalk, ready with gun or phallus, round the surrealistic townscapes of the contemporary American novel."

Lupoff: What a despairing statement!

MacDonald: Isn't it? I think that he arrived at that kind of attitude from the fact that they made him take the last chapter out of *A Clockwork Orange* for publication in this country, because in the last chapter of *A Clockwork Orange* he has the guy, a little while later, getting tired of the violence and deciding he wants a wife and kiddies and they decided that wouldn't work too well in the American novel. Well, heavens, with that novel it wouldn't work too well anywhere. It's sort of an apology for all that's gone before.

Lupoff: Is the English edition published that way?

MacDonald: Yes, it is.

Lupoff: I never knew that. I'll have to look at that. You've given up your time very generously and I'd like to wrap up with just one more question about your own works, and the works of others. Do you have a particular favorite book or books of your own, or a least favorite book or books?

MacDonald: Well, there isn't one I wouldn't like to get back and take another hack at. Excuse the work hack. I like *Slam the Big Door,* reasonably well. I like *The End of the Night* and I like *The Last One Left* reasonably well. Other than that, there are different areas. The one I like the least I've managed to keep from being published any more and that was . . . . Thank goodness for Freud, I've forgotten.

Lupoff: Okay, I'll look for that one then. And, again a hackneyed question but I think it's still a good one. If you were going to be marooned on a desert island with one book, not a John D. MacDonald, what do you think it should be?

MacDonald: A book on survival.

OTHERWISE IT'S JUST HORSE RACES
Changes magazine

When *Kaddish* opened in New York, Allen Ginsberg was in San Francisco at the end of a tour of poetry readings. He arrived in time to appear at a reading of Yevgeny Yevtushenko's poetry which included Lawrence Ferlinghetti as well. Another reading with Ferlinghetti was scheduled for a few days later, following which Ginsberg was scheduled to travel to Australia.

In between, he made time for a quick interview centering on the opening of the play.

"The dramatization of *Kaddish* dates back to 1963," he said. "I had just come back from India, and I was with Robert Frank, the filmmaker. We'd worked together on *Pull My Daisy* with Jack Kerouac and Gregory Corso. It was a sort of home-made *avant garde* movie, really ahead of its time.

"Of course it got tied up legally for a long time, but now it's getting a second chance at distribution, playing at colleges all over the country.

"Anyway, when *Pull My Daisy* was finished, I sat down with Frank to try and do a film script of *Kaddish*. We dealt with a lot of problems involved in translating a poem from print into something visible, manifestible, filmable. I worked on it steadily for three months with Frank at my elbow all the time to make sure I didn't commit any errors in terms of what was practicable for filming."

The starting point was an attempt to make the poem, which involves mental images, flashbacks, simultaneous and overlapping events, more linear for the screen. "I started with a copy of *Kaddish* and a pair of scissors. I cut apart every scene and sorted out the pieces to get the various references to events back together."

But it was impossible to raise the money needed in '63 to film *Kaddish*. Somehow another film *did* come out of the project. "I worked with Frank on a screenplay that was called *Kaddish* for a while," Ginsberg said. "It was a film about Peter Orlovsky's brother Julius, and it finally was released as *Me and My Brother.*"

Meanwhile the screenplay for *Kaddish* remained dormant, although it passed from hand to hand, from would-be producer to producer: Jerry Benjamin had it for a while. Robert Levine had it, but the film never quite came into being.

Finally it was transformed into a play—or, more accurately, a mixed-media drama, with scenes staged, others viewed on a video screen, or both. "The scene of my mother being dragged into the ambulance was filmed in the streets of Paterson, New Jersey," Ginsberg says, "and it's shown on the screen at the same time that actors go through similar actions on the stage.

Allen Ginsberg, author Howl, Kaddish, and many other works (portrait by Gavin O'Keefe)

"I haven't actually gone over the script line for line, but I think it's almost identical to the screenplay of 1963. It must have been as solid as a brick shit-house to work after that long."

Ginsberg has been hugely busy the past few months. "When the play was getting started, I decided that I was going to trust the people doing it. I stayed away from casting, had no hand in that. In November ('71) when they were really working on it, I got involved in other things that occupied me. I did a record album with Bob Dylan, it's called *Holy Soul Jellyroll* and it's due for release on Apple in about a month.

"I think it's good, Dylan liked it enough that he asked me to come back and do another one, and I plan to when I get back from Australia."

The trip to Australia is to last about a month. Ginsberg was invited by the Adelaide Arts Festival. "I'm going to do a couple of readings for $500 apiece to get pocket money," he said, "then just travel around the country, doing free readings, talking to people. I hope to meet the bushmen."

But he had particularly strong feelings about *Kaddish*, still. "I want to emphasize the circumstances of composition," he said several times. "I had no commercial motive when I wrote it, in fact it wasn't published for several years afterward. I wrote it for myself. It was purely meditative, prayer, confessional. I wrote it for God. I wrote it for art, not commerce. Young people keep asking me, 'What do I have to do to be successful?' My advice for a young playwright is to write for yourself. You can't write for commerce, you have to write for art.

"If you write for yourself, that's the important thing, and then if you get commercial success out of it too, that's fine. Write for God!

"If you want commercial success, it's just horse races, just horse races. Write for God."

Ginsberg cites others with whom he's been associated: "Burroughs wrote *Naked Lunch* for himself, Kerouac wrote *On the Road* for himself, I wrote *Kaddish* for myself. We had to write for ourselves. Then commercial success just came."

HOW ARE THINGS ON MARS:
A CONVERSATION
2012

Richard Lupoff: What are you doing for *John Carter of Mars* and how did you get involved?

Michael Chabon: Well, it was pretty neat—it was a lot of chance and just good luck because in the mid-'90s, right around the time I went to Berkeley, about '96 or '97 I think I started, and was still working at the time on an original screenplay called *The Martian Agent*—that was sort of my attempt to work with that sort of John Carter material—the Burroughs Barsoom material, but in my own way. Partly because I didn't have the rights to that material, but also because I wanted to play with it in my own way. It was a screenplay that was set on Mars in the 1890s and was set in the alternate reality where the British Empire, through superior technology, had conquered the entire earth—had reconquered the United States—was the unchallenged master of Earth and was now proceeding to the conquest of Mars. So it was about the British Empire trying to colonize Mars in the 1890s. That Mars was my version of Mars, but it was very much populated with strange creatures, and it was me working with the same type of Victorian adventure stuff that ERB was working with—and H.R. Haggard and all those great Victorian adventure novelists.

It was optioned by Fox and it was supposed to be directed by Jan de Bont, the director who made *Speed* and *Twister*—he was very hot at the time. And they did a million dollars of special effects testing over at ILM. So, when I moved up here I was actually going over to ILM—I went a few times and had a look at the art they were developing—and the thing was going along pretty nicely—and then *Speed 2* came out and it was a disaster. Fox pulled the plug on the project. It just killed everything and in that mass die-off my project got killed and that was it.

I essentially put it away although I did subsequently take the first part of that story and novelized it just as an experiment to see if I could turn it into a novel. I got one chapter into it and then stopped, but that chapter was subsequently published in the McSweeney's anthology that I edited—so that was all there was of that.

Photo by Jennifer Chaney

*My neighbor Michael Chabon —
We had such high hopes for* John Carter of Mars!

Then last Christmas, 2008, I went to a Christmas party at the home of Brad Bird, the director for Pixar Works. He did *The Incredibles, Ratatouille*, and he made the movie *The Iron Giant* as director/writer/animator. And at this party this guy came in a beeline across the room to me saying, "Remember me? My name is Derek and I was one of the production artists on your Mars project back when I worked at ILM." He now works at Pixar, but he remembered me and I remembered him—so we started talking and sort of reminiscing about the project. In the course of that conversation he said, "Do you know Andrew Stanton is doing *John Carter*? Disney got the rights back and he's doing *John Carter of Mars*." And I hadn't heard that—I didn't know that and I got very excited. "That sounds great. Wow! That sounds like a terrific project."

Just a couple of days later, maybe on the Monday following that party, Andrew Stanton himself contacted me and said, "I hear you're really into Edgar Rice Burroughs and Mars. Derek was telling me about this other project you were involved in and I was wondering if you'd like to just come over and check out what we're up to and what we've done? I'll show you what we've got." I had actually met him a couple of times in the past so I knew him slightly. So I went over there and he asked me if I'd be interested in coming on board and doing a rewrite. Their script was in good shape and they'd already been through a few drafts.

Lupoff: Who wrote them?

Chabon: Andrew Stanton and his writing partner, Mark Andrews, who is also a story board/production artist and had worked with Brad Bird on a number of his films—he's a real pillar at Pixar. This might have been his first screenwriting job, I'm not sure, but he and Andrews had written a script together. They actually had worked out and solved many of the thorny story telling issues that the first novel presents.

Lupoff: Is this based on just the first novel?

Chabon: Well, hard to say exactly. I guess I'd say if all goes as planned, the first three films—were there to be three films—would more or less cover the same ground as the first three novels in terms of where they would end it up and what was known to be true.

But the novels were different—serialized novels from a pulp magazine in 1912 and 1915, etc. So they weren't really written with a two-hour, 21st century major motion picture studio film in mind. So there are things that have to be done—so they're not really literal—it's not even like a one to one correspondence like the Harry Potters—it's not like that. Nor is it a complete departure by any means. It's like taking the whole range of things in the first three novels and trying to set them up for an eventual trilogy of films.

Lupoff: Actually a few months ago I went back and looked at what I had said in my first book about Burroughs in 1965 and I discovered that I said *A Princess of Mars* is really not a very good novel. He was learning—it was his first book—and the series got much better. Then I went back and reread *A Princess of Mars* to compare my attitude in 2009 with my attitude in 1964-65—and I said, "This is right—this is not a very good novel."

Chabon: I mean it's clear that he was making it up as he went along and so there are a lot of things, especially in that first book, there were ideas that just get tossed out there and are never followed up on. Like having everyone being telepathic—it turns out he didn't need that—he could tell his story well without that and in fact it would be a disadvantage in many ways. You know at some point you sort of see him realize that, *Crap! If everything is telepathic how am I going to make that? Oh, I know—I'll just say he has a mental block and no one can read him.* It's a very seat-of-the-pants kind of writing.

Lupoff: And you have people fighting with ray guns and swords. Well, if you have a ray gun and I have a sword—you've got it, I surrender. [I was reminded later that they weren't really ray guns, but radar-sighted rifles that shot radium bullets.—RAL]

Chabon: Exactly. The Tharks have their radium rifles and they're clearly meant to be like Afghani tribesmen or something like that. But it's not as if the British army charged the Afghani tribesmen with their swords alone—they had cannons and used artillery and had rifles and Gatling guns and all that stuff.

Lupoff: . . . and they still are.

Chabon: There's a lot more satire that I get. The first time I read the books when I was a kid, I'm not sure if I read all of them, but I probably read eight or nine. This time I'm up as far as *Chessmen* now, which is really good—that might be one of my favorites.

Lupoff: When they're playing Jetan.

Chabon: Yeah, that was fun—but—you know a lot of the wonders of Mars and the marvelous things he's describing are actually sort of satirical exaggerations of American society at the time, whether he talks about racial attitudes or cultural attitudes. He's really just poking fun at human foibles—creating little micro societies that have absurd rules they live by. With the Tharks in the first book there seems to be some kind of an attempt of a critique of socialism.

Lupoff: Have you come across the religious dispute of whether the great truth is "Tur is Tur . . . or . . . Tur is Tur"? That's somewhere later along. It's a great debate.

Chabon: The books remind me frequently of the Wizard of Oz books a lot in terms of the same message . . . dry, dry poking fun at human behaviour, especially when people get into some kind of collective enterprise where they all try to out-do each other or they all try to pull the wool over each other's eyes.

Lupoff: I did a radio show a few years ago with Michael Patrick Hearn, a scholar who seems to know everything there is to know about Baum and Oz. He told me that when Burroughs arrived in Hollywood he was met at the railway station by Frank Baum and they became pals.

Chabon: You know I read something about that too, and I often thought it would be a good subject for a play or film. And they both had their escape: Ozcot and Tarzana that they built on the proceeds of their books. Anyway, that stuff is fun, I think in your memory of the books you sort of forget about that aspect of satire, and when you go back to them it's actually part of the pleasure of reading them but it won't necessarily feed into an exciting action-packed adaptation.

Lupoff: I want to ask you—after reading your Wikipedia chapter, you seem to have got caught in the middle of people throwing rotten cabbages at each other and events between those who say genre fiction is nothing but garbage and those who say that genre fiction is legitimate literature. I haven't read all your works, but I've read most of them and I'm thinking, *Final Solution* with Sherlock Holmes. *Kavalier & Clay*—although it's a mainstream, real world novel, seems completely immersed in the world of comic book heroes. *Summerland* is a sort of fairy tale fantasy. You've done some Lovecraft-related short fiction, and *The Yiddish Policemen's Union* is both an alternate history novel, sort of science fiction without science, and is also sort of a murder mystery. So there you are neck deep in genre work and yet you've had the good fortune to be accepted as a serious literary writer. How do you deal with this?

Chabon: Well I think I was just lucky in that I started out writing more mainstream stuff. And if you look back at it, even the first couple of books that are almost entirely mainstream, naturalistic works of fiction you can see elements of interesting genre fiction. I suppose because I got off to a start that way, I think it a was a lot easier.

It's crazy. It's not that way in movies. You can be taken utterly seriously as an auteur, sycophant, and have made nothing but detective movies or westerns—you can be Hitchcock or John Ford—and nobody ever held the genre against them. In literature that isn't the case. I think it is easier if you sort of start out with kind of mainstream credentials and then move into genre. It's much harder to go the other way. It's much harder once you've been labeled or pigeonholed. It can be done with a writer such as Jonathan Lethem, who never was writing straight ahead science fiction stuff like Larry Niven. It never was like hard science fiction, but he was overtly beset and he was read primarily by people in the industry. Little by little he succeeded in sort of opening a readership, but he did it the hard way. I did it the easy way.

Lupoff: He got a huge break with that *Newsweek* review of *Gun with Occasional Music*. The reviewer thought this was the first time anyone had ever done this, and lots of people had done it. So, you don't let that bother you?

Chabon: I just try to write things I would like to read. I don't read exclusively anything. I have very catholic tastes, lower case "c".

Lupoff: You know Fred Chappell, you know his work?

Chabon: Yes, *Dagon*.

Lupoff: He also has written murder mysteries with a detective called Aunt Shirley Holmes.

Chabon: If writers were like violinists I would trace my lineage to him because he taught a teacher of mine—he taught Eve Shelnutt—a short story writer. He had a huge impact on her and she taught me and had a great impact on me.

Lupoff: I owe Chappell a letter. He wrote a letter to me recently and said he remembered the day when the latest issues of *Astounding Science Fiction* or *Startling Stories* were new on the newsstands . . . and there he is.

Chabon: He's a really good writer. I loved *Dagon*—I've read it a couple of times.

Lupoff: Back to the movie world. Are you aware of the recent movie, *Princess of Mars* with Traci Lords?

Chabon: I've seen the trailer for it.

Lupoff: What's your comment about it?

Chabon: It's hilarious. It made me laugh. When I watched the trailer I burst out laughing. It was not purely scornful laughter—there's a certain element of delight in "over the top." It just looks like a hoot.

Lupoff: Well if it comes on the dish I'll look at it. But *Avatar* on the screens today is a different story. Multi millions and it may be the biggest thing ever. In a number of interviews James Cameron says he was inspired by Edgar Rice Burroughs—five or six references to Burroughs and a couple of references to Haggard. The question then is, what is this going to do, especially the 3-D aspect of it, what is it going to do to the Disney production?

Chabon: As far as I can tell it is very good for *John Carter* that *Avatar* has done so well. If *Avatar* had done badly it would have been very bad for *John Carter*. As far as I know, Andrew Stanton—and I, and everyone involved with the film—are celebrating the success of *Avatar*. It legitimizes and helps solidify the idea that a movie like that with interplanetary romance can be a big commercial success if it's done intelligently. As for 3-D, I have no idea. I don't know if it's going to be shot in 3-D or not. It very well might be.

Lupoff: Have you seen *Avatar*?

Chabon: I liked it. I really liked it. It's fun. It's well made, it's creatively well thought through, it's so rich in detail. The alien creatures and all that have been well thought through and the evolutionary process on that world is clearly worked out.

There's one total throw-away moment when you do see the effort taken. They're stealing the space ship at one point—a flying machine—a military craft—and they're jumping in and they're getting ready to power up the engines and a character climbs up on the back and lifts these fabric covers off the intake ducts—it's just one thought. The manual labor involved in getting this thing ready—they take the two covers off and throw them away and it just shows me that the dream is being dreamed very vividly to get to that part where you're thinking what would be involved in getting one of these things ready. There's a checklist of things that are being done by every character about to take off on this vehicle. I really admire that level of care—it's very carefully thought through.

It's truly right in the line of Burroughs and Haggard in that it's a story of realism and adventure between a doomed, primitive, but in many ways incredibly rich and advanced civilization, and an adventuring imperialistic—as far as we can see in the movie—predominately white empire. It is a very old template in many ways that has been in use since the 1870s and 1880s adventures.

Lupoff: You've surely read *War of the Worlds*.

Chabon: Yeah.

Lupoff: People who think that's about Mars invading Earth are reading or seeing it only on the thinnest surface—which is there, but it's really about the British Empire, most specifically India.

Chabon: Adventure fiction as we most commonly understand it is about imperialism in one degree or another. All the great archetypes, the prototypes from Edgar Rice Burroughs' Tarzan and John Carter, H. R. Haggard, and all the way up to, even the western novel, *The Virginian*, all the way through to James Bond—they're all about empire—the interaction between empires as colonies are colonized. So *Avatar* fits right into that pattern. I wasn't surprised to hear that at all.

But I don't know anything about the 3-D aspect of it. The one thing that I note on the Web—there seems to be a lot of confusion about something that would be nice to lay at rest. People don't seem to know if it is going to be animated and if it is being made by Pixar or Disney. It is being made by Disney and it is a live-action film—it is not an animation made by Pixar. Andrew Stanton is a director who is best known for his work at Pixar and he has never made a live-action movie before. But this is a live-action movie.

Lupoff: How will they do something like the Tharks?

Chabon: I believe it will be the same kind of effects wizardry that they used in *Avatar* or to create Gollum in *Lord of the Rings*. They will use the full panoply—a combination of CGI and models and puppetry and all the new technical things that are available. It is live action. The lead John Carter is going to be played by Taylor Kitsch.

Lupoff: I was just about to ask you that. IMDB gives the full cast and the works and they start shooting January 10th. The release is scheduled for 2012.

My final question—I know you're an incredibly busy person. With the huge success of *Avatar*, you know *Avatar* is the elephant in the room—do you feel that this is a cycle on the order of Jane Austen movies? Everybody loves them, but now it's time for something else. Do you feel that this is going to be some cycle which comes and goes and then it's over, or do you think it's going to be long term?

Chabon: I don't know. There's so much great material out there that's never been filmed—both classic and new. There's Iain M. Banks. Somebody told me there's a plan in the works to film one of his novels. There's so much great stuff that's never been done. What about a movie about *Ringworld*, for example? How awesome that would be. I don't know—with Jane Austen, she only wrote what—six novels and so then you're done, right? They made all of them and then they sort of remade them a little bit again and that's it—we're out of material.

But when you see *Avatar*—if you're a science fiction lover and you watch *Avatar* part of what you're doing all the time is thinking about all the cool things that could be done now. I love Clifford Simak's *City*.

And there's a great Poul Anderson story that has the idea of people being altered to suit the environment of another planet and then deciding they actually prefer to be altered. As I recall, they go out into Jupiter and the people are disappearing. They alter people's bodies so they send them out to survive on the surface of Jupiter and they don't come back. They think they're being killed but then they realize after that they prefer to be Jovians.

Lupoff: Have you read Jack Vance's *The Dragon Masters*?

Chabon: Sure. I thought of making that a movie many times and now they can do it. It could never have been done before.

Lupoff: Well I think this gets back to *John Carter of Mars*. There's been attempts to make this, not just years but for decades—and they always stumbled and fell very early in the process. I don't think anybody ever got much beyond a five minute test.

Chabon: Right, except Bob Clampett. That was the most famous. It seems like Ray Harryhausen could have done it. It probably would have ended up being a little chintzy looking but it still would have been great seeing that.

Lupoff: Kerwin Matthews as John Carter, but again with CGI and the special effects available in the 21st century.

Chabon: *Dragon Masters* is something that's been in the back of my mind a long time. It would be a terrific movie and is short so there wouldn't have to be much weeding out, in fact, you might have to add in a little bit.

Lupoff: I can still see the Jack Gaughan *Galaxy* cover painting of that. Anyway . . . I'm so happy we've done this.

(Transcribed by Bill Hillman)

MISTER PRATHER AND ME

Heading north from Phoenix, the highway passed through flat, arid, desert land that sent heat waves shimmering even in early March. The tall saguaro cactus that has inspired a thousand cartoons stands near the blacktop. It really does look like a caricature of a man. You pass towns with names like Rock Springs, Camp Verde, Rimrock. The land rises, the air grows cooler, and as you turn off the main road to head for Sedona you see something amazing. Towering red rock buttes rise hundreds of feet in the air. Their tops—at least from road level—appear to be perfectly flat. I don't know what geologists say about them, about how those buttes got there. But if there's anything to the "ancient astronauts" theory, it's easy to imagine alien spacecraft silently approaching and leaving those towering rocks, their lights moving like stars against the background of a blazing desert night.

Richard and Tina Prather had just moved to Sedona from Scottsdale, a suburb of Phoenix, when Pat and I visited them in order to tape an interview for radio station KPFA in Berkeley, California. Outside their brand-new one story house stood a baby blue Cadillac convertible, a perfect Shell Scott car. Pat and I parked our rented Buick and Prather bounded across the not-yet-green lawn to greet us. He was dressed in brilliant chrome yellow shirt and trousers, yellow socks and white shoes.

Prather is a slim, dapper man. He wears his hair short and a neatly trimmed pencil-thin moustache. Both in appearance and in energy he seemed far younger than his sixty-five years. Inside the Prathers' house, it was clear that they had not finished unpacking from their move. The Prathers have been married since 1945. Their life has included adversity, but Tina Prather, a mosaic artist, seems to have thrived on it, as has her husband.

When we settled down to record our interview, I introduced Prather by quoting the sales figures blurbed on the covers of his novels over the years. A 1957 Fawcett Gold Medal edition in my collection refers to Prather as "America's fastest selling author." Later editions substitute numbers for adjectives. Over 5,500,000 books sold ... over 7,000,000 books sold ... over 20,000,000 books sold ... over 40,000,000 books sold.

Then the interview began ...

Interview with Richard S. Prather
1987

Lupoff: My first question is, are those numbers for real?

Prather: Yes they are for real and the significant thing about that 40 million copies is that it's United States sales. Nobody knows how many copies have been sold around the world in foreign editions. I know I've probably had six or seven hundred foreign editions of my books, but these are U.S. sales. It staggers me a little to think how many in all.

Lupoff: What's the appeal? First of all, tell a little bit about Shell Scott and what these books typically looked like back in the 1950's when they were first hitting the stands.

Prather: Well, they were published by one of the great publishers, Fawcett Bocks, which at that time brought out a lot of paperback originals and paid the authors on print order, which isn't done these days. I wish it was, because that's the way we make our money, from copies printed, not necessarily copies allegedly sold. Some of the books looked a little bit like the old pulp magazines I read as a kid growing up. They had garish covers and bosomy ladies and guns going off and they had titles like *The Scrambled Yeggs* and *The Case of the Vanishing Beauty* on some of my early ones. They were very much like a transition between the pulps and hardcover-type mysteries which came along later. Some of them were very pulpy, some of mine were pulpy.

Lupoff: Who were the authors you grew up with?

Prather: Well, I read Hammett and Chandler and later of course MacDonald and Spillane and my contemporaries. The most important man to me and in my view the best of all mystery writers was Raymond Chandler. *Farewell My Lovely* and *The Big Sleep* just blew me away and still do. I still occasionally read those books again every three or four years. No other writer affected me more or probably affected my style more. Of course, as I mentioned, I loved MacDonald's work, the late John D. I knew John, met him at some conventions and so forth and I liked him and loved his work. Particularly the early work when he was getting started and I was getting started back in the fifties and sixties.

Lupoff: Do you see a similarity between Shell Scott and Travis McGee?

Prather: Not really, except that they're individuals working on cases for a fee. They're very different people, and I understand that MacDonald actually said in an article that he was my replacement at Fawcett. When I left Fawcett in the early sixties and went over to Pocket Books, I was at that time Fawcett's best selling writer and had a lot of books out in the Shell Scott series. They wanted someone to sort of replace that series and me, so they approached a very fine writer. I'm pleased that they approached someone as good as MacDonald to follow me. MacDonald is the guy that I sometimes think I ought to follow instead of vice-versa. But they got him to try a couple of books and it turned out he wanted to see if he could do a series comfortably, because he'd never done a series before. He started out with Travis McGee, he did a couple of the books, they did very well and that became an astonishingly popular series.

Lupoff: Had you been writing short stories before you went to work for Fawcett?

Prather: No. I started writing novels in the beginning. I wrote a few short stories but usually the short stories and novelettes were because my agent asked me to do them for a magazine or a magazine publisher asked me to do them. I was always thinking in terms of novels and long, long stories. But I've done three books, collections of short stories and novelettes mainly to fill in between the books (novels) because I've always been interested primarily in novels.

Lupoff: Who was your editor at Fawcett?

Prather: Well, primarily, the editor was the late Richard Carroll, who was just a lovely man that I didn't get to meet for many years because I didn't want to meet editors. I didn't want to have anything to do with editors, publishers, or anyone in the business. I just wanted to write books and let the books succeed or fail depending on the books themselves, not upon the people I knew. I finally met him and thought he was a lovely man, and in fact when I did a book with another writer, Steve Marlowe, called *Double in Trouble*, we dedicated it to the late Richard Carroll because he had just died and we were sad about it.

Lupoff: In fact, I'd like to talk about *Double in Trouble* in a little bit, but first I'm trying to pin down how you got started in the business. I mean, it's not the ordinary thing, like you finish your education and become a life insurance sales rep. This is a little bit of an odd-ball profession that you're in, and if you'll pardon my saying it, your way of doing it is a little bit odder than most.

Prather: Yes, I'm oten told that. I'm one of these men who've wanted to be a writer from the time he was a boy in school. I was always going to be a writer but I never did anything about it, and by the end of the forties, close to the early fifties, I was working as a Civil Service clerk at March Air Force Base. I was the chief clerk of the Surplus Properties Disposal Office out there and my wife was working as a cocktail waitress. And I decided, finally, instead of talking about writing, to try it. I had read a lot of mysteries, a lot of pulps, *Black Mask, Dime Detective,* and *Spicy Detective* even, and later novels by people like Chandler and other good guys.

Lupoff: Did you read Robert Leslie Bellem?

Prather: I read Robert Leslie Bellem, yes. I thought he was great. I don't remember Bellem that well, because it was so many years ago since I read him but I was very impressed by Bellem. I'm trying to think of some of the titles.

Lupoff: Well, there was *Dan Turner, Hollywood detective*.

Prather: Dan Turner, yes. People ask me if I was influenced by Bellem because they see similarities between Bellem's work and mine and the private eye type of approach. I was impressed by Bellem, and I read what I could find, but we're talking now before I began writing, before 1949 or 1950. My first book was published in 1950, so we're going back a lot of years to when I read those early books by Bellem and some of the other writers that came out of the pulps.

Lupoff: You were working as a civil service clerk and you just sat down and wrote *The Case of the Vanishing Beauty?*

Prather: Not exactly. I said to Tina, my wife, that I wanted to start writing. We were living in a little house in Riverside then and I did write a book, but it wasn't *The Case of the Vanishing Beauty* They've got a new title on it now, *The Scrambled Yeggs,* I guess, but I called it *The Madame Caper* and it was the first Shell Scott book, the first private eye novel, the first anything I'd ever written. I finished that at the end of 1949 and sent it off to Scott Meredith who then was an agent who advertised in the writers magazines. I didn't know him. I sent him a letter and asked if he would take on the book and send me several thousand dollars. I was egocentric and confident, and eventually he did.

He eventually took the book and put it on the market, and said it was very well done. He liked it, but it didn't sell for about two and a half years. In the meantime I wrote *The Case of the Vanishing Beauty* and also moved from Riverside, California to Laguna Beach. We got a little apartment there and I started writing seriously full time. We gave ourselves a year, both quit our jobs and before the year was up we were established with Fawcett.

Lupoff: Your first five books, up through *Way of a Wanton*, are all Shell Scotts and all published by Fawcett, at least according to the standard reference works.

Prather: Well, yes and no. Fawcett became my publisher but there were a couple of books that they didn't publish in those days. For example, *The Madame Caper* is the first book I wrote and didn't sell for two and a half years. That was brought out by other publishers and later by Gold Medal when they wanted all my titles under one publisher.

Lupoff: You wrote that, under the name of David Knight and Graphic Books published it. Who were they?

Prather: I didn't know then, don't know now. They were just willing to pay me a little money for the book and publish it, and that was enough for me, particularly in those days when every extra buck meant another week of living.

Lupoff: And you had a couple with Lion and one with Falcon. Now these are famous publishers. (laughter)

Prather: Yes, fantastic. Their fame has slipped considerably in succeeding years. (laughter) This was originally *Lie Down Killer*, which was originally not published by Fawcett or Crest. That's one of the books you mentioned. Lion brought out the other one, I think that was *The Peddler*. I'd have to get out my notes, it was so long ago.

Lupoff: According to this list Lion Books did both of these.

Prather: *Pattern for Murder* was Graphic. *The Peddler,* yes, that was Lion, as Douglas Ring. Interesting thing, I love editors when they don't get too eager to change what you've written. This is one of the classic examples. I don't know who the editor was there at Lion Books, one of these very famous publishers of those days that you mentioned. They bought the book, and they wanted to publish it under a pen name because the books by Richard S. Prather were being published by Fawcett.

They really didn't like for anyone else to publish my books, but if they refused the book, they can hardly complain if someone else published it. Okay, I picked out a pen name, Douglas King. I thought, God might be too much, Prince wasn't enough, but King was just right. So I sent it off as by Douglas King. You know what they did? They changed my name and published it as Douglas Ring. Now there's an editor who not only edited the title, and the book, but also the author's name, and I think that's going a bit too far.

Lupoff: Did your trail ever cross with that of Jim Thompson?

Prather: No. But I've read a lot about Jim Thompson and in those days I read some of his books. He's a brilliant writer but sort of brooding and dark and I never—you probably know from reading the Shell Scott books, they're light and happy-go-lucky and you're supposed to feel better when you finish reading one. With Thompson, and a lot of Cornell Woolrich, a man I admire vastly, greatly, I should have mentioned him earlier about the people who affected me and writers I love—they often would make you feel worse. You almost wish you hadn't read the book because you were down and depressed. I don't read much of that if I can avoid it.

Lupoff: Let's talk about Shell Scott himself and the kind of cases he got involved with. Give us a quick physical description.

Prather: He's 6 feet 2 inches tall, weighs 205 or 206 pounds depending on what I put down when I'm writing that book and how I feel. He has short cropped white hair that stands straight up about one inch in the air as if it's repelled by a magnet inside his head and they are wire brushes. He's got steely gray eyes, he likes to call them steely gray. He's very muscular and bronzed, and tan and strong, just a lot like me as you can tell. (laughter)

Lupoff: However your nose has not been broken and reset wrong.

Prather: No, it's set right as you can see. He's had a little clip shot from his ear, he likes rare prime rib, beautiful women, carries a .38 Colt special, a little double action revolver. And otherwise he's just a normal all-American boy.

Lupoff: And he had been in the Marine Corps where you were in the Merchant Marine.

Prather: I was in the Merchant Marine, right, he was a Marine. I thought it was more suitable to a man who was going to shoot a lot of people in my books to not be working the black gang as I did below decks of a ship.

Lupoff: The cases he gets involved with tend to be a little bit offbeat. I read one of your short stories just the other day which involves a beautiful model in a swimming pool full of purple soap suds.

Prather: Oh, yes, "Zing."

Lupoff: With the secret ingredient, SX21.

Prather:Yes, which is nothing but air, and it sounds sexy. The reason, you see, why the books and even some of the stories are a little odd, and hopefully a little different, is because that's my cherished goal. That's what I try to do. That's why it sometimes takes me so long to get a book written. I spend, from a technical point of view—you as a writer would probably be interested in this—I probably spend as much time plotting and not just writing the first draft of a book.

Plotting, plotting, plotting, trying to get something new, fresh and original. Something a little out of the ordinary. They seem unusual and that's what I'm looking for, and I spend most of my time trying to find something that I can write about that the reader will find new and fresh and interesting and actually, if I can't find it fresh and interesting myself I probably can't write it. So it's easier for me if I can find something a little outré, a little different.

Lupoff: I think I know exactly what you're talking about. We get sick of reading or writing the same things over and over.

Prather: Yeah, you're the first reader. The writer has to be the most interested person in the beginning, and if you're not interested and excited by it and you don't think it's real good—whether it is or not—you've got to *think* it's good when you're doing it—or the reader isn't going to think it's any good either.

Lupoff: *Dagger of Fle*sh involves some hypnotism and a man with an invisible parrot on his shoulder who is only there for one hour a day.

Prather: Yeah, well I was very interested in hypnosis back in the early fifties when I wrote the book. It was originally written as a Shell Scott book and then I believe it was Fawcett that wasn't happy with it, so my agent Scott Meredith sold it to another publisher. I had to change the hero from Shell Scott to another name—Mark Logan.

I don't think it has quite the same pizzazz of Shell Scott, but then it wasn't going to be published by the people who published the Shell Scott books. The long story is that later when Gold Medal at Fawcett wanted all my books under the one imprint they bought that book and I changed it from Mark Logan back to Shell Scott.

Lupoff; So there's another version of this book.

Prather: There is another version that's in the garage when I unpack the boxes that all my books are in. Falcon originally published it and this has got to be Mark Logan, so later when it came out as a Fawcett book I did the work and made it Shell Scott again. I think it came out as a Crest in those days because I wasn't being published by Fawcett any more.

Lupoff: Who was Amelia?

Prather: Amelia. She's an absolutely gorgeous, sort of ample lady that someone unknown painted a garish nude of, and Shell Scott found it in a pawn shop and she now graces the wall of his apartment in L.A. In fact, if you step into this bathroom you'll see a sort of Amelia glancing over her shoulders, on the wall.

Lupoff: And Shell Scott keeps fish?

Prather: Tropical fish. Yes. That's partly because we, my wife Tina and I, had a whole lot of tropical fish back in the early fifties. We grew them, raised them, made little babies out of them, fed them brine shrimp and organic foods and made them very healthy and horny and they had lots of little babies. We spawned some neons and some egglayers and a whole lot of live-bearers like guppies. And loved them. Still do. I may get another tank or two and enjoy them like Shell does.

Lupoff: Well I was particularly interested because my wife Pat raises fish and I've got sort of a second-hand education in tropical fish just through what she has in the house.

Prather: They're a great delight.

Lupoff: When I was reading some of the references in your books I thought, now this is not something off the wall, he knows about these fish because he's got it all right.

Prather: Sure, we had them for years and want to get them again.

Lupoff: One of the books you did for Fawcett which you mentioned earlier was *Double in Trouble* written with Stephen Marlowe—who incidentally is Milton Lesser—an older science fiction writer who became the younger mystery writer Stephen Marlowe.

Prather: I knew him only as Stephen Marlowe and I didn't know until there was an interview done by Steve Mertz, I think for *Mystery Scene*, that it was Milton Lesser. I just knew him as Stephen Marlowe, met him as Stephen Marlowe and wrote with him: as Stephen Marlowe. The way this happened, this was the only book I did in collaboration and I probably won't do it again—although it was a good collaboration with Marlowe—or Lesser.

We were both clients of Scott Meredith at that time and I got a letter from Scott Meredith saying that Steve Marlowe, whose books I knew and was also published by Fawcett, were selling very well. They were books about Chet Drum and some others he did. He sort of specialized in exotic and foreign locales in a lot of his books. He did a lot of research in, say, Germany or Switzerland and so on.

The proposal was made to me that we try a book together using both my hero Shell Scott and his hero Chet Drum, alternating chapters, and see what came of it. I was a little dubious but I said, Well, it's always better to say yes and find out later you're wrong than to say no and never do it.

So we said yes and gave it a try. We did it primarily by mail, I'd write a chapter, send it to Marlowe, he'd write a chapter and send it to me, and without going into all the correspondence that went on for nearly a year, we staggered to the end of a pretty fair book. Then when we worked out all we could by mail Steve or Milt flew out to Laguna, we put him in a motel there down on the beach and we got together at my house every day with Tina doing the typing and Steve and I would hack out the problems.

There were problems because I plot out everything in just enormous detail before I write anything and Marlowe worked in a more free-wheeling way. So we had some problems but we worked them out. Tina typed up the book. We read it the last time and made some changes and sent it off. Dedicated it to Richard Carroll, as I told you, and that was it. It had some good reviews and pretty good success.

Lupoff: Did you and Marlowe get along as well personally, as Shell Scott and Chester Drum in the book?

Prather: Well, better, we didn't come to blows.

Lupoff: They almost killed each other!

Prather: They did. I remember Chet Drum hit Shell in the mouth and he felt something drip to the pavement and he thought it was part of his face dripping to the pavement. Something like that, it's been a long time since I read it, or wrote it. But yeah, they wound up friends but they hit each other a lot of times in between. Steve and I got along fine from the beginning.

Lupoff: A major theme of that book is labor racketeering, and I think I detected something about Dave Beck and Jimmy Hoffa era teamsters in there. Did I read that correctly?

Prather: You may have, but not from my point of view. This came about as a contribution of Steve Marlowe's. He wanted this sort of Beck angle, and I went along with it because there were other things that I wanted in there that he went along with just to satisfy me. This is part of the compromise, the working together and the difference in plotting that I talked about a little while ago.

This basic union angle, that was Steve. I said okay and just worked Shell and my characters into that union angle and other angles we had in the book.

Lupoff: That book was very successful. Why didn't you go on and write more such books?

Prather: For one thing, I had a lot of books to do just solo, and it took an enormous amount of time and effort to do the book with another writer. I'd much prefer working alone than working with another writer. That's probably the basic reason. Also, my other books were doing very well and it was less trouble to do them just sitting in my office with the typewriter on my lap, the way I work.

Lupoff: One other book that you did at Fawcett was *The Comfortable Coffin..*

Prather: Well, *The Comfortable Coffin* I didn't write. I had one story in it, but I edited it. This was the Mystery Writers of America Annual, the thirteenth annual of the MWA, which I belonged to since 1950. They're a writers organization representing practically all the well-known and even not well-known mystery writers. They're not a militant organization but at least there's some companionship there and you find out what other writers are doing and what they're up against.

Each year they put out an annual to make money. That's why people write books. And this, the thirteenth, they asked me to edit. So I got the best stories I could from a lot of other mystery writers, included one of my own, wrote an introduction to it, and that was it. I don't know what its sales have been, it's hard to find out what sales are.

Lupoff: You never felt impelled to do any more anthology work either?

Prather: No, and nobody asked me.

Lupoff: Although, I think *The Comfortable Coffin* is a nice book. I've read it and I enjoyed it.

Prather: I loved the introduction. (laughter)

Lupoff: You did something like 26 books for Fawcett, which is a lot of books, from 1950 to 1964. At which time you switched to Pocket Books. Why did you do that? Did you get unhappy with them or they with you?

Prather: No, I didn't get unhappy with them and they didn't get unhappy with me. What happened was that we made pretty good money and had very good sales with Fawcett over those (1950-1962) dozen years.

A suggestion that I leave Fawcett and move to a new publisher, Pocket Books, came absolutely out of the blue with no previous hint or warning to me from my agent Scott Meredith. He and his brother flew out from New York to see me and I didn't know what it was about. It just happened that during that year when they came out and presented this proposal to me, a new contract to go with Pocket Books, in that year we hadn't made very much money up until August or September. I later learned from my friend and publisher Roscoe Fawcett that they had plans to bring out several reissues and a new book during the course of the year which would have increased our income considerably.

At this time we hadn't made much money. And you know, you have to make money in this business, or any business, or you're not going to remain in business. Scott Meredith presented me with a contract from Pocket Books calling for me to deliver a certain number of books to them and in return they would pay me $75,000 a year in advances against royalties. That was a lot of money in 1962.

Lupoff: It ain't so bad now.

Prather: It ain't so bad now, you beat me to it. I was going to say the same thing. But it was splendid money then and all I had to do was write the books and they were expressing what I thought was a lovely confidence in me by beginning to pay me before they had a book in hand. I was very impressed with that. More impressed than I should have been, for reasons that there is no need to go into now because it's ancient history.

But at any rate, the upshot of it was I did sign a contract to go with Pocket Books in 1962 for ten years. When I left Fawcett I talked to the Fawcett people about it. I asked them if they could match the offer. They couldn't at that time, so I left. I don't think it was necessarily the wisest move I ever made but I did it and have no apology for it now. I made a lot of money and wrote quite a number of books—not as many as I was supposed to for various reasons—but that's the story. My agent presented me with a splendid contract and after some soul-searching and problems I signed it and moved to Pocket.

Lupoff: Okay. Now at Pocket Books and Trident Press, which is essentially the same corporation, they publish hardcover instead of paperback....

Prather: They published four of my books in hardcover.

Lupoff: I have books here published mainly up through the late sixties. One in 1970, one in 1971, one in 1975 and then nothing for eleven years.

Prather: That's right. The contract I had with Pocket Books was a ten year contract and ended in 1973 or 1974. I didn't deliver as many books as I was supposed to deliver in those ten years—but then Pocket Books didn't do all the things they were supposed to do either. There was blame on both sides. But at any rate, without going into the details of that, the contract came to an end just before 1975. I guess it's no secret now that I brought suit against them which was initiated in 1975, when they brought out my last book.

Now, I think it's pretty obvious that when you sue your publisher, they aren't going to publish any more of your books. And the lawsuit against Simon & Schuster/Pocket Books took five years, and eventually I guess you could say I won it. The judgment was in my favor, I wound up with a panel of arbitrators who ruled for me. I got all my books back and some other minor considerations. But that took five years.

Lupoff: What was the basis of the suit? What were you complaining about?

Prather: My complaint was that they had falsely reported the sales of my books in the very peculiar royalty statements that they sent to me and had fraudulently concealed that act from me. That was the basis for the lawsuit. As I say, it took five years to prove that, to prove my case let's say.

Lupoff: You say it was eleven years between books. The last book, *The Sure Thing*, was published in July 1975, just about the time I initiated the lawsuit. The lawsuit took five years and then after that was over it took another five years to find another publisher that wanted to bring out the backlog of old Prather books and new Prather books.

Prather: Finally, through the efforts of Richard Curtis, my splendid agent, and Michael Seidman, whom you know also, a marvelous editor, with Tor Books in New York, largely through their efforts and mine and a few other people, Tor finally brought out *The Amber Effect* in October of last year (1986) and will bring out *Shell-Shock* shortly, and many, many more until I get up to the one hundred I want to write.

Lupoff: Now I read something recently by a critic who said that the Shell Scott books were hugely popular and successful in their day but that they became outmoded or outdated and that's why they were all out-of-print. But that sounds to me like a typical critic's theory, which has nothing to do with the business realities that you've been talking about.

Prather: No, and I don't think the books ever did become outdated. They became out-of-print, that doesn't mean outdated. And as I told you, naturally, when I was engaged in litigation with Pocket Books they weren't going to bring out any more of my books. At the same time I got back all rights to other books through different avenues from other publishers, including Fawcett, so I wound up at the end of those 10 years you mentioned between books with all rights to my books, but no publisher, until Tor.

The books just stopped, not because people stopped buying them, they were selling enormously at the very end up until 1975. Interestingly the books with Fawcett were selling more than the new books published by Pocket, which is one of the bases for my lawsuit.

Lupoff: Why do you think that was?

Prather: I don't think I'll get into that right now. I got into that for five years. Suffice it to say the books were selling very, very well, as long as they were on the stands. When they were no longer on the stands, naturally they didn't sell at all. They weren't available.

Lupoff: A painfully familiar tale, believe me.

Prather: Every writer can tell several tales like this, I think, particularly if they've been in the business for a few years which I have.

Lupoff: How did you live? If this is not getting too personal, did you just have a trunk full of hundred dollar bills that you lived on?

Prather: You can get as personal as you want, I can say it's none of your business if I don't want to answer. So feel free. During the years I was with Pocket Books I was making the good advance money that I mentioned for most of that time. Also I was making a lot of money from Fawcett, because as I say, their books were selling in larger quantities than the ones allegedly being sold by Pocket Books. So we made pretty good money, but we also had substantial expenses and you just want to keep to the point where your income exceeds your expenses.

We were getting to the point where that might not happen, so we did a lot of things. For seven years we grew avocadoes, and I think my wife one year picked twenty tons of avocadoes. A lot of avocadoes. We had a ten acre avocado grove in Fallbrook, California, and grew organic avocadoes—probably the only organically grown avocadoes in the state of California. We made a lot of money on the sale of the farm.

Remember the real estate boom? We bought the grove, ten acres and the house, and worked it for seven years and in seven years it appreciated considerably in value and we sold it and made a lot of money. Thank goodness, because I wasn't making any money from writing.

Lupoff: That's exactly what I had in mind. To put it simply, how do you buy the groceries when you're not able to work at your profession?

Prather: You do something else. As a matter of fact, just before the splendid collaboration between Richard Curtis, my agent, and Michael Seidman, my editor, which I'll mention one more time, I had decided that nobody was going to bring out these books. I had this whole backlog of maybe 40 books that publishers could make millions of dollars from if they wanted to bring them out and sell them again. But I decided that wasn't going to happen, so I had some cards printed up—*Freedom Enterprises, Richard S. Prather—Real Estate Investments*.

I was going to become a real estate tycoon. I took some courses, paid three or four hundred dollars for each course, and learned it was very easy to make millions of dollars. And they lied! They lied! And they lied! (laughter) But you say, how do you buy the groceries? You do something else! We grew avocadoes, I decided to work in real estate, that didn't work so well. You just keep trying something until it does work.

Lupoff: In a recent issue of *The West Coast Review of Books*, Michael Seidman lists sales figures on some of your more successful books. Seventeen of them, including two short story collections, which is just about unprecedented, sold over a million copies. And of those, I looked over the specific numbers, ten of the seventeen are over one and a half million in sales and several of them hover right around the two million copy mark. What's the distribution of these books? The old Fawcetts or the later Pocket Books?

Prather: These are all Fawcetts. This is one of the reasons for the problem that arose with Pocket Books. Until 1962 I was with Fawcett and all those books that are between one and two million copies sold are Fawcett books. For one thing, they paid on print order and they had very few returns of my books. Almost none. I checked, not only with the Fawcett people and editors, but with a lot of wholesalers and distributors. Almost none of my books were returned. They were all sold. This situation changed, let us say, with other publishers. They began reporting enormous returns of the same books. So there's something there.

Lupoff: There's something the matter.

Prather: A lot of writers ask these questions. At any rate, all of these books that are over a million and up to nearly two million in sales were published by Fawcett as Gold Medal Books back in the fifties and sixties. They continued printing them all through the sixties and into the seventies. So that's where those big sales came from.

Lupoff: Siedman lists *Darling It's Death* as the top seller with 1,938,000. With foreign editions included that book must have sold just an astonishing total.

Prather: I have no idea. As I said earlier these are all U.S. sales, for all these books, and the totality of the books, 40,00,000 in all U.S. sales. I imagine *The Comfortable Coffin*, the one you mentioned, has had twelve, fifteen, maybe twenty foreign editions. Each of these foreign editions, it might have been a hardcover, it might have been a paperback, I have the records somewhere, but not in front of me, but it might have sold five or ten thousand copies in each edition. So, you just have to guess, and if I give you a figure it would be absolute fantasy, just as any writer who says my worldwide sales are X number of copies. That's fantasy. Nobody knows.

Lupoff: Now after this you sat down to resume writing with a book called *The Amber Effect*, the new Shell Scott. In terms of your own personal feelings and experience when you returned to writing, what was it like?

Prather: It was great. I'd been wanting to return to writing all the time I was growing avocadoes and looking at real estate. So it was great. But let me correct the history a bit here. When I returned to writing, *The Amber Effect* was already written. *The Amber Effect* was the book that I wrote clear back in 1973 or so and sent to Pocket Books before the lawsuit. As part of the decision in my favor at the end of that litigation I was awarded a little bit of money and all of my books—including the unpublished manuscript of *The Amber Effect*. So that was available for another publisher.

Lupoff: You must have revised *The Amber Effect*. I say this because it involves some sections bordering on science fiction with some highly advanced laser hologram technology and computer technology which couldn't have been written in the early seventies.

Prather: It *was* written in the early seventies.

Lupoff: That's astonishing.

Prather: Well, Shell Scott is astonishing. All I did when I revised it for Tor was check automobile names and dates. I did very little rewriting and almost no rewriting of the technical stuff about lasers and holograms.

Lupoff: That's amazing. That's just startling to me that this is not a newly written book. It reads so up to date, and in fact, ahead of date. Now we go on to *Shell-Shock*—is that correct?

Prather: That's right. That's the book I finished writing last year (1986). It was sent to Michael Seidman in about September. He asked for some changes and revisions and particularly some cutting, because it was an enormously long book. I think it was about 135,000 words, twice as long as most of my books and the longest thing I've ever written. So I cut it down eventually from 135,000 to 120,000 and added about 5,000 words in revision so it's about 125,000 words. It's in the schedule at Tor. They've got a beautiful new cover for it, I've seen the jacket for it here, and it will be out later this year (1987).

Lupoff: Does this book go in a new direction for you that it's that much longer?

Prather: No. Maybe it was so much fun writing again after eleven bloody years that I couldn't stop. And I just kept going and going. It was fun. Of course not all fun, because you're a writer yourself and sometimes you sit there and nothing comes out beautifully, it sticks, it hurts and it's painful, but a lot of it came out smoothly and sweetly, so that part was fun.

Lupoff: What's the appeal of Shell Scott?

Prather: I wish I knew for sure because then I could create three or four more characters that would be just as popular. I think mainly it's the idea that he's a self-starting, self-motivated individual. He's not waiting around for the government to do anything for him, or give him a handout.

He's going to solve his own problems and believes whatever comes to you is your own fault, just as I do, or your own benefit. You get the praise or the blame for whatever happens in your life. And he's strong, a little witty, self-reliant, he encompasses what I call those lovely Emersonian virtues, and I think people like strong, self-reliant individuals who make mistakes, get hit on the head, and don't even get a bump.

Lupoff: He also seems to be very, very attractive to beautiful women who don't wear too many clothes, and occasionally he's twenty-nine years old, once in a while thirty, but he never seems to go past that.

Prather: No, he will be thirty for the next hundred years. When I die at 130, he'll still be thirty. True, he does have an eye, two eyes—if he had nine eyes, he'd have nine eyes for the lovely ladies. He likes these beautiful, bright, busty—lots of B's here, I could think of a couple more but I won't—lovely ladies, and this also gives me something to write about that's fun to write about. Who would want to write about Grandma Moses in all the books? Not that there's anything wrong with her.

Lupoff: This is not politically incorrect or old-fashioned or immoral of you, or is it?

Prather: Politically incorrect? Are you talking about the ladies that Shell likes and the hoods he doesn't like? Well, that doesn't have anything to do with political. Once in a while, in a couple of the books I get political, like *The Trojan Hearse* and *Pattern for Panic*, but mainly I just want people to feel better when they finish one of my books. Maybe a little healthier and happier.

Lupoff: How much do you know about your readers in terms of the ordinary person who plunks down his money and buys your book?

Prather: In the beginning I didn't know anything about them. Except, I know about me, and they're not going to be too much different from me. Over the years I've had a lot of input from people who've read my books, from fans, and fan letters that told me a little bit more. One of the most gratifying things in my life is the pleasure that I apparently have given these people through my books.

I know at the Bouchercon last year a fellow came up to me and thanked me for writing the books that he read to his dying son. They read the books aloud together and laughed and had some good times while he was still alive. It was important to him. That makes it important to me. If just a few people have been affected in a positive, a beneficial way, because of the books I've written then that's just about all the reward you need—along with a lot of money, hopefully.

Lupoff: One of the critics I read recently, referring to the Matt Helm films with Dean Martin, said that based on having read the

Matt Helm books, this was a mistake that was made in Hollywood. Dean Martin should have played Shell Scott and there should have been a Shell Scott series instead. How do you feel about that?

Prather: Well, that's very interesting. I wish there had been a Shell Scott series and Shell Scott movies because oddly enough with all those large sales over the years there's never been a series on TV or a movie made. There have been nibbles and bites, and interestingly that you had mentioned Dean Martin. Back in the late 50's I guess it was, maybe early 60's, a fellow named Marty Jareau, a movie producer, was interested in doing *Find this Woman*. As you know in Hollywood there's just a lot of talk and very little actually happens.

But they were talking about Shell Scott played by either, now get this, Robert Mitchum or Dean Martin. The movie was never made so I don't know if Mitchum would have been better or Martin would have been better, but Martin was suggested as Shell Scott in the movies. I would have settled for Mickey Rooney.

Lupoff: He'd have a little trouble playing Shell Scott.

Prather: That's true.

Lupoff: Who would you pick today if there were such a series?

Prather: I wish I could remember. There was a short-lived series on TV about three years ago in which there was a blonde, good-looking young guy. I think his name was Marshall Colt. He was the sort of second lead on the cop show. If I got his name right, he would have been great. Other than that I think a new face, a new character so he's not identified with other roles. But he'd have to be big, and young, and strong and laugh a lot.

Lupoff: That sounds right to me. That combination, somebody with the big, brawny physique, but with the light touch in his character.

Prather: Yeah, a happy guy. He's got to be happy and joke a little and not take life too seriously.

Lupoff: Now that Richard S. Prather has returned to the delight of us fans from your prior incarnation, how have your new readers responded to this? Are they buying *The Amber Effect*? Is it getting reaction?

Prather: You'd have to ask Tom Doherty, or Michael Seidman or somebody back at Tor Books because one of the big problems in the business from the writer's point of view is that all kinds of things go on in New York, or across the country, with an author's books, and the author is not informed except once every 6 months when he gets his royalty statement. So I don't really know how it's doing. I confidently expect that it is chugging along just like the other books did in the three decades and more since 1950. I expect particularly when they get into paperback, the sales will be like those you were referring to that I had with Fawcett almost thirty-five years ago.

Lupoff: When will this paperback edition be out?

Prather: The paperback of *The Amber Effect* will be out later this year (1987) but again, writers are not informed as fully as they should be. It's one of my crusades that I have temporarily set aside.

Lupoff: Thank you for a most enlightening and amusing interview.

THE SWORD OF ALDONES

Despite a quarter century of producing science fiction, Marion Zimmer Bradley has only recently been recognized by any organized branch of the science fiction community. This community has become widespread, encompassing such diverse forms as publishing, television, motion pictures and recording. However, for present purposes the community may be regarded as comprising three major groups: the professionals (primarily authors, but also editors, illustrators, publishers, and critics); the fans (who may be defined as those readers whose enthusiasm leads them to participate in organized activities such as conventions and clubs); and the academics who have in recent years so enthusiastically albeit belatedly chosen to embrace science fiction as literature.

Bradley has never won a Science Fiction Achievement Award, or "Hugo," the major token of recognition given by the fans since 1953 at their annual World Science Fiction Conventions. She was a finalist among the nominees only once, and that was for *The Sword of Aldones* (1962). She has never been designated Guest of Honor at a World Science Fiction Convention nor has she received a Nebula Award, the annual presentation of the Science Fiction Writers of America for literary achievement.

She has been the recipient of two of the less widely publicized and prestigious trophies of science fiction. One is the "Invisible Little Man," a presentation of the Elves, Gnomes and Little Men's Science Fiction, Chowder and Marching Society. This organization, less formally known as the Little Men, draws its name from the classic comic strip *Barnaby* by the late Crockett Johnson. The organization has a long-standing informal tie with the University of California at Berkeley. The "Invisible Little Man" is reserved specifically for persons who have been inexplicably overlooked in the presentation of other science fiction-related honors.

Coincidentally, Bradley received both the "Invisible Little Man" and the "Forry" in 1976. The latter award, named for pioneer science fiction enthusiast Forrest J Ackerman, is presented by the Los Angeles Science Fantasy Society, also as recognition of those otherwise overlooked.

Finally, in a period when academic dissertations, critical monographs, full-length studies and cooperative symposia have been devoted to many science fiction authors, Bradley has been virtually ignored.

Yet on a popular level—and despite the failure of the fan community to do her honor on other than a local and rather low-keyed basis—Bradley is an author of consistent and growing acceptance. Her books invariably sell well and are avidly collected. They generally get a favorable reception in the fan press, though professional reviews have been limited by Bradley's own preference for paperback publication. This preference is based on a desire to gain rapid access to a mass audience, as well as on a long-standing loyalty to one editor, Donald A. Wollheim, who has been associated with paperback publishing since the beginning of Bradley's career as an author.

In past years the ephemeral quality of paperback publishing has caused most of Bradley's books to go out of print, creating a premium market for them among used book dealers. More recently, however, almost all of Bradley's books have been reissued, to the relief of her younger fans. It is a not uncommon sight at science fiction conventions and at signing parties sponsored by booksellers to see fans approach with stacks of books seeking Bradley's signature on their often tattered title pages.

Although this disparity between the lack of official recognition and Bradley's great popularity with readers is puzzling at first observation, there are several reasons for it.

First there is the nature of Bradley's works themselves. Virtually every science fiction novel she has written (and Bradley is primarily a novelist, although she has produced several dozen short stories in the course of her career) is basically an action-adventure story. They concentrate on plot and physical action rather than on the examination of character or society. There is also an emphasis on the color and "wonder" of the setting.

Although there is nothing illegitimate or disrespectable about using the action-adventure format for a novel, especially a science fiction novel, it is not the type of story which attracts heavy academic or critical attention or literary honors. More often than not, these rewards are reserved for works that place their primary emphasis on character development, social analysis and commentary, moral and philosophical questions, or on ethics and problems of political and social policy.

In fact, the strong adventure-story orientation of Bradley's novels and her failure to employ overt sexual descriptions or use strong language in dialogue or internalization has led to the categorization of these books, by such critics as have taken note of them at all, as quasi-juvenile fiction.

This criticism—if criticism it be—is not wholly without merit. One observer has described the typical Bradley fan as "a fat 13-year-old wearing a cape." If this is an apt description, it certainly does not in itself make Bradley's works unworthy of attention; rather, it behooves the observer to ask *why* Bradley's books are so popular, and *why* they attract the audience they do. For starters, the books offer images of adventure, excitement, and romance which would appeal naturally to readers encountering the pains and dislocations of early adolescence. A similar audience has been attracted from time immemorial by certain books, and whether these books were overt juvenile fiction like Robert Louis Stevenson's *Treasure Island* or Madeleine L'Engle's *A Wrinkle in Time,* or allegedly adult fiction like J. R. R. Tolkien's *The Lord of the Rings,* the literary merit of these works is surely not diminished by their appeal to young readers.

A second reason for the lack of critical attention to Bradley's books has been her choice of publishers. Bradley's long-proven commercial appeal suggests that many publishers, including those who publish hardcovers, would be pleased to issue her future works. Nonetheless, only one of her science fiction novels has been issued by a house other than Ace or DAW. This was *The Colors of Space* (1963), published by the now-defunct Monarch Books. The reason for this break, Bradley explained in a recent interview, was that she had done a number of non-science fiction books for Monarch, and that publisher asked her for some science fiction as well. Her regular science fiction publisher at the time was Ace Books, and she felt that she had been providing material to Ace as fast as it could be used—thus, the one book for Monarch.

Bradley's editor at Ace was Donald A. Wollheim. She felt an intense loyalty to Wollheim, and when he left Ace to found DAW Books—the name of the company is an acronym of his initials—she was quick to follow. Unfortunately for Bradley's critical recognition, neither Ace nor DAW is widely regarded by critics and readers as a prestigious or even as a "serious" publisher.

Yet both of these houses—especially Ace Books during the late 1950s and early 1960s—provided early exposure, encouragement, and financial support for many beginning novelists. Some of these, of course, fell by the wayside while others achieved a minimal level of competence that they have maintained ever since. Only a few outgrew their humble origins to achieve significant success and recognition, and in the course of doing so, they moved on to more prestigious, "serious" publishers. These few "alumni" include Robert Silverberg, Harlan Ellison, Samuel R. Delany, Ursula K. Le Guin, R.A. Lafferty, and Thomas M. Disch.

It is instructive to trace the path followed by one of these "Wollheim alumni," Ursula K. Le Guin. Le Guin's first appearance as a novelist was as the author of half of an Ace Double. (These are a line of books invented by Wollheim, in which two novels or collections are printed and bound back-to-back and upside-down, so that the reader sees the "front cover" any way he holds the book.)

From the Ace Double, Le Guin graduated to a single Ace novel, still under Wollheim's editorship. From this she progressed to an Ace Special, a premium paperback line edited by Terry Carr that placed a greater emphasis on literary values and less of the flavor of the old pulp magazines (Wollheim's origin) than the standard Ace product (note that the publisher chose to segregate "serious" books under a separate rubric).

Finally, Le Guin outgrew Ace altogether. Her recent juveniles have appeared under the imprints of Atheneum (in hardcover) and Bantam Books (in paperback). Her adult books have been issued by Harper & Row and by Berkley/Putnam (hardcover) and by Avon and Berkley Medallion (paperback). Le Guin's progress to increasingly prestigious publishers has paralleled (or has been paralleled by) increasing commercial and critical success.

Marion Zimmer Bradley, by contrast, has placed all of her science fiction books with Ace or DAW with the exception of her one placement with Monarch—and all because of Bradley's strong sense of personal loyalty to Donald A. Wollheim.

For many years the editor-in-chief at Ace Books, Wollheim gave Bradley her initial encouragement and exposure as a novelist in the United States. Consequently, she remained loyal to him (except for one temporary estrangement, which will be addressed) throughout his association with that publisher. When Wollheim left Ace Books in 1971 to found DAW Books, one Bradley manuscript *(The Endless Voyage)* was already "in the mill" at Ace, and was issued by Ace after Wollheim's departure. All of Bradley's science fiction written since *The Endless Voyage* has been issued by Wollheim's DAW Books. Had Bradley moved on to more seriously regarded publishers upon leaving Ace, she might herself have become more seriously regarded as a novelist, despite her preference for action-adventure stories.

A final possible reason for Bradley's failure to attain due recognition—in the science fiction community at least—lies in her own roots. Within a few years of the founding of *Amazing Stories* (1926) and a series of similar periodicals, "science fiction fandom" as a self-aware and relatively cohesive institution had come into being. It was as a member of that fandom in the 1940s that Marion Zimmer Bradley first became visible in the science fiction community. She participated in local fan clubs, published "fanzines," attended science fiction conventions, was a member of the Fantasy Amateur Press Association and other fan organizations. One of these organizations was a juvenile club called Young Fandom. In addition to Bradley, its members included Rick Sneary and Lin Carter, later well known as an author and editor of fantasies.

Many recent and present science fiction writers have emerged from within the ranks of fandom, as have a smaller number of editors, illustrators, agents, booksellers and even publishers. On the face of the matter, one would assume that a member of the fan community, making good as a science fiction writer, would be regarded as a celebrity, even as a hero or heroine, by the mass of fandom. In fact, however, the response tends to be less one of "home town boy (or girl) makes good," than of the famous verse from Matthew, "A prophet is not without honor, save in his own country."

In his autobiographical essay, "Sounding Brass, Tinkling Cymbal," Robert Silverberg makes precisely this complaint—i.e., that it took him many years of professional authorship before the fans would take him seriously as a writer because he had previously been one of them. He was not regarded as a "real" pro. Similarly, Marion Bradley mentions that it has taken her many years to be regarded as a "real" professional writer, rather than "just a fan who got lucky."

While the "fan-turned-pro" procedure is thus seen to have in it perils to recognition, it is not wholly negative in its impact on the writer. Of course, it is entirely possible for an outsider to come to science fiction bringing a fresh perspective, and to write science fiction of commercial and/or critical worth. Examples in recent years include Michael Crichton, Kingsley Amis, Howard Fast, and (Bradley's own favorite example) the author and critic Joanna

Russ. However, in contrast, the fan-turned-pro is a "second generation science fiction writer," while the newly arrived outsider is "first generation."

The second generation writer is one who grew up reading science fiction and participating in fandom; in the case of Bradley and other writers of her (chronological) generation, this meant reading the science fiction of the pulp magazines. Some or all of the formative cultural influences of Bradley's generation of SF writers were science fictional in nature, and when they began to write it was not with the idea of creating or discovering a new thing of some sort, but with the feeling of carrying on a tradition—and these differences in attitude and influence show in the writing. What will be introduced with ruffles and flourishes, and what will be taken for granted; what will be placed at center stage, spotlighted, exclaimed over and explicated in full detail; and what will be regarded as merely part of the stage setting?—these factors will be treated differently by a Crichton and a Silverberg, by a Russ and a Bradley.

Born June 3, 1930, Marion Zimmer was raised on a farm just outside Albany, New York. Bradley was her married name for some years. Although that marriage ended in divorce and she is presently married to Walter Breen, she retains the name Marion Zimmer Bradley for professional purposes.

As a schoolgirl she found little of interest in the usual round of dates, dances and football games that preoccupied her contemporaries. Consequently she sought friendships through correspondence with people outside the usual circle of schoolmates. She presently recalls her closest friends of this period as being Steve Weber, Thyril Ladd, Dorothy Quinn, and Rick Sneary.

Through Weber in particular she became an admirer of Mary Gnaedinger, one of the first women to edit a pulp magazine in the field of science fiction and fantasy. Gnaedinger was the editor *of Famous Fantastic Mysteries* and its spin-off publication *Fantastic Novels. Famous Fantastic Mysteries,* despite its name, was not a mystery magazine in the usual sense, but a magazine of science fiction and fantasy, with emphasis on the latter. The bulk of its contents consisted of reprinted (and often condensed) novels of fantastic adventure. Through a corporate succession, most of the files of the old Frank A. Munsey pulps were available to Gnaedinger for reprinting. These pulps—*Argosy, All-Story* and *Cavalier* being the most prominent—featured material by many significant fantasy writers, including Abraham Merritt, Max

Brand, George Allan England, Austin Hall, Homer Eon Flint, Murray Leinster, Otis Adelbert Kline, Francis Stevens, Charles B. Stilson, J.U. Giesy, and Ray Cummings. In addition, Gnaedinger reprinted outside material by authors ranging from Ayn Rand to Franz Kafka to H. Rider Haggard.

Steve Weber was a sometime science fiction fan and a fantasy book collector who provided much source material for Gnaedinger's use in *Famous Fantastic Mysteries*. Thyril Ladd, Dorothy Quinn and Rick Sneary were all science fiction fans.

Dorothy Quinn, Bradley recalls, saw *The Sword of Aldones* in its earliest manuscript form, long before Bradley had the courage to show it to any professional editor (and long before she felt that it was in any condition to be shown).

Sneary, a longtime fan residing in the Los Angeles area, became a correspondent of Bradley's when they both sent letters to the old *Planet Stories*. The magazine included correspondents' addresses in its readers' columns, and many such relationships developed through this medium. The friendship between Bradley and Sneary developed such warmth that Bradley dedicated *The Sword of Aldones* to Sneary, even lthough it was years before the postal friendship resulted in a face-to-face meeting.

As is the case with many science fiction fans, Bradley sought to emulate the writers she admired (in the sense of entering their profession, not imitating their styles or themes). Her favorite authors of the then-burgeoning pulp school included Catherine L. Moore, Henry Kuttner, Theodore Sturgeon, and Jack Vance. These authors she read in magazines oriented toward colorful adventure—like *Planet Stories* and *Startling Stories*—rather than in the most famous science fiction magazine of that era, *Astounding* (later renamed *Analog*). *Astounding*'s orientation was more heavily technological.

In the area of pure fantasy, Bradley remembers that she never liked *Astounding*'s companion magazine, *Unknown* (later *Unknown Worlds)* "because I don't think the writers ever really liked or believed in fantasy." She preferred the longer-lived *Weird Tales*.

Favorite works included the Jirel of Joiry and Northwest Smith stories of Moore, *The Ship of Ishtar* (1926) by Merritt, and *The Dying Earth* (1950) by Vance. She states that "Henry Kuttner formed my mind ... what I tried to do in *The Sword of Aldones* [was] to make you feel that these are *real* people, that this is a world that might actually *be* someday. This is what happened when I started reading Henry Kuttner. There was just enough scientific rationalization that I could feel, *My God, these people are real.* Even if some of them were werewolves and things. It was a *real* werewolf, a man who had something weird changing his bones so that he could actually change."

Other writers whom she admired at the time were H. Rider Haggard, Sax Rohmer, the members of the Order of the Golden Dawn, and Mary Renault, in the earlier years of her output.

Bradley's first two sales were to a short-lived magazine titled *Vortex Science Fiction.* (This magazine had a brief career in 1953 and is not to be confused with *Vertex Science Fiction,* published in Los Angeles in the early 1970s, or with another *Vortex Science Fiction* published in Great Britain beginning in 1977.) Bradley's recollection is that the original *Vortex* operated on so small a budget that no major literary agent would deal with its editor. That editor, ironically, was Chester Whitehorn, who had served as editor of the pulpwood *Planet Stories* in 1945-46.

Whitehorn appealed to a number of minor agents, including Bradley's, to "send us anything you have and we'll put it all in a pile and read everything we get and keep the least worst." Whitehorn bought Bradley's story "Keyhole" for $12—her first professional sale. Shortly Whitehorn accepted another story, Bradley's first expressing any form of feminist concern. This story was written as "For Women Only," but was published under the shortened title, "Women Only." Both "Keyhole" and 'Women Only" appeared in *Vortex's* second (and final) issue, October, 1953. "Women Only" dealt with a female android. Androids, although endowed with sexual capacity, were regarded as universally sterile, yet the one in Bradley's story was able to bear a child.

Her first *significant* sale, in Bradley's judgment, was the novelette "Centauras Changeling." This story was also sold in 1953 and appeared in the April, 1954 issue of *The Magazine of Fantasy and Science Fiction,* which was by that time Bradley's favorite magazine.

The history of her first published novel, *The Door Through Space* (1961), is more complicated. Originally entitled *Bird of Prey,* it was written at novel-length, revised into a shorter format and then published in *Venture Science Fiction* in May, 1957. *(Venture,* now defunct, was a companion publication of *The Magazine of Fantasy and Science Fiction.)* It was then sold to a publisher in Europe and appeared in a German translation. Still later, after Bradley had established herself with Wollheim at Ace Books,

Wollheim asked to see the novel. In the interim, Bradley's carbon copy of the manuscript had been lost, and she had to reconstruct the novel by retranslating the German version to English. The book appeared, eventually, under the title in English *The Door through Space.*

Another novel, *Seven from the Stars,* had appeared in *Amazing Stories* in 1960. This was Bradley's first Ace book and her first book published in the English language.

Despite the bibliographic citation *of Bird of Prey/The Door through Space* as Bradley's first published book, and of *Seven from the Stars* as her first English-language book publication, she herself regards *The Sword of Aldones* as her first book— "absolutely first" in her own words.

She conceived the book, she states, at the age of 15. This would place the event in 1945 or early 1946, seven or eight years before the *Vortex* sales and eleven or twelve years before any form *of Bird of Prey* was published. *The Sword of Aldones* gestated for over three years before the author actually began writing it. She was then age 19. The first complete draft was finished in 1949— this was the version seen by Dorothy Quinn.

In 1956 Bradley "sold" *The Sword of Aldones* to Raymond A. Palmer. Palmer had been a pulp science fiction author (and fan) as early as 1930. He had been tapped to become the editor *of Amazing Stories* when that magazine was taken over by the Ziff-Davis Publishing Company in 1938 and remained with Ziff-Davis until 1949, when he left to found his own publication, *Other Worlds Science Stories.* Operating on a budget that would make even *Vortex* look generous, Palmer often failed to pay his authors even token rates. Palmer also had the regrettable habit of holding stories in inventory for very lengthy periods, thus affording the authors not only no payment, but not even the publicity value of publication. Palmer held *The Sword of Aldones* for fully five years.

By 1961, Bradley's earliest novels had been well received as "halves" of Ace Doubles. Consequently, when Bradley sold Ace *The Planet Savers,* editor Wollheim asked her if she had another novel with which he might make up an Ace Double, rather than pairing Bradley with another author. She retrieved *The Sword of Aldones* from Palmer, revised it for Wollheim, and the double volume of *The Planet Savers* and *The Sword of Aldones* was issued in 1962.

The revisions of 1961 were mainly general polishing, but a major new element was introduced as well: the loss of one hand by the protagonist Lew Alton. In the preceding versions of the novel, Alton's face had been scarred, but Bradley had used the device of facial scarring in other works by 1961, and to provide a newer (and obviously far more powerful) element, she introduced the further injury.

Although *The Sword of Aldones* was published as the "back half" of *The Planet Savers,* it proved the more popular work almost from the outset. It was a finalist in the Hugo nominations the following year. The other nominees were *A Fall of Moondust* by Arthur C. Clarke, *Little Fuzzy* by H. Beam Piper, *The Man in the High Castle* by Philip K. Dick, and *Sylva* by "Vercors" (Jean Bruller).

Bradley did not expect to win the award, and in fact campaigned for another candidate by asking fans to cast their votes for *Little Fuzzy*. However, neither Piper's book nor Bradley's gained the award, which was won by *The Man in the High Castle*.

Bradley does not consider *The Sword of Aldones* a particularly good book. In 1972 she wrote a critical article in which she stated some of her own objectives in the writing of the book and attempted to gain an understanding of its great popularity (despite her own feeling that it "was not a very good book"):

Bradley:

"I explored one theme, rare before and since in SF and even rarer in fantasy or sword-and-sorcery; the idea that, as the hero has more capabilities than the average man, he also has more capacity to feel strongly about what happens to him. Lew Alton, in this book, is living with the knowledge that years ago, saving his people from an extra-dimensional horror, his young and much-beloved wife had been killed in the crossfire.

The usual 'hero,' needless to say, usually regarded this sort of catastrophe as just part of the scenery. Conan's various girls get stabbed, eaten by dragons, or strangled by Bems with monotonous frequency; he never seems to remember the litter of bodies in the wake of his sword. The villains seem to care even less. Yet I reflected that one side's evil rebel is the other side's valiant freedom fighter; the villain of any given story would be the hero of his own. If they happened both to genuinely love the girl who died, the seeds of a resolution to their blood-feud lay in that very fact.

"So I seem to have originated the villain who is not evil or wicked, but just the hero of the counter-establishment. I hoped, actually, to provoke comment as to whether the villain was not a better man, fighting for a more worthy cause, than the hero, and the hero simply a good man fighting misdirectedly for a lost cause. Robert E. Lee is a hero, but nevertheless he fought on the side of tyranny and slavery.

"I was also sick and tired of the hero who took all his slashes and scars for granted. In most books the interesting scars on the faces of the heroes are just what the old manuals on how to write fiction used to call "a tag of character"; it never occurred to anyone that a scarred hero might actually suffer self-conscious agonies about how messed-up he looked. And also, Lew Alton had lost a hand, and I went right out of the hero tradition by making him resent it and even have trouble actually handling things."

To the extent that Bradley achieved these objectives *The Sword of Aldones* is successful as a novel, from the viewpoint of art. From the commercial viewpoint, the yardstick is presumably some product of total sales and years in print. *The Sword of Aldones* has done amazingly well by both of these measurements.

As for the failings of the book as seen by its author, Bradley recently characterized these broadly as "puppy fur problems." This is completely understandable if it is remembered that *The Sword of Aldones* is the conception of a 15-year-old mind. The book is full of the romanticism, posturing, and overstated dramatics to which the adolescent mind is subject. Even though the book was not actually written until the author was 19, and revised for publication when she was past 30, it is still the book conceived by the-author-as-15-year-old.

From a more literary-technical point of view, Bradley assesses the shortcomings of the book in these words:

Bradley:
"Especially in the beginning of the book, too many episodes are happening. In the first three chapters of the book too many people keep turning up for all the wrong reasons. And disappearing again. And you never really did find out why it was so urgent to get the gun away from Lew. You never found out what all the sound and fury was about.

"It was ill-conceived and not too well thought out. It was a lot of adventure but there wasn't too much behind [it]. It was all busy-work."

And yet, the book has its appeal. Once more, Bradley assesses this as a function of its *urgency.* This she attributes in part to the first-person narration (the narrator, Lew Alton, seems to live in a state of uninterrupted crises) and in part to the emotion, unusual if not unique in adventure science fiction at the time of *The Sword of Aldones* (and not overly common today). "There's the poor man bleeding all over the page," Bradley says, "you *have* to care."

~ ~ ~ ~ ~

Today it is not uncommon for women to write science fiction from the viewpoint of male characters. Bradley does so frequently although not exclusively. The basis for this custom lies in the marketing and readership of science fiction. This audience for science fiction has been, traditionally, overwhelmingly male, just as the readership of romances and neo-gothics has been overwhelmingly female. While the proportion of female science fiction readers has increased dramatically in recent years, the audience is still predominantly male, and gender bias in stories continues to reflect this fact.

Exceptions have appeared, from Judith Merril's *Shadow on the Hearth* (1950) to Joanna Russ's *The Female Man* (1975). The use of a female protagonist in a science fiction or fantasy novel by a male author is even more unusual, although exceptions are not unknown: *The Witches of Karres* by James H. Schmitz (1966), *Rissa Kerguelen* by F.M. Busby (1976), and *Lisa Kane* (1976) and *Sword of the Demon* (1977) by the author of this Introduction.

Bradley recalls her early attempts to break the stricture of male protagonists only, in adventure-oriented science fiction—and the result: "In those days (late 1950s and early 1960s) you couldn't write science fiction from a woman's point of view and have any real chance of getting it published. I tried it once and couldn't get it published. That was a novel called *Window on the Night.* It's never been published and it never will be. The science became obsolete."

In regard to the artistic challenge of writing from the viewpoint of the opposite sex, Bradley has stated: "Can a man write from a woman's point of view? Can a woman write from a man's point of view? If anyone still has the nerve to ask that question after reading a story by Hal Clement in which he writes from the viewpoint of a disembodied alien, I think they should be ashamed of themselves."

Quite aside from its intrinsic values, its virtues and faults as a piece of literature, *The Sword of Aldones* is of special interest because it was the first novel Bradley wrote. In it she felt constrained to abide by the rules of heroic adventure writing as they stood at the time it was conceived, 1945.

Thus, the action is carried by Lew Alton and Robert Kadarin, both men. Female characters, in the heroic adventure tradition, existed primarily to be threatened, frightened, captured, rescued—in short, their roles were totally *passive*. In addition, they might provide emotional support and occasional physical assistance to male characters, and they might offer a small degree of sex appeal for the mild titillation of adolescent male readers. There was almost never any "real" sex in such stories; this had to be supplied by the reader's imagination.

Bradley maintains that this female passivity is no longer a feature of her works, and cites the transitional novel for this point as *Winds of Darkover* (1970). Nonetheless, even in *The Sword of Aldones,* Bradley chafed under the requirement. She gave her female characters as much freedom and rebelliousness against the traditional submissive role of women in this type of story as she felt able to do in the era and the category in which she worked.

Thus, when the Comyn or ruling council of Darkover debates the arrangement of a politically expedient marriage for the young woman Linnell Aillard, her guardian—also a woman—Callina Aillard, hurls defiance at the council. And she does so not on the grounds that the council's prospective direction is unwisely chosen, but on the grounds that the council has not the power to dictate to herself or the younger woman. "Linnell is *my* ward!" Callina asserts. "This is no matter for council meddling!"

Further, while there is no explicit "onstage" sex in the novel, Bradley makes it clear that the attractive young woman Dio Ridenow takes lovers of her own selection and without official sanction. This in itself was revolutionary for a science fiction novel of the time of *The Sword of Aldones.* And to make it even more so, Bradley portrays Dio neither as a slut nor as a scheming adventuress utilizing her wiles to gain unworthy ends, but as a sparkling and thoroughly sympathetic figure who ultimately "gets the leading man" by marrying Lew Alton!

For these reasons *The Sword of Aldones* offers valuable insights into the early attitudes and later development of its author, and into the standards and conventions of adventure science fiction during the 17-year period from the novel's conception to its publication.

Mention was made previously of the long and loyal relationship between Bradley as author and Donald A. Wollheim initially as editor and later as editor and publisher. Bradley has written material other than science fiction for editors other than Wollheim. She mentions having written "a whole lot of gothics," and without providing a bibliography mentions that these appeared from a number of publishers, including Berkley Medallion and the now defunct Lancer Books, under the Marion Zimmer Bradley byline.

She was also the author of a number of "vaguely risqué" volumes for the now long-defunct Monarch Books in the late 1950s and early 1960s. Bradley does not object to mentioning the existence of these books, but declines to reveal their titles or the byline or bylines under which they appeared. She does state that they were *not* credited to Marion Zimmer Bradley.

This does leave one anomaly, *The Colors of Space,* which was also published by Monarch (1963). This book was written by Bradley and sold to Monarch approximately at the time of her temporary falling-out with Wollheim. To the suggestion that the sale of the book to Monarch was connected with a dispute with Wollheim, Bradley responds with a denial: "Not really—[it was] just that they asked for a book and I needed the cash."

But a dispute with Wollheim did take place, and its circumstances are worth noting.

The estrangement resulted from Wollheim's tampering with the conclusion of the American edition of *Bird of Prey/The Door through Space.* This was published by Ace Books under Wollheim's editorship. What Wollheim had done was to extend the final paragraph of the book by two sentences. While this sounds like a minor, even a trivial, case of tampering, the additional sentences serve to reverse totally the philosophical charge of the novel. It is not surprising that Bradley was furious. For the record, then, and with the enthusiastic concurrence of Marion Zimmer Bradley, the following lines, with which *The Door through Space* concludes, should be noted as *not* her work. Further, she disclaims, disowns and denounces them:

> *Now, after all my years on Wolf, I understood the desire to keep their women under lock and key that was its ancient custom. I vowed to myself as we went that I should waste no time*

finding a fetter shop and having forged therein the perfect steel chains that should bind my love's wrists to my key forever.

Eventually, Bradley and Wollheim became reconciled and she resumed writing for him. In fact, she states that the reconciliation did not take very long, once Wollheim had explained the problems on his part which led to his adding the two sentences. "I didn't stay *mad* long . . . " Bradley states, "more upset."

Nonetheless, she has never become reconciled to those two sentences.

AN INTERVIEW WITH RICHARD LUPOFF
by J. Alec West (*Murderous Intent* magazine)

Mel Blanc was known as the man of many voices—Lon Chaney as the man of many faces. Dick Lupoff's multifaceted interests surely qualify him as the man of many hats. He's received nominations for Hugo and Nebula Awards in science fiction, edited fiction and nonfiction books with topics ranging from Edgar Rice Burroughs to comics, penned literary criticisms, interviewed authors and others in the entertainment industry, created the world of Hobart Lindsey and Marvia Plum in a current mystery series . . . the list goes on and on.

~ ~ ~ ~ ~

West: Your multifaceted career path bears a remarkable similarity to that of Anthony Boucher. Did this path come about by conscious design or merely a result of going with the flow?

Lupoff: Anthony Boucher sent me my first rejection slip, 45 years ago. I still have it. I was an ambitious schoolboy and I sent a couple of stories to *The Magazine of Fantasy and Science Fiction*. The rejection slips I received from Boucher—and from his partner, J. Francis McComas—were so wonderfully sympathetic and encouraging that I carry a warm spot in my heart for Tony and Mick. So I find the comparison flattering, but there was certainly no conscious *patterning* of my career on Tony's.

West: Your entry into the mystery genre dates back, at least, to short fiction published in *Mike Shayne Mystery Magazine*. What first drew you into the genre and why?

Lupoff: My first published story featured a private eye named Nick Train. This was published in a mimeographed newspaper at summer camp when I was somewhere around nine years old. When I was in my teens I drifted into the science fiction fan community, so when I started selling fiction it was naturally science fiction. But I always had a fondness for mysteries, and in recent years I've moved back (mostly) into the mystery field. That story in *Mike Shayne* came about in the summer of—I think 1974—

when Michael Kurland and I were collaborating on a novel. We spent a whole summer on the project, researching, planning, and writing. This included some "hot-chair" sessions: one author types until he's exhausted, then the other takes over.

There I am proudly displaying my Cody's Books sweatshirt — another great brick-and-mortar store gone!

One day while sitting on a basement sofa in Michael's house, awaiting my turn, I picked up a calculator and started tinkering with it. A story idea dawned on me, and when I got home I wrote the story, "Killer by Calculation." Next day I showed Michael the manuscript. He did a second draft, adding characters and doubling the length of the story. This version was sold to *Mike Shayne's Mystery Magazine* and appeared as "The Square Root of Dead." We earned $80. Our agent got ten per cent and Michael and I split the remaining money, so we each earned $36. Our collaborative novel failed to find a home, so "The Square Root of Dead" was the sole product of our summer's efforts.

West: Besides writing in the genre you've interviewed other notables in the field like J.A. Jance and Mary Higgins Clark for KPFA in Berkeley, California. I know you do your homework but did they or others you've interviewed ever astound you with information you didn't expect . . . and if so, what information astounded you the most?

Lupoff: My producer and on-air partner, Richard Wolinsky, and I always try to do our homework, and our guests appreciate it. Sometimes by asking unexpected questions you get fascinating answers. For example, Arthur Hailey's story about his RAF fighter-flying experiences in World War Two ... Tony Hillerman's story about stepping on a land mine and suffering leg injuries and temporary blindness ... Margaret Atwood rhapsodizing about her fondness for the "Victorian proto-feminist fantasies of Rider Haggard" ... meeting Don Westlake for the first time in thirty years and picking up a conversation in mid-sentence. Once in a great while we'll have a guest who comes pre-programmed with pat answers, and who refuses to stray from them in an interview. But 99% of our guests are flattered that we've both read their books and researched their careers, and they're almost always forthcoming with wonderful stories.

West: Your "Killer" series of Hobart Lindsey/Marvia Plum mysteries was first introduced years ago but has maintained a popular following. Do you have any clues as to what attracts readers to your particular style?

Lupoff: I don't think it's the writing style of the "Killer" books that makes readers like them. They're written in a deliberately—what Samuel R. Delany calls a "transparent" style. That is, the prose doesn't make a show of itself, doesn't come between the reader and the subject matter of the story. The reader can *see through* the prose and *see* the characters, their actions, feelings, and so forth.

The "Killer" books are—I hope—multi-dimensional, and offer the reader rewards on several levels. They're not just about who knifed Uncle Walter. I try to make my characters real ... give them emotional and intellectual lives, families, interests, desires, fears and aspirations. The late James Blish used to speak of *whole characters* and *functional characters.* The latter have just the qualities and characteristics needed to function in the story. The ship's captain, for instance, is courageous, knowledgeable, experienced, knows how to read a chart and handle his ship.

But a *real* ship's captain *also* has a favorite flavor of ice cream. He's religious (or he's an atheist). He loves opera and hates rock & roll—or vice versa. He collected stamps when he was a child, and he still has a stamp album at home. His all-time favorite movie is "Citizen Kane" and his favorite book is "Go Dog Go" which he read to his children when they were toddlers. You see what I'm driving at?

Now, from the viewpoint of an author, you can't get so carried away with the minutia of your characters' lives that the story gets lost. I made that mistake on one of my early books, and wound up with a manuscript a foot high. My editor wanted me to cut it drastically and I had so much trouble doing that, I finally went back to my outline and wrote the whole book over. That editor was Clyde Taylor, and I learned more about writing from a couple of bloody fights with him than from four years of college. The book finally came together and it was a success, thanks to Clyde's tough attitude. So the relationship between Bart Lindsey and Marvia Plum *matters* to readers.

One woman finished reading *The Cover Girl Killer* and caught up with me in a bookstore and punched me—hard—because of a turn in that ongoing relationship. Several readers have approached me and wanted to discuss Bart's mother and her mental problems. I think, when your readers care that much about your characters, you're doing something right.

Another element in these books is the historical research and background. Some of the *history* in my books, I remember. Some. I participated in. The rest, I can research in ways that others cannot. Let me give you a few examples. The first "Killer" book, *The Comic Book Killer*, deals with comic books of the 1940s and 50s. I spent many hours with Otto Binder, Will Lieberson, Julius Schwartz, and other writers and artists and editors who *made* the comic books of that era. And more recently, of course, I've written for the comics myself. I think the authenticity of my treatment of that subculture gives the book a richness and a credibility that appeals to readers.

The Bessie Blue Killer deals with the Tuskegee Airmen—African American pilots who fought in World War Two—and with survivors of the Port Chicago explosion, a disaster that took place at a naval munitions station in 1944. In researching this book I crawled around inside a B-17 Flying Fortress, a B-24 Liberator, and a B-29 Superfortress. I walked over the ground at Port Chicago where the explosion took place. I interviewed a number of World War Two aviators including Tuskegee Airmen and a Port Chicago survivor who happens to live very near me. I picked up anecdotes and technical details that no other author has ever mentioned.

The Cover Girl Killer deals with the Abraham Lincoln Brigade, the American volunteer unit that fought in the Spanish Civil War between 1936 and 1938. I spent hours taping the recollections of a onetime machine-gunner in the Brigade, and more hours with a fantastic woman who served with the Lincolns as a field-hospital nurse. Her stories could make *M*A*S*H* sound like a church picnic. That all went into the book. Well, I won't go into every book in the series, but every one has involved this kind of research, and I think that readers can *feel* the reality of what's there, the life-changing and heart-changing experiences that these people lived through, and that's far more important, I think, to readers, than "Who Knifed Uncle Walter in the Drawing Room."

West: You seem fascinated with the wartime years of World War Two and I know you grew up during that period. Your personal recollections, please?

Lupoff: Most of the males in my family, especially of my own generation, served their country. We speak that phrase with a wry grin nowadays, but when I was young it was taken seriously. My cousin Aaron was in the Lincoln Brigade and died in Spain. My Uncle Eddy was a B-17 mechanic in England, in World War Two. My brother was in the navy in the 1950s, and I was in the army. My cousin Wally, my cousin Andrew, my cousin Raymond, were all in the army or the navy. None were career military. We all considered it a matter of duty, and we all served. We didn't have to ask what we could do for our country. We knew it, and we did it.

West: Could you expand on your characters, Hobart and Marvia . . . their origins as characters?

Lupoff: Hobart Lindsey was created first, and he was created out of a set of negative characteristics. What I mean is, I wanted a private eye—sort of— but I wanted to *play against type.* The classic hardboiled PI is tough, brave, smart. He packs a gat, drinks hard, and womanizes. He can get beat up tonight and bounce back for more tomorrow. He never questions himself or his actions. Even his name is tough—Spade. Hammer. Stone.

My PI was designed to be an Everyman. Maybe even a little bit less. He's a reluctant dragon. He lives with his mom. He doesn't own a gun, doesn't know how to use one, and doesn't want to learn. He has doubts about himself. And when he gets beaten up and shot in the foot he winds up in a hospital bed. I've always been convinced that the story of an ordinary person facing an extraordinary challenge is far more interesting than that of an extraordinary person facing an ordinary challenge.

Look at the earliest Superman stories. He fought bank robbers. He could outrun their getaway car, stop it with his bare hands, they could shoot him and the bullets would bounce off his chest, and he could knock them silly with one punch. No suspense there. No story.

But when W.C. Fields—Egbert Sousé—in *The Bank Dick* had to catch the robbers... here's this commonplace, mildly addle-pated and frequently tipsy Everyman going up against tough, gun-wielding criminals. There was a story!

Of course, Lindsey has grown a lot over the course of six novels, largely through the influence of Marvia Plum. Marvia was a walk-on character in the first draft of *The Comic Book Killer*. My agent saw the manuscript and called me up:

"Lupoff," he said, "how long have I been your agent?"

"Since the start of my career."

"And I've read everything you've written, haven't I?"

"Pretty much."

"Well I'm telling you that Marvia Plum is the best thing you've ever done, and you *have* to get her onstage more. I don't care how you do it or what she's doing. Let her walk past eating an ice cream cone. Anything. But give her scenes."

And we went from there. Marvia was a composite of three black women I knew over the years. One was a friend of mine in the Army in the 1950s. Another was a co-worker at IBM in the 1960s. A third woman was a co-worker at a government agency in the early 1980s. Each contributed qualities—playfulness and *joie de vivre,* moral courage, professional competence and commitment. And there was Marvia Plum.

West: Hobart's job guarantees him contact with people in positions of wealth and power, common attributes found in novels of bestseller caliber. Are you comfortable continuing a popular mystery series or are you perhaps trying to elevate the series to bestseller proportions?

Lupoff: There are some very serious problems in the marketplace, and I will confess to you that if my wife, Patricia, didn't have a steady job, my income from writing these books would not keep our household afloat.

West: Ah—the official motto of Mystery Writers of America—"Crime doesn't pay—enough."

Lupoff: Exactly. If I could write a bestseller—or even earn a decent living rather than scratch along at sub-minimum wage—I would be thrilled. I'm having a great time writing mysteries. The community of writers, readers, editors, and collectors is full of the most wonderful people I've ever known. I have no trouble with the title of "mystery writer." I just wish I could make a buck.

West: Can you give us a hint on the next baffling case for Hobart and Marvia?

Lupoff: Before I get deeply involved in any major new projects I want to complete the Lindsey/Plum cycle. This is not an open-ended series, but a single mega-novel, eight volumes in length. Each volume—in effect, a long chapter—is a complete murder mystery, with the proverbial beginning, middle and end.

But the mega-novel is not a murder mystery at all. It's a very different kind of story, and you'll have to read all eight books to grasp it fully. Five volumes have been published. The sixth, *The Silver Chariot Killer*, is in production right now. And I've been working on the seventh and eighth. Now, the first seven books are fairly conventional mysteries.

They're all single-viewpoint narratives. They all have very linear plot structures. The crime is discovered on Thursday, the clues are collected on Friday, the suspects are questioned on Saturday, and the solution is revealed on Sunday. All of the historical material is presented in present time by such devices as interviews, reminiscences, and documents. The seventh book, *The Radio Red Killer*, has as its background a radio station, and remember that I've worked in radio since the 1950s, so I know this field pretty well.

But the eighth book will be very different. Its background is the theater and the production of a "lost musical." My friends Lori Leigh Gieleghem and Greg Tiede have got me access to the backstage world in San Francisco, and producer/director Greg MacKellan has agreed to let me sit in on a full production cycle—from casting auditions to opening night. This will actually be a mainstream novel. There will be multiple viewpoints and the story will take place in multiple time-periods, from 1919 to the present day.

The book will include the dual biographies of singer-actress Arabella Ainslee and composer-lyricist Melville Clarke, and will involve Tinpan Alley, Broadway and Hollywood, World War Two, and contemporary America. And there will be a murder and a solution in there, to boot. It's going to be one hell of a novel. And, yes, you *can* interpret that two ways, can't you? It's going to be a big challenge and it's going to be a big gamble. I might crash and burn with this book, or I might get the best book of my life. I'm betting on the latter.

West: And will that be the last we'll see of these characters?

Lupoff: A while ago I did a bookstore appearance with Joe Gores and Linda Grant. The program was moderated by Patricia

Holt, the book editor of the *San Francisco Chronicle*. We got through with a really fine panel discussion and Q&A session, and then Pat Holt surprised the audience by saying, "I have just one more question." Everyone listened attentively. She looked straight at me and said, "Are Bart and Marvia going to get married?"

I said, "I know, but I'm not telling."

She said, "What if you die before you finish writing the series?"

I said, "Don't worry. It's all taken care of." Actually, it wasn't. But I went home that night and opened a computer file and wrote the last paragraph of the last Lindsey/Plum book. My wife and my son both know how to find it.

~ ~ ~ ~ ~

The man of many hats will don two of them quite soon. His next in the Hobart/Marvia series, *The Silver Chariot Killer* is forthcoming from St. Martin's Press. Also, Fedogan & Bremer will release *Before 12:01 and After,* a short-story collection spanning over four decades of Dick's work. Keep an eye out for them at your favorite bookstore. And, keep an eye out for Dick in St. Paul, Minnesota. His science-fiction/ fantasy/horror hat will be apparent when he attends Arcana 1996, and a week later, his mystery hat at Bouchercon 27.

[2013 Update: The Tinpan Tiger Killer *never got written. I started the book, hit a wall, and never did get rolling again. Instead, the eighth-and-final Lindsey and Plum novel was finally published in 2012. It's called* The Emerald Cat Killer *and in my opinion it's the best book in the series. And if I live long enough I may take another crack at that backstage novel, but it will not include Hobart Lindsey or Marvia Plum, both of whom are now enjoying their well-deserved retirements, — RAL]*

ESSAYS

NICE MYSTERIES
(FREDRIC BROWN)
1985

Last Saturday I drove into the city and squeezed into a parking place around the corner from Bruce Taylor's shop. Taylor runs the San Francisco Mystery Bookstore.

It's a tiny store, crammed with a gorgeous jumble of breathtaking collectables and tattered reading copies. A while after I arrived I was invisible, burrowed into a cranny searching for a lost treasure. Like the proverbial fly-on-the-wall I could peer out and observe and overhear a conversation without the speakers noticing that I was there.

Two archetypal little old ladies were giving Taylor their joint want-list. Taylor was telling them about his experience meeting a popular mystery writer whose private eye often uses marijuana and other marginally illegal relaxants.

"That's terrible," one of the little old ladies scolded. "I certainly wouldn't want to read about that, and I can't imagine why anyone would want to write about it."

"But it goes on all the time," Taylor said gently. Taylor is a huge man with a fierce black moustache. He looks a lot like Robert B. Parker. Like many such brawny types, he has developed a startlingly gentle manner of speech and movement.

"It's in the newspaper every day," he said. "Why shouldn't authors write about it? Why do you object to reading about it?"

"Because," the second little old lady asserted through pursed lips, "we like to read *nice* books about *nice* mysteries!"

~ ~ ~ ~ ~

They didn't go into detail as to what "nice mysteries" are, but then there was really no need. The two little old ladies were talking about the kind of genteel, traditionally English, tea-with-the-vicar mystery novels associated with Agatha Christie, Doris Miles

Disney, Georgette Heyer, and their whole school, down to P.D. James and Marion Babson.

But this is fantasy.

It is as much fantasy as are the works of Tolkien and T.H. White, Marion Zimmer Bradley and Katherine Kurtz and Piers Anthony. A different *kind* of fantasy, but these *nice* mysteries have as little connection with real crime and detection as tales of unicorns and trolls and wizards and fairies (or "faeries") have to do with real life and struggle and death.

Fredric Brown — why do the tough writers look so mild?

Chandler said it first and best, of course, writing about a contemporary: "Hammett took murder out of the Venetian vase and dropped it into the alley.... Hammett gave murder back to the kind of people that commit it for reasons, not just to provide a corpse; and with the means at hand, not with handwrought dueling pistols, curare, and tropical fish."

The pulp tradition of mystery writing falls somewhere between that grim and brutal reality, and the genteel fantasy of tea with the vicar. (And, aside, is it not puzzling that little old ladies *want* murder to take place in their genteel fantasies? I will not offer my theory as to why this is so, although I have one.)

The pulp story in general and the pulp mystery in particular represent a distinct approach to writing, with definite standards and requirements. Subtlety was a vice, characterization was performed with broad fast swipes of strong pigment, *plot* was rudimentary in the sense that complex relationships or moral ambiguities were eschewed in favor of white hats battling black hats, but *story* was all-important in terms of the requirement that things kept happening all the time.

The ideal was to grab the reader by the nose in paragraph one and start running at top speed and never let go until you had reached the end.

The very best writers outgrew the pulps. Hammett and Chandler of course and also John D. MacDonald and Cornell Woolrich and Horace McCoy, and if better researchers than I are to be believed, Stephen Crane and Jack London and Upton Sinclair and Mackinlay Kantor and Sinclair Lewis and Ray Bradbury. Whether their stories continued to appear in pulp magazines or not, they had triumphed over the form.

And the worst pulp writers—well, citing Mickey Spillane is like shooting fish in a barrel. What does Mick care, he doesn't even have to laugh all the way to the bank any more. They send a bonded messenger in an armored truck to make Mick's pickups.

Fredric Brown went to neither of these extremes. He did not transcend the pulp form, but neither did he pander to it or to the baser instincts of his readers. Within the limits of the established pulp form he worked with high competence and responsibility. He gave his editors and his readers honest value for value tendered. He was an honest story-teller, he respected the traditions and the formulas of the fields in which he worked. Yet he brought a pleasant tincture of originality to many of his stories. He mixed a touch of the macabre with a dash of sardonic humor.

The result was a menu of essentially standard dishes, yet each served with a distinctive and often elusive flare that was Fred Brown's own trademark.

This we find in his mysteries, his science fiction stories, and in his occasional forays into other realms.

In 1956 Brown contributed an essay titled "Where Do You Get Your Plot?" to Herbert Brean's compilation, *The Mystery Writer's Handbook*. Brown claimed that all writers constructed their stories the same way; it was just that some of them did it on a subconscious level while others did it consciously. Brown wrote this:

> "A writer plots by accretion. If you've forgotten what the word means I'll save you a trip to the dictionary—it means *increase by gradual addition*.

"It can start with anything—a character, a theme, a setting, a single word. By accretion it builds or is built into a plot."

In his essay Brown goes on to construct a story from a single word, "goldfish." Although he doesn't say so in "Where Do You Get Your Plot?" the goldfish story was apparently one that he had written several years earlier. In somewhat transmogrified form it seemingly became "A Cat Walks" in *Detective Story Magazine* in 1942.

Locale was important in many pulp stories, immaterial or even anonymous in others. This of course is equally true outside of the pulps. Stories of show biz centered on Broadway or Hollywood for obvious reasons, although in at least one yarn Brown used a "little theatre" background that could be set in any city. Writers of high adventure clung to the glamorous and mysterious trappings of Tibet, Yucatan, or Cairo.

In the detection field, at least until Chandler added Los Angeles to the list, most stories took place in London, San Francisco, New York, Paris, or Chicago. I suppose Paris appears on the list because so many of the para-fictional crime memoirs of the nineteenth century took place there, as did the immortal Poe's stories of the Chevalier Dupin.

Doyle deserves credit for London's popularity, I suppose, but he has to share that with Dickens and Collins and the wonderful shrouding fog. And that fog, I think, is a major reason for the laying of so many tales in San Francisco.

But New York and Chicago were the gang capitals of the nation during the heyday of the pulps, and the placing of gangster stories there was as natural in that day as is the flashing of spy-thrillers between Washington and Moscow today.

The stories in the present volume don't rely heavily on Chicago settings even though Fred Brown was an old Chicago boy himself. The major yarn, "The Freak Show Murders," has as its background an itinerant carnival; although various towns are visited in the course of the story, it's the carnival itself that is the real setting for the tale.

The killings themselves are somewhat bizarre. They come close to the "Venetian vase . . . handwrought dueling pistols, curare, and tropical fish" that Chandler scorned. But there is nothing here of the genteel vicarage school of writing. "The Freak Show Murders" is, in at least one scene, chillingly anticipatory of Graham Greene's "The Third Man." And in overall tone, "The Freak Show

Murders" resonates with William Lindsay Gresham's jolting and unforgettable *Nightmare Alley*—which it predates by three years.

Brown had other strings on his bow.

"Double Murder" (published under the pseudonym John S. Endicott) features one of the neatest bits of misdirection you'll come across in a library full of mysteries.

And "Two Biers for Two," a tough gangster story of the classic style, features one of the most powerful—and bloody—images you're likely to encounter this year. It also includes some neat and unexpected foreshadowing. The reader gets that little surge of pleasure that comes when all the pieces slip neatly into place.

Memorable characters are not numerous in these stories, for two reasons which converge to prevent their growth.

One is the nature of pulp writing. James Blish said that pulp characters typically possessed only those characteristics needed to function in their roles in the story. A ship's captain in a pulp story (starship captain in a science fiction story, steamship captain in a modern romance, pirate captain in a swashbuckler) had only those elements required to play his part. Intelligence, courage, technical and tactical knowledge.

But in a well-executed literary work, that captain would have a childhood and education behind him, a chosen flavor of ice cream, a religious preference, and very likely a favorite poet, baseball team, and brand of beer.

Blish's notion wasn't altogether invalid, but it also wasn't altogether fair.

The problem of the short story versus that of the novel must also be considered. Philip K. Dick said that the short story was about things that people did while the novel was about people who did things.

There just isn't that much room in a short story, to develop character. That's true as a generality in both pulp and literary short stories, but it is intensified and re-intensified in the pulp short story with its requirement for constant action.

Fred Brown's characters aren't really badly drawn, they're just a trifle too sketchy. I find myself wanting to know Mortimer Tracy better—and George Hearn of the Springfield police department as he tries to figure out if the murderer was a rooster wearing silk pajamas—and private eye Carey Rix.

When Brown did stretch out more, as in "The Freak Show Murders," he *did* develop his characters more. We learn, at least, that carnival barker Pete Gaynor is 36 years old, was passed over by the World War Two draft board because he has just a touch of hemophilia, and wants very much to marry beautiful Stella the snake girl.

Pulp writers got around the problem of undercharacterization in their short stories by writing series about the same people. Readers liked that because they became fond of the characters and wanted to see them return. Editors liked it because that boosted sales. And authors liked it because it tended to provide some stability in a terrifyingly unreliable marketplace. It also saved them the trouble of dreaming up a whole new cast of characters every time they set out to do a new story.

Thus there were Carroll John Daly's Race Williams, Robert E. Howard's Breckinridge Elkins, Johnston McCulley's Zorro, and of course Hammett's immortal Continental Op.

Fred Brown had Ed and Am Hunter, an uncle-nephew private eye team. Their adventures filled volumes.

But the stories in *this* book rest not on character but on Brown's wry and ingenious way of constructing and then revealing the structure of his crimes and their solutions. While far from the grim and violent stories we have learned to expect from some of our more modern practitioners, Brown's stories still have at their heart that ultimate crime: murder.

I'm sure that those two little old ladies twittering away at poor gentle Bruce Taylor would not care for this book. They would not consider Fredric Brown's crime stories, *nice* mysteries.

But the trouble, damn it all, is that crime is seldom nice and murder is *never* nice.

Say, has anybody used that yet as a title?

NOT EXACTLY A SHOE SALESMAN

For a long time the only image I'd ever seen of Day Keene was a typical book-jacket photo. There isn't a lot of biographical data available on Keene and I don't know when or where the photo was made, but it has the look of a small-town studio run by a photographer who specialized in documenting weddings and young children for posterity. Photog might have scored big once every twelve months doing graduation portraits for the local high school's yearbook.

These shots were marked by standard poses and proper lighting. They were technically flawless and utterly unimaginative.

One glance and you'd guess that Keene was a shoe salesman, employed by a shop on the main street of that presumed small town. After twenty years of service—or maybe thirty—Keene would have been promoted to assistant manager, a job which he would hold with pride until reaching retirement age. He was probably a faithful member of Kiwanis, a Mason, and possibly a deacon of the nearby Presbyterian Church.

Bet he drove a six-year-old Plymouth.

Thinking about this some more, he might have been a high school biology teacher rather than a shoe salesman. The kids in his class always giggled a lot when they came to the unit on sexual reproduction. He likely was a scoutmaster as well.

All of this on the basis of one book-jacket portrait.

In it we see a smallish man with thinning, slicked-down hair, a neatly-clipped moustache, and horn-rimmed glasses. He's wearing a white shirt, a really silly polka-dotted bow tie, and a dark jacket. Probably had that photograph taken on his lunch break from the shoe store. Or on Saturday when he didn't have to teach.

In fact, he looked like a cross between H. T. Webster's immortal comic strip character, Caspar Milquetoast, and the brilliant, prissy movie actor, Clifton Webb.

You'd never take him for the prolific author of some of the toughest, nastiest crime fiction of his generation.

And then—*mirabile dictu!*—I came across another photo of Keene. In it he's at least a decade younger than he was in the previous shot. Hair much thicker. Moustache bushier and less disciplined. No horn-rimmed glasses. And—heaven help us!—no ridiculous bow tie!

Yeah!

That was the Day Keene who wrote *My Flesh is Sweet, The Big Kiss-Off, Bring Him Back Dead, Passage to Samoa, Home is the Sailor,* and dozens of other tough crime novels, most of them flavored with more than a tincture of twisted sexuality.

Yeah! That was Day Keene.

Day Keene – why do the tough writers look so mild?

Before going any farther, let's talk about by-lines, especially that peculiar one, Day Keene. It piqued my curiosity when I was a teenager back in Harry Truman's day, and I didn't find out what lay behind it until I got involved in the mystery field myself, not very many years ago.

Biographical data on Day Keene is regrettably sparse. Such fine scholars and critics as Bill Pronzini, Kevin Barton Smith, Al Guthrie, and even the great Bill Crider provide only minimal information. For as prolific and visible an individual as Keene was professionally, he seems to have been remarkably elusive in his personal life.

At least one website asserts that he was born on March 28, 1904, probably in Chicago. His legal name was Gunnar Hjerstedt or maybe Gunard Hjertstedt. He broke into the pulp field with a short story, "Pure and Simple," in *Detective Fiction Weekly* for October 31, 1931. He maintained a steady output of roughly one story a month for five months, all of them published in DFW. In Steve Lewis's fine bibliography, there is then a gap until May, 1935, when our boy pops up in *Clues Detective Stories* with "Case of the Bearded Bride."

Then another gap, until he reappeared in *Ace G-Man Stories* for September, 1940 with "It Could Happen Here!" bylined Day Keene. If you've been following the Keene renaissance you will have seen several stories that he wrote under the name John Corbett between 1942 and 1950. And after that he never stopped running, turning out literally hundreds of criminous yarns for the crime pulps, with an occasional foray into general fiction mags like *Short Stories, Adventure, Argosy,* and slicks or semi-slicks like *Adam, Esquire* and *Man's Magazine*. He even sold stories to *Western Short Stories, Fifteen Western Tales, 10-Story Western,* and *Jungle Tales.*

But what was he doing between May, 1935 and September, 1940? The answer—or at least a partial answer—is provided by golden age radio scholar Victor A. Berch, who discovered that Hjerstedt wrote at least eight dramatic scripts for a radio series called *First Nighter.* He wrote at least one episode for *Behind the Camera Lines.* He wrote scripts for the *Little Orphan Annie* radio serial, and may have penned as many as several hundred scripts for *Kitty Keene, Incorporated,* a radio series about a female private eye.

The story of how Gunnard Hjertstedt (or however we're spelling it at the moment) was transformed into Day Keene has many variations. Here's the consensus version:

Our boy was visiting the office of one of his pulp publishers, maybe to plead for an advance check. That kind of thing happened all the time. The office was almost certainly that of Popular Publications on 43rd Street in Manhattan. Throughout his career, Popular Pubs was Hjertstedt's favorite outlet. For instance, of the eleven stories in the collection at hand, six were first published in *Detective Tales,* four in *Dime Mystery,* and one in *Popular Detective.* All three magazines were issued by Popular Publications.

That company was headed by Harry Steeger. The top editor was Rogers Terrill, and in all likelihood the person Brother Hjertstedt was there to see was Terrill. I imagine their conversation went something like this:

Terrill: Gunnard, I really like your story "It Could Happen Here!" I'm going to use it in *Ace G-Man Stories* and I want to blurb it on the cover, but your by-line, you know, isn't really very commercial. Half of our customers won't be able to read it and the other half won't be able to pronounce it. Please, buddy, give me a different by-line I can slug on the front of the book.

Hjertstedt: Uh, I dunno, Mr. Terrill, sir. Maybe—uh—do you have any suggestions?

Terrill: How about a family name? What was your mom's maiden name, that's usually a good one.

Hjertstedt: Keeney. Her name is Daisy Keeney.

Terrill: Hmm. Possibilities. Definite possibilities. But it needs work. How about cutting it a little? We certainly don't want a name like Daisy on the cover of *Ace G-Man Stories*.

Hjertstedt: Right. Let's drop the last syllable of each word. That leaves us with Day Keene. What do you think?"

Terrill: "Okay, I think that's it. Now, how much do you need? How soon can you give me another story? I can't just go writing advance checks to every writer who wanders in here with his hand out!"

And so it was. Or at least, that's how it might have been. Gunnard also wrote as Lewis Dixon, William Richards, and Daniel White. All pretty generic by-lines. But Day Keene is the one he used for the greatest bulk of his work, and it's the one by which he is remembered.

Unlike many of his pulp-writing colleagues who established popular series characters and returned to them frequently, Keene created few recurring characters. Doc Egg, the Times Square druggist who pops up in several of Keene's New York stories, is an intriguing figure. It's unfortunate that Keene didn't make more use of Doc. And Keene brought back the Chicago private eye firm of McPherson, McCreedy and McCoy more than once, but these characters were never particularly vivid and the stories were carried by their not-especially-startling plots.

By the end of the 1940s the handwriting was on the wall for the pulp magazines, and while many of them survived well into the 1950s—and a few even into the early '60s—most of the better pulpers headed for safe harbor elsewhere. Some, like Howard Browne, wound up in Hollywood writing for the movies or for that new medium called television. Others, including Henry Kuttner,

Edmond Hamilton, Alfred Bester and Otto Binder became comic book scripters either full- or part-time.

But the greatest number skedaddled into the book biz, especially the burgeoning paperback field, where Keene eventually wrote something like 50 novels. Exact count is hard to pin down, as publishers came and went pell-mell, sometimes changing titles as they scrambled to survive.

The great majority of Keene's novels were criminous in content, generally set in the more-or-less realistic contemporary world of the 1950s and early '60s. However, he did experiment with other genres.

World Without Women (1960), co-authored with Leonard Pruyn, was Keene's sole foray into science fiction. In this novel, a plague wipes out most of the women in the world and leaves almost all of the survivors sterile. Only a few fertile women remain, and hope for the survival of the human species depends on them. The novel focuses on the husband of one of these surviving fertile females. Think half of Philip Wylie's *The Disappearance* (1951) flavored with a tincture of Richard Matheson's *The Shrinking Man* (1956).

Seed of Doubt (1961) is set in a wealthy Florida town. As Keene's plot evolves, a leading male citizen proves to be sterile and his wife conceives through artificial insemination. Why this development should be treated as a shameful secret and lead to a series of melodramatic and violent events, is better left unexplored at this late date.

Chautauqua (1961) was co-written with Dwight Babcock, the latter writing as Dwight Vincent. In 1969 this became a filmic vehicle for Elvis Presley, and I think I need say no more about it than that.

Guns Along the Brazos (1967), a Western set in northern Mexico and Texas, concerns a onetime rancher and former Confederate army doctor who emigrates to Mexico after the Civil War. Upon returning to Texas to reclaim his ranch he finds that his wife and their foreman have been plotting to betray him.

But let's get back to Day Keene's mainstay, the novel of crime and suspense. Typically, these books are not detective stories or even mysteries as we commonly think of such. A Keene protagonist is most often a well-intentioned twenty- to thirtyish male who falls under the spell of a sexually dynamic woman of devious motives. Devious to the reader, that is. Keene's hero is so smitten that he follows his new sweetie-pie into trouble that keeps getting deeper and nastier by the page.

A favorite Keene device is to have the mob commit a heinous crime, then frame Keene's protagonist for the dirty deed. Keene's hero tries to determine who really committed the crime and hang the label of guilt upon the real criminal. That's the only way he can clear himself. Of course the mob don't want the crime to be solved, they want to frame some sucker, which will take the heat off them, so they go after our hero.

At the same time, the cops (variously corrupt, inept, and brutal) are also chasing him. At various times in the book he'll be caught by either the police or the mob and beaten within an inch of his life, only to escape and resume his seemingly hopeless search. All of this action—and tension—is subjected to occasional brief intermissions during which he gets to practice belly-to-belly gymnastics with one or another lubricious young lady.

Keene could occasionally pull a switch on the reader. An example of this was *Who has Wilma Lathrop?* (1955) a convoluted story of treachery, double-dealing, suspense, and—for once in a Keene opus—some major surprises. It's one of his better efforts.

Trying to pick the best of Keene's many novels is a daunting task, but certainly a leading candidate would be *Death House Doll* (1953). In this book Sergeant Mike Duval, a veteran of both World War Two and Korea, returns to the US on a mission. His brother has been killed in action, and Duval is to visit his deceased sibling's widow. Mike is still in the army, and he has obtained a leave of limited duration.

Problem is, the woman in the case has been convicted of murder and faces electrocution within a matter of days. Duval gets to see her, courtesy of an understanding warden who appreciates Duval's military service. Mike meets the widowed Mona Duval and becomes convinced that she is innocent of the crime for which she is to be executed.

He leaves the prison determined to prove Mona's innocence despite her refusal to cooperate. Before long Mike is being chased by the mob (they want Mona to take the rap), the military police (Mike has overstayed his leave and is technically AWOL), and the regular cops (okay, so he did beat up a few guys).

The result is a madcap hunt-and-chase novel. Keene somehow manages to keep things under control (sort of) and to tie up a spaghetti-bowl full of loose ends in a mere 140 Ace Double pages.

The book is absolutely stunning, unforgettable, Day Keene at his very best.

I should also mention that he created only one continuing character in his novels. This was Johnny Aloha, an LA-based Irish-Hawaiian private eye. Aloha appeared in *Dead in Bed* (1959) and *Payola* (1960). There's a light, tongue-in-cheek feel to these two books. I have a feeling that Keene had encountered the great Richard S. Prather's Shell Scott capers, which were immensely popular at the time. Keene decided to try his hand at something similar. He substituted Aloha's occasional usage of Hawaiian cultural references for Shell Scott's fondness for tropical fish as a character tag or "funny hat." Otherwise, they're just about interchangeable. Big, tough, ex-military, cynical, sexy.

Apparently Keene found the genre uncongenial, as he dropped Aloha after just two outings.

Having moved to the Gulf Coast of Florida, where several of his later books are set, Keene joined a congenial group of hard-boiled writers who had settled in the Tampa Bay area. To all evidence (of which there is, alas, far too little) he enjoyed the tropical lifestyle and the company of his colleagues. Somewhere along the way he had married and fathered a son. His last book, *Acapulco G.P.O.,* was published in 1967. He died in Los Angeles on January 9, 1969.

As for the stories in the present collection, I am indebted to our series editor, John Pelan, who tracked down the pulp magazines in which they originally appeared, and assembled them. All else aside, John has made my job incalculably easier by finding the stories in this collection (like many others!). All I've had to do is sit down and enjoy them. And believe me, Day Keene understood the first commandment of the commercial fiction writer: *Give the Readers Something they'll Enjoy!*

In the classic pulp era the sign over every successful editor's door read, *Fiction is a Medium of Entertainment.*

Anything else, if there had to be anything else, was secondary. If you want to sell your readers on your philosophy of life, if you want to explain to them your brilliant insights into the human condition, if you want them to understand a turning point of history, if you want to teach them something about the wonders of chemistry, physics and astronomy . . .

. . . all of those goals are okay, provided you show the customers a good time.

In reading several dozen of Keene's hundreds of stories, I've been deeply impressed by the growth in their quality, from his apprentice-work "Hjertstedt" stories of the 1930s to the many productions of his mature years. The fact is—and let's be brutally honest about this!—Keene's earliest stories are pretty weak. The ideas are slight; e.g., a dart gun hidden in a camera, a crooked bartender who feeds his customers mickey finns and rolls them for their cash. The characters are very thinly established, e.g., red hair or bald, tall and massive or short and energetic, given to slang or committed to "proper" English speech. The pacing is jerky and there are technical flaws in the prose that any good high school composition teacher would have red-lined, e.g., changes in narrative viewpoint whenever convenient for the author.

In fact, it's a wonder that Hjertstedt sold those earliest stories at all. I've got a theory which I'll share with you. The pulp magazine field was huge in the 1920s. In the '30s, with the Depression growing ever deeper, there was some shrinkage in the field but the volume of production remained high. Prices, however, dropped. Cover price of many pulps slid from 25¢ down to 20¢, 15¢, 10¢, and in a few cases even to 5¢. Payments to authors dropped from several cents per word to a penny or even a fraction of a cent. Writers' magazines of the era contained letters from pulp authors complaining that publishers were retitling and reissuing their earlier works while making no payments to them at all.

And yet the hungry presses kept churning out mountains of magazines every week. Titles came and went literally by the hundreds. Of all the pulp categories—westerns, science fiction, horror, love stories, sports stories, war stories and so on—mystery and detective magazines were the most popular and consequently the most numerous.

If an average pulp contained ten stories, that meant that the demand for fiction ran to literally thousands of stories every month. In this market, as science fiction writer Robert A. Heinlein theorized a decade later, virtually any story with the faintest glimmer of merit could find a home somewhere, in some periodical, providing only that the author keep it circulating in the face of form rejection slips.

That, at least, is how I believe Gunnard Hjertstedt got his start. Now, more than three quarters of a century later, we can be grateful that he didn't give up. As he learned his craft he learned to create characters with depth and pathos and plots with subtlety and complexity. And he honed his once clunky and graceless prose into a keen-edged instrument to be envied by generations of successors.

It's also my personal belief that Keene's experience writing radio scripts contributed to the development of his talent. Audio drama has the same major ingredients as printed fiction—character, plot, setting—but it also has its own array of requirements. Terseness and clarity are paramount among them. The reader of a novel or a magazine story can linger over a convoluted sentence; the listener cannot. And timing is vital in radio drama. The novelist can go on for another ten pages or another hundred if that will make for a better book. The radio writer must wrap in time for the proverbial message from his sponsor.

Above all, Day Keene understood that principle, that principle that whatever other purposes to which it could be put, fiction always was and still remains a medium of entertainment. For a demonstration of how well he understood it, simply turn the page and start reading the stories in this book.

MISTER BURROUGHS AND ME
1965

When I was a schoolboy and a science fiction fan—I'm talking about the mid-to-late 1940's—I kept coming across the name Edgar Rice Burroughs. The letter columns of the professional magazines and the fanzines included frequent mention of him, along with demands from readers for more of his stories. Such were not to be had. Burroughs had served as a war correspondent in the Pacific until his health failed, following which he was largely inactive for the remaining years of his life. There were a few late novels—*Llana of Gathol, Tarzan and the Foreign Legion*—but these were very minor Burroughs.

Certainly of interest to completists and collectors, but far from his best or even his average output.

To me, the name Edgar Rice Burroughs was connected with Tarzan, not with science fiction. And even Tarzan had to do with mainly low-budget adaptations. Movies that featured an overweight and overage Johnny Weissmuller, a so-cute-you-could-puke chimpanzee named Cheetah, and the same three or four stock shots of African wildlife year after year. Comic books that didn't interest me very much; I loved the comics as a medium but the crudely-drawn Dell version of Tarzan was not to my taste. Big Little Books I didn't often bother with; I was already into the pulps.

And then one afternoon I had an epiphany. My dictionary defines an epiphany as "a usually sudden manifestation or perception of the essential nature of something." There are several other definitions, but that's the one that applies to my experience.

It was a perfect afternoon late in spring of the year.

Probably in the month of May. I can't tell you the year—1945? 46? 47? The sky was china blue, puffy white clouds drifted overhead. I sat on a splintery old bench beneath a willow tree that sighed—it did not weep—in the breeze. On a nearby tennis court players practiced their game. The *pock*-pause-*pock* of ball colliding with racket made a pleasant, rhythmic background sound.

This all took place in the small town in New Jersey where I was attending school. A local resident kept a row of hen-houses behind his home, and the same breeze that pushed those pretty clouds along and that made the willows sigh, also carried the distinctive sharp odor of chicken droppings to my youthful nostrils. Unpleasant, but part of the memory nonetheless.

What a great portrait of the grand storyteller —
by Al Williamson and Reed Crandall

I had come across a Big Little Book edition of *Tarzan and the Ant Men*, and out of curiosity I made an exception to my practice of ignoring Big Little Books. I read *Tarzan and the Ant Men* and I experienced a "sudden manifestation or perception of the nature of something." The "something" was the appeal of Burroughs. For *this* Tarzan was not the flabby, inarticulate character I knew from the screen, nor was the story the childish pastiche that I had read in the comics. This Tarzan was an intelligent, noble adventurer, a real hero. And the story was full of wonders—tiny people, size-changing, immortality, marvelous cities shaped like bee-hives lighted and ventilated by wonderful candles that burned carbon dioxide and emitted oxygen.

Edgar Rice Burroughs died in 1950, and I never did get to read one of his science fiction stories—in that era.

A decade and more passed. I went to college, then into the army. After I completed my military service I began a career in the then-fledgling computer industry. I was married and started a family. I still read science fiction and kept up some contacts in the fan community, but Burroughs was far from my mind.

Illustration by Mahlon Blaine for A Fighting Man of Mars by Edgar Rice Burroughs

Then in the early 1960's, Burroughs books began to appear once more. These were reissues, of course. There had been no Burroughs in the bookshops for many years, except for some old and (to me at least) unappealing Grosset & Dunlap Tarzan reprints. But the new books that were appearing from a company called Canaveral Press were real science fiction, with fascinating and impressive titles: *The Moon Maid, At the Earth's Core, A Fighting Man of Mars.* They were illustrated by a strange artist named Mahlon Blaine, whose drawings were weird and peculiarly erotic.

I was buying my science fiction in those days from Stephen Takacs, a dealer with a little shop on Second Avenue in New York City. Steve was a handsome, beefy man with a shock of wavy gray hair and a lugubrious manner. Business was always terrible, he was forever on the ragged edge of bankruptcy, his favorite expression was not a word at all but a moan of despair.

When I read the first Canaveral Press editions I became wildly excited. These books weren't the kind of science fiction I was accustomed to reading in *Galaxy* and *F&SF*. They weren't quite like *anything* I could recall reading. There was an intensity of color and excitement to them, a feeling of *freedom* from the bonds of everyday reality and the drabness of the here-and-now.

Instead of dressing in a three-piece suit, riding the subway to sit at a desk in a huge office building grinding out technical documentation to accompany programming packages for the Univac SS 80/90 or the IBM 1401, I was riding across the wind-swept plains of Barsoom on the back of my faithful six-legged *thoat*, dressed only in warrior's leather harness, sword in one hand, radium-pistol in the other, pursuing the foul-hearted villain who had carried off my gorgeous and mostly naked princess to face a fate worse than death.

Or was I plunging through the Earth's crust with David Innes and Abner Perry, *en route* to a weird, timeless world within a world. Or I was visiting a strange future in which our planet has been conquered by centaur-like invaders from the moon and heroic survivors fight to free themselves from their alien overlords . . .

How could a young man, stifling in the mundane world of business, resist?

I couldn't wait for the later titles to appear. Publication schedules were announced, and when the books were not in Steve's shop on the promised date I was distraught. Every few days I would take the IRT downtown from my home on 73rd Street in futile pursuit of *Tanar of Pellucidar, The Monster Men, The Land that Time Forgot*. I made such a pest of myself that Steve decided to get rid of me. If I wasn't satisfied to wait, he told me, I could just go ask the publishers why the books were late. I was terrified at the thought.

But Steve encouraged me to go ahead. In fact, he insisted. The offices of Canaveral Press were located just a couple of city blocks from Steve's shop.

So, wearing my courage like a cloak, I headed for the offices of Canaveral Press—which turned out to be a cubbyhole in the surplus stock attic of another bookshop, Biblo & Tannen's. Once there I met everyone in the establishment—Jack Biblo and Jack Tannen, the owners; Alice Ryter, the secretary and business manager; and David Garfinkel, a retired academic who hung around and performed miscellaneous jobs out of friendship and the sheer love of books. David had grown up on the dime novels that preceded the pulp magazines, and was forever eager to reminisce about Old Sleuth, Baseball Joe, or Buffalo Bill.

The two Jacks had been partners in the book business since the 1920's. They were physically similar, both men of medium height with dark hair and receding hairlines, bushy moustaches and horn-rimmed eyeglasses. They could have easily passed as brothers. Jack Tannen was a little heavier and a little more outgoing. Jack Biblo was slimmer, more softspoken and retiring. In addition to operating a wonderful used book store, they had been in the business of reprinting books on art and archaeology, mainly for the library trade, and historical novels, mainly for school use.

Over the years, they told me, the most requested of all out-of-print authors had been Edgar Rice Burroughs—especially his science fiction. They had attempted to contact Edgar Rice Burroughs, Inc. to inquire about reprint rights, and received no cooperation at all. Operating purely on a hunch, they had searched copyright records through the Library of Congress, and discovered that approximately half of Burroughs' works were in the public domain!

This was under the "old" copyright law, of course. Under our present law, a literary work is copyright for the duration of its author's life plus fifty years. But under the old law, the copyright was good for only twenty-eight years, and could then be renewed for a second, like term. But the renewal was not automatic—it had to be filed for, and Burroughs' personal secretary / business manager / administrative assistant had failed to file for renewals!!!

[2013 update: Congress keeps tinkering with the copyright law. Last time I looked, copyright ran for the author's lifetime plus ninety years.—RAL]

I'm afraid that I made a pest of myself again, hanging around the offices of Canaveral Press and complaining about the lateness of books. (There were scheduling problems at the bindery, it turned out; there was nothing the publisher could do about it.) Finally one of the Jacks said, "Listen, if you're so concerned about this, why don't you come to work for us as an editor."

The money they offered was too little for me to live on, no less support a by-now growing family—but I wasn't going to pass up this opportunity, either. So we agreed that I would keep my job in the computer business and work for Canaveral Press on Saturdays. Was I ever thrilled!

Following Canaveral's lead, other publishers had started to get into the act on Burroughs books. Don Wollheim at Ace Books had had the same frustrating experience trying to obtain reprint rights from ERB, Inc. He had published Burroughs imitators like Otis Adelbert Kline and Ralph Milne Farley as a poor substitute for the real stuff. Now Ace, too, began reprinting public-domain Burroughs books.

Dover Books issued several giant Burroughs omnibuses.

Ian Ballantine, then still running the company that bears his name, flew to California, met with surviving members of the Burroughs family, and finally got them to resume active management of the company.

And Monarch Books, a small company in Connecticut—rumored to be owned by the Mafia and used as a money-laundering device—began publishing a series of *new* Tarzan books written by the pseudonymous "Barton Werper."

After Ian Ballantine returned from California there followed a series of meetings, mainly with lawyers. Hulbert Burroughs flew to New York to participate in these. Hulbert Burroughs was most concerned over the new "Werper" books, and I helped him with some research to provide his lawyer with ammunition, should the case ever go to court.

The outcome of the maneuverings was as follows: Monarch and Dover did no further Burroughs titles and Burroughs, Inc. did not bring suit against them for alleged offenses already committed. Ballantine and Ace divided the paperback rights with Ballantine getting the Tarzan and Mars titles and Ace getting the Pellucidar and Venus books. The other, miscellaneous books were similarly apportioned. Canaveral Press would continue to have rights to publish Burroughs in hardcover.

So much for Burroughs *reprints*.

But then there arose the even more exciting topic of first editions. There were a number of Burroughs stories that had appeared in magazine form but had never been gathered into books. And when an inventory was conducted of manuscripts in Burroughs' old office safe, Fate sprang the greatest surprise of all: completely unpublished stories turned up. Some were early works, stories that had failed to sell. These might be of historic interest. But there were others—a complete Tarzan novel, a Pellucidar novelette that would round out a series published in the early 1940's, a sequel to the novelette *Beyond the Farthest Star,* even an historical novel set in Imperial Rome!

These were to appear in Canaveral Press editions, and I was to be the editor. What a far cry from that splintery wooden bench where the odor of chicken droppings filled the air!

Working with the two Jacks, Alice, and David, I set out on the task.

Mahlon Blaine, already an old man when he had illustrated the first few Canaveral Press editions, had retired. We worked with new artists including Al Williamson, his wife Arlene Williamson, the great Roy Krenkel, Frank Frazetta, Reed Crandall, and Larry Ivie. Most of these artists had been associated with the old EC comic book line of the 1950's—illustrators whose work I had admired in my teens. Now, ten years later, they were working for me!

There was a lot of variety in their personalities as there was in their drawing styles. Reed Crandall, for instance, came across as a Midwestern farm boy, straw hat and all. Modest, sweet-natured, cooperative. Al Williamson was a handsome, exotic figure who had been born in Chile of Scots parents, travelled to the United States to pursue his career and learned English as a second language. Arlene Williamson was an exceptionally beautiful woman who created maps and calligraphy for some of our books. They lived in a farmhouse in the Catskill Mountains, and Pat and I would visit them from time to time and Al would play Woody Herman and Artie Shaw records from his collection.

Frank Frazetta was hugely talented and completely businesslike. Give him an assignment, give him a schedule, and on the appointed day you would have the work—and it would be superb! Roy Krenkel was equally talented but utterly unbusinesslike. He refused to have a telephone in the home he shared with his aged parents. If you wanted to confer with him you would send him a letter enclosing a dime and ask him to call you. If the weather was pleasant and the mood struck him right he would walk to a candy store and call you from the pay phone. He was a perfectionist in his work, and would not turn in an assignment until he was satisfied with it. You could admire his dedication, but his perfectionism also made it almost impossible to work with him. Schedules meant nothing.

I remember having lunch with Don Wollheim one day in the early 1960's. Wollheim had been getting Krenkel covers for Ace Books, and he asked me if we were planning to continue using

Roy for Canaveral Press. I said that I loved Roy's work—and Roy himself, a delightful person—but that I would have a very hard time giving him any further assignments. Don said that he had the same problem.

The books that eventually appeared in Canaveral Press first editions were *Tarzan and the Castaways, Tarzan and the Madman, Tales of Three Planets, John Carter of Mars,* and *Savage Pellucidar.* The Roman novel, *I am a Barbarian,* was eventually published by Edgar Rice Burroughs, Inc. All of them were eventually issued in paperbacks by either Ace or Ballantine—sometimes with stories reshuffled, titles changed, and other unpublished material added. Nightmares for collectors and bibliographers, the greatest of whom was Henry Hardy Heins, whose magnificent Burroughs bibliographies in time became highly prized collectables themselves.

Most of these books carried either introductions or bibliographic notes that I was called upon to write. One of them, at least—*Savage Pellucidar*—had dust-jacket copy by Edgar Rice Burroughs himself! He had written it back in the 1940's, and it had lain gathering dust for twenty years!

I was concerned over the total length of some of our books, in particular *John Carter of Mars*. There wasn't very much John Carter material—two novelettes, one of them of dubious authenticity—and I worried that it just wouldn't bulk up enough to make a commercially viable book. The Jacks told me to make up the difference by writing an introduction. A long introduction. I went home and started work on as essay titled, as I recall, "Edgar Rice Burroughs: Science Fiction Writer."

When I finished my work I proudly marched into the Canaveral Press office and dropped off the manuscript. Neither Jack was present, but Alice said she'd give it to whichever of them came in first.

The next time I visited the office I was confronted by an angry man in horn-rimmed glasses and a bristling moustache. He brandished a fat manila envelope beneath my nose. I knew what was in the envelope—it could only be my manuscript!

Jack (which of the two Jacks, I do not remember) waved the envelope menacingly and demanded to know, "What's this?"

"It's my introduction for *John Carter of Mars,*" I said.

"This? But—look at the *size* of it!"

"You said to make it long."

"Not *that* long!"

I had fallen into a shaggy dog story!

"What do you want me to do?" I asked.

"Go home and do another introduction for *John Carter of Mars*. And make it *short*!" And he shoved my fat manila envelope, the product of long and painstaking research and uncounted hours of work, into my hands.

I accepted the envelope. Heartbroken, I asked, "What should I do with the old version?"

"Take it with you," Jack said. "And when you finish writing the new, *short* introduction for *John Carter of Mars*, you can start researching the Tarzan stories and the rest of Burroughs' works. Then you can write the rest of your book. If it's as good as the first half," and he pointed at my manila envelope, "Canaveral Press will publish it!"

~ ~ ~ ~ ~

I wish I could say that Canaveral Press was a roaring success and that my association with it was a long and happy one. Well, my association was certainly happy. We all got along fine; the two Jacks were like fond uncles to me. We published something like twenty Burroughs books, plus a novel by Edward Elmer Smith and a non-fiction book by L. Sprague de Camp and Catherine Crook de Camp, and every project provided education and pleasure for me. Certainly working with "Doc" Smith and Sprague de Camp, two more of my boyhood heroes, was a thrill.

I finished expanding that essay on Burroughs and it became *Edgar Rice Burroughs: Master of Adventure*. Two Canaveral Press editions sold out, and I have seen copies on sale in recent years for as much as $200.00 or more. At one science fiction convention, a book dealer tried to sell one to me at that price, obviously not knowing who I was. I examined the copy and recognized it—it was one that I had inscribed for my old friend Steve Takacs. Takacs had since died, and the book had passed from his estate through who know how many hands before being offered back to me! *Edgar Rice Burroughs: Master of Adventure* was reprinted by Ace Books and the paperback edition went through at least three printings.

A companion volume, *Barsoom: Edgar Rice Burroughs and the Martian Vision*, was commissioned by Ballantine Books some years later. Unfortunately the manuscript got caught up in a squabble between my editor, Don Benson, and his boss, Betty Ballantine, and kept coming back for revisions time after time. I'd tweak the manuscript to please Don and Betty wouldn't like it. I'd tweak the manuscript to please Betty and Don wouldn't like it Finally we parted company, the book was returned, and eventually published by Mirage Press after still another rewrite. It has since been reprinted in Japanese.

[2013 update: Edgar Rice Burroughs: Master of Adventure *is now in print from the University of Nebraska Press under the title* Master of Adventure: the Worlds of Edgar Rice Burroughs. Barsoom: Edgar Rice Burroughs and the Martian Vision, *is in print from Gary Lovisi's Gryphon Books.]*

My relationship with Canaveral had remained active and extremely friendly as long as I lived in New York City. However, in the mid-1960's I was transferred to Poughkeepsie by my employer. That meant a 90-mile drive any time I wanted to visit Biblo & Tannen's bookshop instead of a fifteen-minute subway ride. Then, in 1970, I moved to the West Coast, and was forced to give up my connection with Canaveral Press altogether.

If Canaveral had been as successful as hoped, the Jacks might have replaced me and continued to produce books. But instead they decided to shut down the operation, maintaining their stock until all the books were sold. Eventually they were, and today every Canaveral Press title is itself a collector's item. Perhaps the chief prize is *Tarzan and the Tarzan Twins,* which was intended for younger readers and has never seen a paperback reprint.

My last visit to Biblo & Tannen's store in May of 1970 was a sad parting, and when I returned to New York on a research trip in 1976 I went to see my old friends. Characteristically, Jack Tannen asked about my research project and gave me an important book I had not been able to find elsewhere.

David Garfunkel had died several years earlier. The last time I heard from Alice Ryter she was living in Los Angeles, operating an antiquarian book business. Jack Tannen later retired to Florida to become curator of a private library. And Jack Biblo is still living in Brooklyn, operating Biblo Books.

[2013 update: Alas, all are now deceased.—RAL]

While Canaveral Press was far from a failure, it was not nearly the success that the two Jacks—and the rest of us—had hoped it would be. The greatest potential, we all believed, lay in those five

Burroughs "originals." We felt that we should have at least a year's head start before these books appeared in paperback. But the Burroughs people insisted on retaining full control of those books, and they authorized paperbacks so fast that they appeared virtually on the heels of our hardcovers. A Canaveral edition would no sooner arrive in the bookstores than a paperback at one-tenth the price would go into competition with it. We could determine the date and time of publication of these paperbacks almost to the hour, just by tracking the disastrous collapse of the sales of the hardcovers.

There are just so many first-edition collectors out there—and a great many more readers or casual collectors who don't require hardcovers and firsts. We could never get that message across to the Burroughs people, and we paid bitterly for their insistence.

The other Canaveral Press books—the de Camp and the Smith—preformed adequately if not spectacularly for a small company with limited facilities to promote and distribute its publications. When the company ceased publishing new titles we returned properties already in house. These included a novel by James Blish and Norman L. Knight, *A Torrent of Faces*, later published by Doubleday, and a really excellent novel by Ed Ludwig. I don't know what became of that book or of Ludwig.

[2013 update: He's dead. –RAL]

Other properties that had come to Canaveral and been turned down for one reason or another were very varied. Some, I regretted having to turn down. Others were—well, let me give you a few examples.

Jerry Siegel, the writer who created Superman, offered to do a series of books for us. I would have loved to take them, but Siegel required a substantial advance that we just couldn't afford to pay, so that project, unfortunately, went a-glimmering.

Sprague de Camp offered us the revised and collated Conan series. This proposal was turned down mainly on my judgment, on the grounds that the old Gnome Press edition had saturated all possible readership for Conan. Was I ever wrong!

We were offered an "unauthorized" Burroughs biography called *The Big Swingers*. We turned it down and it later found a home elsewhere.

I wanted to issue the collected Captain Future stories by Edmond Hamilton, in hard cover. I was overruled on that one, but I still think that I was right. A later paperback series came out with very bad covers and no support from the publisher, yet today even these poor editions are sought after. I think that an attractively produced, matching set of the books would have been an achievement.

[2013 update: Haffner Press has begun issuing the Captain Future novels in a series of omnibus editions. They are splendid books, and reside proudly in my personal library.—RAL]

There were other experiences, some of them pretty unsavory, others just silly. For instance, there was the self-identified pornographer who was going to produce a "great" science fiction novel for us. He sent in a portion and outline, and the book was just dreadful. It went back like a shot! And there was the elementary school teacher who wanted us to publish a volume of poems by fourth-grade students. We declined politely. And there was the literary agent, since deceased, from whom I tried to buy a book by Avram Davidson. The agent didn't answer his mail, and whenever I phoned him he was too drunk to carry on negotiations. The book later appeared as a paperback original.

Back in those days of the early 1960's, when Ace Books was issuing Burroughs titles from the public domain list, Don Wollheim asked various Burroughs fans to write introductory notes for them. I did several of these, and also one for a book called *Lieutenant Gullivar Jones: His Vacation*, by Edwin Lester Arnold. This was a forerunner rather than an imitation of Burroughs' Martian novels, as I pointed out in my introduction. In *Edgar Rice Burroughs: Master of Adventure* I expanded on the theme of Burroughs' antecedents and sources, which struck me as both an interesting and a valid area of investigation. To my dismay, a number of fanatical Burroughs fans thought that this comprised *lese majeste*, and my name became mud for them.

Then a fellow named Irwin Porges announced in *The New York Times Book Review* that he was going to write an "authorized" biography of Edgar Rice Burroughs, and asked for documents, materials, etc. This is a very common practice. Since my own book on Burroughs had already been published, I sent Porges a letter offering my assistance. In reply, I received an extremely curt, icy note rejecting my offer.

Some years later Porges' book appeared. It was a massive tome, apparently a hodge-podge of everything Porges could throw together on the subject. Whole passages seemed to derive from existing works, mostly my own *Edgar Rice Burroughs: Master of Adventure,* and Henry Hardy Heins' superb bibliographies. Porges even reproduced the frontispiece from *Edgar Rice Burroughs: Master of Adventur,e* a wonderful portrait of Burroughs surrounded by his most famous creations.

And he did this without paying the artists, without obtaining their or my permission, and without acknowledging the original publication of the picture. Porges even went out of his way, in his text, to state that he had used primary sources only, thereby slapping in the face all those who had gone before him, and whose works he had used as source material.

At about the same time, I was contracted by a friend who reads Japanese. My friend mentioned that Edgar Rice Burroughs, Inc. was authorizing Japanese editions of Burroughs' works and including my introductory essays, to which Burroughs Inc. had no title. Again, without payment, permission, or even the courtesy of providing me with copies!

Needless to say, all of this soured the relationship between me and Burroughs Inc. I wrote to them repeatedly seeking to make an arrangement whereby they would provide courtesy copies and make payment—even token payment—for the materials they were using. They never budged an inch. Finally, rather than give anything, they volunteered to drop the frontispiece drawing from later editions of Porges' book. I don't know whether they ever actually did or not, but that wasn't the point. I wasn't trying to suppress the picture—it was a *marvelous* picture!—I was trying to get recognition and payment for the artists—Al Williamson and Reed Crandall—(and, I will confess, a credit line for myself). The last I knew, the Porges book had been remaindered, so I guess there were no later editions.

My lawyer looked over the situation and said, "You're in the right and you can't afford to sue them so go home and forget it!"

In a sense, that was the end of my association with Edgar Rice Burroughs.

But some years later, I had an intriguing telephone call from a newly hired editor at Ace Books. By this time I had become a successful fiction author myself, and one of my publishers was Ace.

"I've been looking through our contract file," my editor told me, "and I found this ongoing contract between Ace and ERB Inc. There's a clause in it that says, 'No word by Richard A. Lupoff, nor any mention of his name, may ever appear in an Ace edition of any book by Edgar Rice Burroughs.' I've never seen such a thing before. Do you have any idea why it's there?"

So I told her the story.

Of course, no one at Burroughs Inc. had ever told me anything about that clause.

A real class act, hey?

~ ~ ~ ~ ~

In 1977, when Harper & Row published my fantasy novel *Sword of the Demon*, I received a telephone call from a producer at radio station KPFA in Berkeley. They were planning a new program to be called "Probabilities Unlimited," a talk show devoted to science fiction and fantasy. Would I appear on their inaugural broadcast, to talk about *Sword of the Demon*?

I agreed, and the show ran with good response. The producers asked me back several more times, then asked me to become a guest interviewer, and finally a permanent member of the program's staff. "Probabilities" (the title was shortened before very long) has now been running for well over a decade, and has become quite a fixture of the local literary community since we broadened our coverage from science fiction to include mysteries and other literary forms.

Not long ago, on a program devoted to reviewing recent books, I attacked a paperback space opera as unworthy of having been published. One of my colleagues, Richard Wolinsky, challenged me. "It's just a space opera," he asserted, and I was wrong to judge it as if it had been a serious novel.

I insisted that this was not the basis of my complaint. Space opera or any other pulp form could still be written in valid English, not the garbled gunk that the book I'd reviewed was written in.

Wolinsky knows my fondness for many of the old pulp writers. "When did you last read Burroughs or Doc Smith?" he challenged me, over the air.

Before our next broadcast I took down Burroughs' *The Moon Maid*, Smith's *Grey Lensman*, and—for good measure—Lester Dent/Kenneth Robeson's *The Man of Bronze* from my bookshelf. I brought them to the studio and read the first sentences from each. The three authors had different approaches to writing and very different styles, but all three were excellent. Three books anywhere from forty to sixty years old, and all of them held up.

I don't regret the time I devoted to the pulps or to the pulp authors.

[2013 update: In 2010, after fifty-five years in radio, I more-or-less retired from that field. But Richard Wolinsky carries on, and occasionally invites me back into the studio for a guest appearance. –RAL]

THE LONG ROAD TO BARSOOM
2012

Part I: On the Road
(with apologies to Jack Kerouac)

Introductory comments to a benefit showing of John Carter *in San Francisco, August 11, 2012:*

A couple of days ago I was in my car and a bus pulled up alongside me in traffic and I looked out my window and saw a replica *John Carter* poster on the side of the bus. I guess they'd overlooked that one when they took down all the *John Carter* promos and replaced them with signs advertising cell phones or automobile tires or the newest crop of TV sitcoms.

It made me very sad.

The first interplanetary romance that I know of was *The True History,* by old Lucian of Samosata (circa 120-185, CE). Lucian is beloved of science fiction historians eager to acquire for their favorite branch of literature the respectability that goes with extreme old age.

Lucian described a ship caught up in a whirlwind and carried off to the sun and the moon, both of which were inhabited by odd creatures. As I remember, there were talking cabbages in this story, but I read it a very long time ago and I might have the details wrong.

Of more relevance to us, there wasn't much talk or literature about other worlds and their inhabitants for a long time after Lucian. But in the Nineteenth Century a surprising alliance of science and religion served to revive interest in the subject.

The science of optics was making great strides. Improved telescopes made it possible to see other planets as actual places rather than just points of light. And once people started thinking of Mars, Venus, and the other planets as actual places, they started to wonder if there was anybody home.

Thinkers had posited the existence of remote, inhabited worlds other than the Earth for many years, but now that it was possible to actually see such worlds, the question arose, *If God went to the trouble of creating many planets, would he put people on only one?* Well, probably not. And if there were people on the other planets, all sorts of intriguing questions would follow.

This was known as the multiplicity of worlds theory.

To this day, I believe, some theologians are undecided as to whether the Gospel of Christ and his sacrifice applies to aliens as well as to Earthly humans. Was it the duty of Christian missionaries to carry the Good News to other planets, or might Original Sin apply only to the children of Adam and Eve, thus precluding the need to wash away the stain from those talking cabbages of old Lucian.

Along came the great Italian astronomer Giovanni Schiapparelli (1835-1910) who observed Mars and detected markings which he interpreted as "canali"—channels, often mistranslated as canals. And the American Percival Russell Lowell (1855-1916) who built upon Schiapparelli's ideas in several books, the most notable of which was *Mars as the Abode of Life* (1908).

Lowell had been propounding his theories for decades, and he is sometimes cited as the inspiration of both H.G. Wells' *The War of the Worlds* (1898) and Edgar Rice Burroughs' Martian novels, starting with *Under the Moons of Mars* a.k.a. *A Princess of Mars* (1912), which we celebrate tonight.

There were no science fiction magazines in 1912—*Weird Tales* was eleven years off and *Amazing Stories* was fourteen years in the future—but there were "variety" pulps which shuffled detective stories and westerns, swashbucklers and sports stories and love stories and science fiction stories like the suits in a deck of playing cards.

Burroughs reputedly considered his tale so fantastic that readers would think the author was crazy, so he used the pseudonym "Normal Bean" as his byline; this was altered to "Norman Bean" before the story was published. *Under the Moons of Mars* was successfully serialized in Frank A. Munsey's *Argosy* magazine and we were off and running. Burroughs wrote a long series of sequels to this book, and in fact was still at it at the time of his death in 1950, at the age of seventy-four.

I entered this scene in the early 1960s. My Beloved Spouse and I were little past the newlywed stage, and I came home one evening to find her reading a somewhat battered red-covered novel. I asked what it was and she told me it was *Tarzan of the Apes*. I'll confess that I sneered. Pat had recently received her degree in

English literature, and I expected her to be reading Thomas Hardy or Edith Wharton. To me, Tarzan was an overage and overweight Johnny Weissmuller yodeling through a series of low-budget potboilers, or some crudely drawn comic books by a fellow named Jesse Marsh.

But Pat insisted that *Tarzan of the Apes* was a much better book than I thought. She convinced me to read it, and she was absolutely right, and I was hooked.

Now you must understand, Pat Lupoff is a sensible person whose reading can bounce from a jungle adventure by Edgar Rice Burroughs to a Regency romance by Georgette Heyer to a fantasy epic by Mervyn Peake to a murder mystery by Francis and Richard Lockridge.

I, on the other hand, will "discover" an author and have to read his or her entire *oeuvre*. Thus, John D. MacDonald, thus Margery Allingham, thus Edward Elmer Smith, Ph.D. And thus, Edgar Rice Burroughs.

Yes.

Around this time a little company in New York called Canaveral Press had begun reissuing long out-of-print Burroughs books. I became so involved that I wound up working for Canaveral Press. I became Edgar Rice Burroughs' posthumous editor and eventually wrote a couple of books about him.

Now, if you have read *A Princess of Mars,* I think you will agree with me that it is not a very good novel. It was Burroughs' first novel, and it suffers from the shortcomings common to first novels. Its plot is rather haphazardly constructed and it is very badly paced. John Carter travels to Mars by astral projection which Burroughs tells us is not astral projection. Arriving on Mars, John Carter discovers that he has telepathic powers but the author apparently forgets all about that after a while. The Martians use radar-aimed rifles firing radium-tipped bullets but they conduct their wars with swords. You'll remember that something in the Arizona cave from which John Carter departs for Mars scares the daylights out of a band of fierce Apaches. Looks as if the author has something planned there, but he never does return to the theme.

Doesn't make a hell of a lot of sense.

But *A Princess of Mars* succeeded nonetheless.

My friend Michael Kurland suggests that this is because Burroughs' vision of Mars, his planet Barsoom, is so detailed and so convincing, that reading this book is like reading a long letter home from a friend who is visiting a strange, fascinating, and exotic land.

And the books in the series got better—a lot better—as the years went by. They certainly have had their impact.

Ray Bradbury wrote an essay about his childhood called "Take Me Home," published in *The New Yorker* for June 4, 2012. I will quote from it:

> "I was always yelling and running somewhere, because I was afraid life was going to be over that very afternoon.
>
> "My next madness happened in 1931, when Harold Foster's first series of Sunday color panels based on Edgar Rice Burroughs' 'Tarzan' appeared, and I simultaneously discovered, next door at my uncle Bion's house, the 'John Carter of Mars' books. I know that 'The Martian Chronicles' would never have happened if Burroughs hadn't had an impact on my life at that time.
>
> "I memorized all of 'John Carter' and 'Tarzan,' and sat on my grandparents' front lawn repeating the stories to anyone who would sit and listen. I would go out to the lawn on summer nights and reach up to the red light of Mars and say, 'Take me home!' I yearned to fly away and land there in the strange dusts that blew over dead-sea bottoms toward ancient cities."

Bradbury died on June 5, 2012.

An adjunct of the multiplicity of worlds theory was a notion called "planetary evolution." Charles Darwin had published his revolutionary *Origin of Species* in 1859 and created a wave of turmoil that has still not fully subsided. Of course Darwin was writing about biological evolution. His ideas were met with hostility which has still not totally dissipated. But the general notion of evolution was in the air, and the theory of planetary evolution dealt with geological events, not biological.

The idea was that the planets were not all the same age, created by God or formed from the whirling dust cloud that surrounded the early sun. Instead, the sun popped them out at intervals, rather like a hen laying eggs.

Each planet began life close to Mother Sun, warmed by her rays, moist and fecund. As the years passed, the planet would slowly migrate away from the sun, its orbit becoming longer and longer. As it did so it would become cooler and drier and less hospitable to life.

By Burroughs' time, 1912, the three planets closest to the sun were believed to be Venus, Earth, and Mars. Mercury would remain undiscovered until 1930.

Venus, being closest, was warmest. Its thick, opaque cloud cover proved that there was plenty of moisture there. It must rain a lot. Thus we knew that the planet had deep oceans teeming with giant marine creatures, and its land masses would be covered with tropical rain forests inhabited by huge beasts.

Earth was farther from the sun, and older. It had cooled to a more temperate state and the giant beasts had given way to more modestly sized birds and fish and mammals.

And Mars, the oldest of the three, was now cold and dry, a dying world on which the decimated remnants of ancient civilizations struggled to survive.

The Mars that Burroughs called Barsoom was more like the Mars of several million years ago, maybe several hundred million, so that—this is my theory, anyway!—John Carter crossed not only space but time, as well, when he made his disembodied journey to Barsoom.

By the middle of the Twentieth Century the theory of planetary evolution had largely faded from scientific thought. Mars, we were told, was cold and dry with a vanishingly thin atmosphere and no life whatsoever. And that's the way it had always been and always would be.

There was hope for Venus, though. Those clouds kept the surface hidden but we knew that Venus was almost identical to Earth in size. And with water from those clouds and energy from Mother Sun, there might indeed be rain forests and warm seas full of spectacular species.

But fast forward to the Twenty First Century. We've put satellites into orbit around Venus and Mars, and landed scientific instruments on the surface of both worlds.

Venus, alas, turns out to have been a false hope. Those clouds aren't made of water vapor and the rain isn't water rain. We're talking about hydrochloric acid. The surface is hot, yes, but not hundred-degree hot; it's more like 500 degrees. And the atmosphere is so dense, if you could somehow stand on the surface of Venus it's a question of whether you would be cooked, poisoned, or crushed to death first. Maybe all three.

But talk about a reversal of fortune!

Our satellites that orbit Mars and our rovers that explore its surface are telling us that Mars did indeed once have great seas and rivers, a rich atmosphere, and a salubrious climate. Astonishing! This sounds rather like the ancient Barsoom.

No it doesn't. Wait a minute. It sounds *exactly* like the ancient Barsoom!

Did Eager Rice Burroughs know something that it would take a hundred years for the rest of us to find out? Was he that clever and foresightful, or was it all just a lucky guess?

~ ~ ~ ~ ~

There have been many attempts to film Burroughs' Martian novels. Most foundered on the problems of special effects. The most advanced, of which a very good test strip survives, was by animator Bob Clampett. I don't know why his project did not go forward. My guess is that Clampett was unable to obtain the funding that he needed.

There was a full-length, live action film of *A Princess of Mars,* released direct to DVD in 2009. Traci Lords, onetime porn queen, plays Dejah Thoris. Anthony Sabato is John Carter. Pat and I stumbled across this film on a movie channel, decided to subject ourselves to a few minutes of it, and wound up watching the entire thing.

I won't say that it was a good movie, but it was nowhere nearly as bad as I'd expected. This may be the reward of having low expectations.

But now we have the big-budget Disney version, titled simply *John Carter.* I chatted with my neighbor Michael Chabon about this film when he was script-doctoring it, and Michael was enthusiastic. I also asked him if he was worried about *Avatar*. That film was of course a monstrous success. Did Michael think that *Avatar* might suck up all the interest in alien-planet science fiction adventure films and leave nothing for *John Carter?*

No, Michael opined, the success of *Avatar* would only whet the appetite of audiences for more such films, emphatically including *John Carter.*

Your lips to God's ear, Michael, I thought.

Toward the end of the production cycle I was invited to a Pixar installation called Barsoom Productions to record a lengthy interview for inclusion in the DVD package.

First thing I had to do was sign a release promising not to get cranky and sue them if my footage wound up on the cutting room floor. Which apparently proved to be the case. The Pixar people showed me some clips from the film—the final version was not ready—and asked my opinion. I told them that the special effects were very impressive but I hoped they would not overwhelm the characters and plot.

They also borrowed some books from me, and promised to return them and send me a copy of the DVD as soon as it was available.

So far—no books, no DVD.

Hooray for Hollywood.

The picture opened nationwide and was pronounced an instant flop. What's interesting is that the reviews tended to be cool but not disastrously hostile. And the word-of-mouth—at least what I've heard and what I've seen in the blogosphere—has ranged from warm-and-friendly to over-the-top enthusiastic.

What went wrong?

I haven't seen the picture yet. That's one of the reasons I'm grateful that Rina invited me here tonight. But I'm really surprised that Disney was unable to make this a success. They're the masters of promotion and marketing, and *John Carter* simply disappeared without a trace.

Maybe it's a bad movie, but I don't expect that.

Maybe it was just the wrong picture at the wrong time.

Maybe Disney should stick to princesses and fairy tales and talking cars.

~ ~ ~ ~ ~

Part II: On the Road Again
(with apologies to Willie Nelson)

A few Days Later:

Now that I've seen *John Carter* I am more distressed than ever by the failure of this film at the box office, and by Disney's decision to trash-barrel it after just ten days rather than work to make it successful.

John Carter is a good movie. Maybe even a very good movie. It is certainly not a great movie. It will never displace *The Maltese Falcon, Gone with the Wind, Singin' in the Rain, The Great Dictator, Bride of Frankenstein, Nosferatu, The Gold Rush, Psycho, All about Eve, 2001: A Space Odyssey, Casablanca* or *The Wizard of Oz* from my list of Dozen All-Time Movie Favorites. You probably have your own list of favorites. I'm quite sure it's not the same as mine. I doubt that *John Carter* will be on it but I could be wrong.

Top 100? Maybe. I don't have such a list, but if I ever do . . . maybe.

But it's a very worthwhile science fiction flick. The script by Andrew Stanton, Mark Andrews, and Michael Chabon is not bad. A trifle incoherent and choppy, but good fun. The idea of casting Daryl Sabara as Edgar Rice Burroughs was clever and it was surprising. Of course showing Burroughs as a somewhat weedy twenty-something in 1881 doesn't quite match up with the Great Man's biography. He would have been six years old at the time. But we already know that the "Burroughs" in *A Princess of Mars* isn't exactly the same Burroughs who wrote *A Princess of Mars*.

And there's a real story in the film, with a very nice framing sequence set in New York. I didn't care for the flash-forward or whatever it was, of the Battle of Helium, that opens the film, but everything settles into place pretty soon.

There's some divergence from the books, not surprisingly. The role of the Therns is somewhat different from Burroughs' version, and the shape-shifting of Matai Shang, the chief bad guy in the film, is an innovation. But it works well. And while we see the hatchery of Thark eggs and some great scenes featuring the hatchlings, no mention is made of the fact that the "human" Barsoomians, Dejah Thoris emphatically included, are oviparous.

But never mind. Let's judge the film on its own merits.

Taylor Kitsch as John Carter looks like a slightly scrawny, younger Brad Pitt. He plays the role with a mixture of humor and action-heroism that works well and keeps the film from being just another dumb Arnold Schwarzenegger muscle flick. Lynn Collins as Dejah Thoris is breathtakingly beautiful. She has the indefinable quality that makes one look at her whenever she's on screen, regardless of what may be going on around her. Mark Strong as Matai Shang, the Thern, was suitably sinister. Reminded me more than a little of Voldemort in the later Harry Potter movies. The rest of the cast are at least adequate; in fact, far more than adequate.

The sets and special effects were flawless. The costumes looked a little bit too much like leftovers from a Roman Empire swashbuckler, I thought, but that's a minor quibble. The CGI green Tharks are terrific, the white apes are impressive and Woola the calot—Barsoomian dog—is a joy to behold.

Personally, I would have liked the film to spend more time exploring the characters and their relationships, the history of Barsoom and the conditions in which John Carter finds himself. I'd gladly have traded off a few minutes worth of battle scenes in exchange for this. But that's just me.

So again I ask, What went wrong? Any number of explanations have been offered. One is the *Avatar* theory—that is, that the mega-successful *Avatar* drained all the water out of the pond and left none for *John Carter*. Another: some people have suggested that the title *John* Carter was a mistake. My friend Grania Davis commented, "John Carter? Wasn't he a peanut farmer from Georgia?"

The recent flop *Mars Needs Moms* might have spooked Disney out of using the word *Mars*. At the end of the film the title flashes on-screen, *John Carter of Mars*. Huh. Maybe Disney was too smart by half. By leaving out the "of Mars" part in all their promotional material they may have taken most of the zing out of their marketing campaign. If there even was one.

When I was invited down to Pixar to give my inputs on the film—too little, too late, by far!—the people there referred to this film as "Jay-Com." Bet you can figure that one out. And the operation was called Barsoom Enterprises. They knew what they were about.

Somebody back in Hollywood clearly did not.

So now, Rina Weisman (who set up the San Francisco screening) tells me, the film has been embargoed by Disney. Meaning, withdrawn from all markets, locked away in the film vault, and a memory-wipe administered to everyone who worked on the project.

What a shame!

~ ~ ~ ~ ~

Part III: The Long and Winding Road
(with apologies to Paul McCartney)

After the Burroughs Centennial Dum Dum, August 15-19, 2012.
This was the Centennial Year. 2012. The hundredth anniversary of the first publication of both *Under the Moons of Mars* and *Tarzan of the Apes*. This year's Dum Dum, the annual gathering of the Burroughs Bibliophiles, was a truly gala event.

Held in ERB's adopted hometown of Tarzana, California (well, technically in neighboring Woodland Hills, but who's counting?) and sponsored by ERB Inc., this was a glorious assemblage of the faithful and celebration of the centennial of Edgar Rice Burroughs' two most influential works.

Speakers were fascinating and informative. The program also included a Tarzan Yell contest that was great fun, there were tours of the ERB Inc. offices, a heart-pounding dedication of the Edgar Rice Burroughs postage stamp, and a huckster room filled with lovingly produced reference works and collectible Burroughsiana. An actual Martian flying boat looked so damned realistic, my Beloved Spouse had to grab my shirt-tail to keep me from climbing into it and heading off into the wild black yonder.

There was even a goodie bag filled with wonderful items—a Bibliophiles polo shirt, a Burroughs coffee mug, a portfolio of spectacular Burroughs art, books, buttons and bows.

Our special guest, primatologist Jane Goodall, was available to meet-and-greet, and could bound from hilarious to inspirational at will. I'll be personal: I got to share my banquet meal with former Tarzan Ron Ely and with Johnny Weissmuller's granddaughter. The only adjective that I can think of is, *thrilling*. Jeez, here I am well into my eighth decade, the author of sixty-odd books, and suddenly—there I was, a wide-eyed fan again!

There was just one sour note to the weekend.

No, I take that back. "Sour" isn't exactly the right word. "Melancholy," I think, expresses it better.

This was the year that *John Carter of Mars* was going to be a huge blockbuster. After all, it had the might of Disney Studios behind it, the technical brilliance of Pixar Productions, the wallop of a quarter-billion dollar budget, and the creative genius of the Old Guy himself.

Somehow on its way from the studio to the theater the words "of Mars" disappeared from the title. The pre-release buildup sounded more like the squeal of an ulsio than the roar of a banth. Initial box office results were disappointing but a great big Disney promotion campaign would almost certainly had pumped up those numbers. Instead, Disney pulled the plug after just ten days.

Ten days!

Both ERB Inc. President Jim Sullos and Pixar Executive Jim Morris made remarkably candid presentations on the subject. There was no spin, no attempt to put on a happy face. They gave the brutal facts.

Except the facts were not nearly as brutal as I had expected. *John Carter* is a big hit, world-wide. In Moscow—biggest box office opening ever! In London—fourth biggest opening ever. In China—a major success.

DVD sales—number one in the US, first week of release. And also, number one most pirated DVD, for whatever that means.

But what went wrong? I think the most telling statistic had to do with publicity releases for *John Carter* as compared to those for its obvious box office competition, *The Hunger Games* and *The Avengers*. My thanks to Michael Sellers for the actual numbers:

The Avengers	1,497
The Hunger Games	1,119
John Carter	45

The conclusion seems inescapable. *Disney didn't want this film to succeed.* Something happened in the executive suites, some corporate knives were bloodied, and somebody—I don't know who, I'm not in the world of Hollywood corporate politics—somebody decided to torpedo this ship. To sink it without a trace.

And succeeded.

~ ~ ~ ~ ~

Part IV: Let me Sit in a House by the Side of the Road
(With apologies to Sam Walter Foss)

August 27, 2012—After the Tarzan Centennial Celebration in Sacramento, California.

It was a striking contrast. The Dum Dum was relatively big, very slick, professionally produced and a grand success. Just a week later Beloved Spouse and I found ourselves a few hundred miles north of Tarzana, attending a weekend-long Tarzan festival sponsored by the Northern California Mangani chapter of the Burroughs Bibliophiles. The event was modest in size, mildly disorganized, and totally grass-roots.

I loved both events. Loved 'em equally, although in very different ways. And although the Sacramento event had an Ape Man theme, there was plenty of side-chatter about *John Carter*. Everyone present either liked the film or absolutely loved it. Obviously, not an unbiased audience, but still, knowledgeable viewers might well bring harsher judgments than casuals. There was more talk of what had gone wrong, but by now the major facts are clear.

John Carter never had a chance. The title was wrong, the trailers were poor, the promotion campaign was virtually nonexistent (see statistics above). I'm not a lawyer—except to the degree that every author becomes a sort of jack-lawyer with a specialty in intellectual property rights—and it seems to me that ERB Inc. might have grounds for a very interesting lawsuit against Disney.

At the very least, ERB Inc. ought to demand a sit-down and an honest accounting from Disney of what they did and why and how they did it. Clearly, ERB Inc. has every moral right to demand that Disney repackage and re-release *John Carter* as *John Carter of Mars* and proceed with the second and third films for which they have an option.

If Disney refuses, then I think ERB Inc. should sue for the cancellation of the options and find another studio to proceed with *The Gods of Mars* and *The Warlord of Mars*.

But then I'm not an attorney-at-law. I'm just an humble novelist. Maybe a little bit like Edgar Rice Burroughs.

~ ~ ~ ~ ~

Postscript: Death Don't Have No Mercy
(with apologies to the Reverend Gary Davis)

June 15, 2013—While reviewing the above events.
Michael Sellers' book *John Carter and the Gods of Hollywood* told the above story in horrifying detail—and, to what I thought was its conclusion. Alas, how wrong I was! Several months ago Disney announced the purchase of LucasFilms for enough gazillions of dollars to buy Luxembourg. George Lucas, already immensely wealthy, is now somewhere up in the Warren Buffett / Bill Gates / Koch Brothers class of riches beyond imagining.

Of more concern to us, however, Disney now owns the Star Wars franchise. All the back-list films, merchandising contracts, books, videos, and—perhaps most important of all—the rights to make future films in the series.

If Disney had ever contemplated undoing the damage its mishandling (not to say deliberate sabotage) of *John Carter* had caused, and either repackaging and re-releasing the 2012 film or extending the series, or both, we can pretty well forget about it. It was unlikely anyway. Disney doesn't seem interested in undoing its errors. The folks there would rather bury their mistakes and move on to new enterprises.

But now that Disney owns Star Wars, there is no way in the entire known universe that they would try to resuscitate John Carter.

Maybe some other Burroughs science-fiction property that ERB Inc still controls—and there are plenty of them!—can still make it onto the big screen. The Venus series is the most obvious candidate.

Scrub *John Carter of Mars.*
Bring on *Carson Napier of Venus.*
Could happen. Honest to God, it really could happen.

IN ANOTHER GALAXY
2004

Robert A. W. Lowndes was known as "Doc." He wasn't a medical man; as far as I know he did not hold any kind of doctorate. But he had a scholarly air about him and was, indeed, a deeply thoughtful person. He spent a lifetime editing books and magazines, generally with microscopic budgets and nonexistent staff support, yet he always managed to produce remarkably good publications.

I once asked him what he would do if he ever had a decent bank account to work with, and he admitted that he would probably be lost. "I'm so used to making bricks without straw," was the way he put it, "I don't think I'd know what to do with real money."

One of Doc's great virtues was his terrific sensitivity as a "slushpile" reader. He could look at a stack of manuscripts, almost all of them by hopeless amateurs, and pick out the one or two or three that had real merit, and whose authors had real talent. If you have any doubt of that, think *Roger Zelazny*. Think *Stephen King*. If that doesn't convince you, think *Philip K. Dick*. And if you still need convincing, think *Jim Harmon*.

Jim Harmon?

James Judson Harmon, a twenty-one year old sometime science fiction fan and would-be author, made his professional debut in the November 1954 issue of *Science Fiction Quarterly*, with a story he'd written two years earlier, at the age of nineteen. *SFQ* was one of the last of the classic-style science fiction pulps. Jim Harmon's story was called "Voting Machine." Lowndes was the magazine's editor, the pay rates were as usual tiny, but young Jim Harmon, eager to join the hallowed ranks of Heinlein, Bradbury, Asimov, and Clarke, had made it. He had surmounted the barrier that separates the masses of wanna-be "writers" from the real professionals.

It was almost two years before Jim Harmon's next story appeared. This was a little gem called "Name Your Symptom." Most of the science fiction magazines were now in the smaller digest size, and Jim moved up to one of the top periodicals in the field,

Galaxy Science Fiction, the superb monthly created by the difficult, cranky, brilliant Horace Leonard Gold and continued, after Gold's retirement, by the highly talented Frederik Pohl.

"Name Your Symptom" was a perfect *Galaxy* story, an extrapolation of social trends carried almost to the point of *reductio ad absurdum* and injected into the reader's bloodstream with a sharply pointed needle and a healthy dose of sardonic humor.

Jim Harmon – we became friends circa 1960, and stayed friends for the rest of Jim's life

From his home in Mt. Carmel, Illinois, Jim produced slowly and carefully, but steadily: two stories in 1957, one in 1958, then five in his breakthrough year of 1959. Thereafter he continued to appear in the science fiction magazines until 1967. His favorite market was *Galaxy,* a magazine that specialized in psychological and sociological themes, with occasional forays into *Galaxy's* sometime companion magazine, *Worlds of If,* and into the highly-literate *Magazine of Fantasy and Science Fiction* when that periodical was under the brief tutelage of the erudite and sometimes acerbic Avram Davidson, and *F&SF's* companion, *Venture Science Fiction.*

Jim's stories were marked by wit and concern. His most successful story was probably "The Place Where Chicago Was," a gimlet-eyed examination of the implications of enforced pacifism. This story, first purchased by editor Frederik Pohl, has been anthologized over and over. Other stories in Jim's career are marked by a nostalgic fondness for the mass culture icons of his boyhood, and by questions of identity and reality comparable to some of the best stories of his near-contemporary, the late Philip K. Dick.

The years of Jim Harmon's science fiction career were some of science fiction's finest, with an amazing array of authors producing a steady stream of brilliant stories. But in this same era, paradoxically, the science fiction magazines were dying off. Jim's favorite market, *Galaxy,* was among the casualties. From the capable hands of Horace Gold and Frederik Pohl it passed to a series of increasingly cynical publishers and decreasingly competent editors. It disappeared, reappeared in a new format, then disappeared once more.

After a lengthy hiatus, *Galaxy* finally returned still again, this time under the aegis of Eugene Gold, the son of *Galaxy's* founding editor. But, alas, the magazine's time had passed. It still exists today, after a fashion, as a Website—an electronic simulacrum of its once robust ink-and-paper self. It's the kind of thing that might have happened, once upon a time, in a story in *Galaxy.*

From a peak population of more than forty titles in the early 1950's, the science fiction magazines dwindled to the handful that survive, just barely, to the present day.

What killed the rest?

A combination of factors, including the collapse of the traditional system of distributing periodicals, and the competition of the new medium that science fiction had so long predicted, television. But mainly, I think, it was a matter of size. Just as the pulps had given way to the smaller and more convenient digests, the latter were replaced by the still smaller and more convenient paperback book. Two major paperback science fiction lines made their appearance in the early '50s—Ace Books, edited by pulp veteran Donald A. Wollheim, and Ballantine Books, guided by canny publishing mogul Ian Ballantine.

Most of the leading science fiction writers switched from short stories, which the magazines had gobbled up in huge numbers, to novels, which the paperback houses preferred. Those who were unwilling or unable to make the switch soon faded to minor status in the field, or else disappeared entirely.

But Jim Harmon did neither. Instead, he moved into several very different realms. He did write a number of novels, but rather than science fiction they were of a more esoteric nature. Now out of print, they are eagerly sought by avid collectors who stand in line at antiquarian book shows to get Jim's autograph and to meet the man who wrote such treasured volumes as *Vixen Hollow, The Celluloid Scandal,* and . . . *and Sudden Lust!*

Jim edited several magazines dealing with motion picture history, then found his true *metier,* popular culture and cultural history. In this latter realm he is the author of several highly-regarded works including *The Great Radio Heroes, The Great Radio Comedians, The Great Movie Serials,* and *Radio Mystery and Adventure.* He presents his scholarship with the same entertaining and witty flair that marked the best of his stories.

As for myself, I first had the pleasure of meeting Jim Harmon in 1960, at the World Science Fiction Convention in Pittsburgh, Pennsylvania. Jim was one of the bright new stars in the field; my wife, Patricia, and 1 were a couple of excited young fans. To our delight, shortly after returning to our home in New York, Pat and I received a visit from Jim Harmon.

That's Jim and me at a book show in Southern California — great, great fun!

Not only did he visit us at our apartment, he actually stayed there, sleeping on our living room couch, while he was in New York. We couldn't have been more thrilled and flattered if President Eisenhower had arrived and asked permission to pitch his pup-tent in our parlor.

In retrospect, Jim was probably just saving the price of a hotel room—but we didn't see it that way in 1960, and I still treasure my memories of that generous visit by the famous professional writer to the home of two admiring aficionados.

In the years that followed, Jim and I maintained a sporadic relationship, entirely by correspondence. He commissioned me to write an article for one of his film magazines, and I was happy to earn the few dollars that the magazine paid. In return Pat and I commissioned Jim to write an article for our fanzine, *Xero,* and when a collection of articles from *Xero* was published later Jim received some monetary return for his own efforts.

He even talked me at one point into trying my hand at the literary agent business. Jim was my first and, it turned out, my only client. I earned a fat zero dollars for him, and dutifully took my commission, ten per cent of zero. It was a profession in which I was not cut out to shine.

We didn't see each other for nearly forty years. Then our paths crossed once more in the late 1990's at a mystery convention in Monterey, California. By now we were both living on the West Coast, and have managed to get together from time to time ever since even though our homes are several hundred miles apart.

At one of these meetings we were joined by Sean Wallace of Cosmos Books. I urged Jim to assemble a collection of his science fiction stories, urged Sean to consider taking on the book for Cosmos, and, to my inexpressible delight, both agreed.

The result is the book you are holding now.

Maybe I should have hung on in the literary agent business after all.

Most of the stories in this book are from Jim's era working for the science fiction magazines—*Galaxy, If, F&SF, Venture*—but others come from rather different and perhaps unexpected sources. There's one from Jim's magazine, *Fantastic Monsters,* one from Jim's book, *Radio and TV Premiums,* and one, a reconstruction of a "lost" collaboration with the great Robert Bloch, from *Scientifiction,* the journal of an organization of veteran science fiction fans.

A special treat is "Pyramid of the Visitors," newly written for the present book but actually a skillful and deliberate throwback to the days of radio adventure shows, a subject on which Jim Harmon is a world-class authority.

Somewhere in another universe there may be a planet almost identical to our Earth, where the only difference is this: the "paperback revolution" of the 1950's never quite got off the ground. As a result, *fictionmags* galore elbow one another for display space on the sales racks. The forty science fiction magazines that existed in 1953 are still going, along with several dozen more.

The science fiction short story, instead of being a minor companion piece to the novel, is still the chief focus for writers, editors, publishers and readers.

Galaxy Science Fiction is the world's most popular magazine, with planet-wide circulation of some fifty million copies every month. Maybe every week, who's counting? The magazine's pay rate starts at ten dollars per word, and its most popular author is Jim Harmon, who of course receives a huge bonus rate over the standard ten bucks a pop.

I'm not sure who sits in the editor's plush office these days, beneath a copper bust of H. L. Gold. Maybe me.

I like to think of that universe as *Harmon's Galaxy*.

A HANDFUL OF DARKNESS
(PHILIP K. DICK) — 1978

A Handful of Darkness (1955) was Philip K. Dick's first collection of short stories and his first book to appear outside the United States. It enjoyed reasonable success, being reissued in the UK by the (British) Science Fiction Book Club, and still later as a Panther paperback. The paperback edition, however, omits several of the stories from the original hardcover. Perhaps surprisingly, the book has never been published in the United States prior to the present Gregg edition. A number of the stories it contains have been available in later Dick collections—notably *The Preserving Machine* (Ace, 1969), *The Book of Philip K. Dick* (DAW, 1973), and *The Best of Philip K. Dick* (Del Rey/Ballantine, 1977).

Fully nine of the fifteen stories *in A Handful of Darkness* are available in none of the three later collections, and short of a file of quarter-century-old pulp magazines, this book is the preferred source for the text of the stories.

The importance of Philip K. Dick is increasingly recognized, and will almost certainly continue to grow in recognition through the 1980s. Dick is a classic example of late recognition. Not of "late blooming," for his work has been distinctive, striking, powerful and incisive from the start. This is not to say that his later works fail to show growth over the earlier ones. On the contrary. His novels of recent years —*Flow my Tears, the Policeman Said* (1974) and most notably *A Scanner Darkly* (1977)—are clearly superior works. The latter in particular exhibits Dick's talent for sensitive characterization, startling rendition of social milieux, dizzying reorientations and pessimistic portraiture of a distorted but still recognizable reality; all of this punctuated by the author's astonishing and deadly interjections of black humor.

For many years Dick labored in relative obscurity, his earliest days marred, perhaps, by his own prolificacy which caused him to be labeled (inaccurately) as a hack. In recollection of those days, Dick recently stated, "I had had a lot of stories published. In 1953

I published 27 stories, and almost as many the next year. In June of '53 I had seven stories on the stands simultaneously."

The great Philip K. Dick

[Interview with Philip K. Dick, conducted by Richard A. Lupoff at Sonoma, California, November 27, 1977. The interview was tape-recorded and all quotations are transcribed from the tape. Paragraphing and punctuation provided by the interviewer.]

His very first sale had been to Anthony Boucher, then co-editor with J. Francis McComas of *The Magazine of Fantasy and Science Fiction.* The story was "Roog," which appeared in the February, 1953 issue of the magazine. Dick's first published story, however, in distinction to his first sold, was "Beyond Lies the Wub," in *Planet Stories* for July, 1952. This was followed in print by "The Skull," *Worlds of If,* September, 1952.

Within three years of his first publication, Dick had published the better part of 100 stories in almost every science fiction magazine extant at the time. "But no American publisher approached me to do a collection. This was before I did any novels. And Rich and Cowan in England approached me with the idea of putting out a collection of stories.

"They were incredibly primitive. I sent them several fantasies that had been published in *F&SF*. And because the fantasies dealt with children, Rich and Cowan said they were stories for children. So I suppose the audience for Agatha Christie's mysteries should be axe murderers. My original idea for the collection included more of the *F&SF* fantasies but Rich and Cowan rejected all those. The ones that were picked were substantially science fiction.

"I made the selection, by and large. Every story that they looked at was one that I submitted to them rather than one they found on their own. But they continually kept rejecting stories and I kept sending more, so it took three or four separate batches of stories before they agreed on the contents. And the contents were quite satisfactory to me at the time."

Regarding these same stories, Dick offered a somewhat different assessment in later years. "These do represent the earliest stories of my career, and at the time they definitely seemed to me to be the best stories that I had published.

"I feel that they are very minor works now. Looking back on them, there is very little there of substance compared to my later stuff."

But despite the author's later dismissal of his early works, they are of great interest to the reader, indicating the point of departure for Dick's later works and demonstrating in prototypal form such persistent concerns as:

~ The treachery and danger implicit in reliance upon machinery. In "Colony" a microscope strangles its user; an automobile literally eats its driver (and in an early display of Dick's black humor, comments, "Glub").

~ The question of establishing identity and of distinguishing between human and robot or android beings. In "Impostor" a man is accused of being a robot impersonating himself, and struggles desperately to prove his identity until he himself comes to doubt it.

~ The mixture of Eastern mystical philosophy and Western scientific speculation, and the interplay, conflicts, and possible dialectical synthesis of these, as later developed in Dick's first major success, the novel *The Man in the High Castle* (1962). In "The Turning Wheel" a probability scanning device is used to predict the next incarnation of a bureaucrat—on another planet.

~ The destructive power of obsessive love. In "Upon the Dull Earth" a man's unwillingness to accept the death of a loved one leads to universal disaster.

All of these themes can be traced in later and more developed works of Dick's. Their presence in these early stories provides an illumination of his grasp of the themes in an earlier form.

To obtain a clear perspective on the stories in *A Handful of Darkness,* it will be useful to pursue Philip Dick's own views of himself, his surroundings, and the literary field of his choice. Fortunately there are available two autobiographical sketches by Dick published in 1953. These will be followed by a reminiscent view of the same era, as given during a November, 1977 interview.

In the February, 1953, issue *of Imagination,* Dick published an autobiography as one of a series of features titled "Introducing the Author." This is its text:

> Once, when I was very young, I came across a magazine directly below the comic books called *Stirring Science Stories.* I bought it, finally, and carried it home, reading it along the way. Here were ideas, vital and imaginative. Men moving across the universe, down into sub-atomic particles, into time; there was no limit. One society, one given environment was transcended. Stf was Faustian; it carried a person up and beyond.

Dick: I was twelve years old, then. But I saw in stf the same thing I see now: a medium in which the full play of human imagination can operate, ordered, of course, by reason and consistent development. Over the years stf has grown, matured toward greater social awareness and responsibility.

I became interested in writing stf when I saw it emerge from the ray gun stage into studies of man in various types and complexities of society.

I enjoy writing stf; it is essentially communication between myself and others as interested as I in knowing where present forces are taking us. My wife and my cat Magnificat, are a little worried about my preoccupation with stf. Like most readers I have files and stacks of magazines, boxes of notes and data, parts of unfinished stories, a huge desk full of related material in various stages. The neighbors say I seem to "read and write a lot." But I think we will see our devotion pay off. We may yet live to be present when the public libraries begin to carry the stf magazines, and someday, perhaps, even the school libraries."

In the September-October 1953 issue of *Fantastic,* Dick published this brief note:

> "Appeared on terra just twenty-three years ago, in Chicago, Illinois. Very cold, rainy day. Moved quickly to Berkeley, Cali-

fornia to get back in the sun. Grew up slowly over the years, listening to Bach, reading dusty second hand fantasy magazines, writing little sinister stories. Married a girl anthropology student from the University and bought a house and a cat. Have finally arrived as a writer. Droves of small boys, all aficionados of science fiction, greet me on the street. Ah, Fame!"

[Dick attended the University of California at Berkeley in 1950, enrolling as a philosophy major, but shortly thereafter dropped out.]

A certain wry ambivalence toward the science fiction fan population is visible in the *Fantastic* autobiography; this ambivalence was not apparent in the *Imagination* autobiography. In a 1977 Sonoma interview, a far more negative reaction to the *aficionados* is apparent, its expression arising as a side-issue to Dick's enumeration of his own reading experiences and education as a writer:

Dick: "After going to Cal I was working part-time in a music store. I finally got to the point where I was manager of the record department and I would work half a day and then write the other half day. I made my first sale to Tony Boucher at *F&SF* in November of '51. I attended a writing course that he gave. I submitted 13 different stories simultaneously. I figured I stood a chance of selling one, perhaps, of the 13. Which is exactly what I did, and I had to revise it considerably for Tony.

"There's no substitute for good prose models. I like the stories of Maupassant very much. And the short stories of James T. Farrell had a tremendous influence on me. In the novel form, the French realists—Flaubert and Stendahl and Balzac and Proust. And the Russians, Turgenev and Dostoyevsky, and some of the playwrights like Chekhov, for example."

In response to the question, Did he not then grow up on the works of science fiction pulp authors like E.E. Smith, Dick said:

Dick: "I did that too, but the culture in Berkeley, the milieu in Berkeley in the late '40s, required you to have a really thorough grounding in the approved classics. If you hadn't read something like *Tom Jones, Moll Flanders, Ulysses,* you were just dead as far as being a guest anywhere. If you went to a party and you hadn't read Dos Passos' *USA* . . . .

"I had read plenty of science fiction but the pressure of the milieu—you have to bear in mind that in the late '40s and early '50s, science fiction was so looked down upon that it would have been tantamount to suicide in a group of people to come forward and say, 'Boy, did I read a marvelous story recently!'

"And then they say, 'Well, what was it?'

"And then you say, 'It was *The Weapon Shops of Isher* by A.E. van Vogt.'

"I mean, they just would have pelted you with half grapefruits and coffee grounds from the garbage, if they could have deciphered who you meant anyway. They just wouldn't have known the name.

"I wasn't faking it that I enjoyed things like *War and Peace*. I did read *War and Peace* all the way through and it was truly exciting. I really loved it.

"Of course, there was a kind of fandom, there was the Little Men's Science Fiction, Marching and Chowder Society and I knew the people in it. But they were all real weird freaks. They were unpalatable to me because they did not read the great literature. There wasn't anybody that read both. You could either be in with a group of freaks who had read Heinlein, Padgett and van Vogt, and nothing else, or you could be in with the people who had read Dos Passos and Melville and Proust. But you could never get the two together, and I chose the company of those who were reading the great literature because I liked them better as people. The early fans were just trolls and whackos. They were terribly ignorant and weird people.

"So I just secretly read science fiction, and then I would write it, and people in Berkeley would say, 'But are you doing anything serious?' And that used to make me really mad. Then I would all of a sudden drop my posing and I would just get furious and I would say, 'My science fiction is *very* serious!'—if I said anything at all. I just got so mad I could hardly talk."

Philip K. Dick wrote a special foreword for his later collection *The Preserving Machine*. Ironically the foreword did not appear in that book, but instead in a scholarly journal. In it, Dick draws an intriguing distinction between the short story and the novel:

> A short story may deal with a murder; a novel, with the murderer, and his actions stem from a psyche which, if the writer knows his craft, he had previously presented. The difference, therefore, between a novel and short story is not length . . .
>
> There is one restriction in a novel not found in short stories: the requirement that the protagonist be liked enough or familiar enough to the reader so that, whatever the protagonist does, the reader would also do, under the same circumstances . . . or, in the case of escapist fiction, would like to do. In a story it is not necessary to create such a reader identification character because (one) there is not enough room for such background material in a short story and (two) since the emphasis is on the deed, not the doer, it really does not matter—within reasonable limits of course—*who* in a story commits the murder. In a story, you learn about the characters from what they do; in a novel it is the other way around: you have your characters and they do something idiosyncratic, emanating from their unique natures. So it can be said that the events in a novel are unique—not found in other writings; but the same events occur over and over again in stories, until, at last, a sort of code language is built up between the reader and the author . . .

While this assessment may have been formulated after the fact—by 1969 Dick almost entirely abandoned the writing of short stories to concentrate his efforts on novels and occasional essays—it casts light upon his earliest works, including those in *A Handful of Darkness*. There are no memorable characters in these stories; rather their strength lies in the striking events (and/or situations) depicted.

Three of these stories—"The Preserving Machine," "The Little Movement," and "Expendable"—were originally sold to Dick's mentor and sponsor, Anthony Boucher, and appeared in Boucher's magazine. It was Boucher's practice to write lengthy (or relatively lengthy) introductions to stories in his magazine, rather than the brief blurbs of most pulps. His comments on Dick's stories are of particular interest.

For "The Preserving Machine" he said:

> In November of 1951 Philip K. Dick sold his first story (to *F&SF*, we may add proudly), and within a very few months thereafter he had established himself as one of the most prolific new professionals in the field. By now he has appeared in al-

most every science fiction publication—and what's more surprising, in each case with stories exactly suited to the editorial tastes and needs of that particular publication: the editors of *Whizzing Star Patrol* and of the *Quaint Quality Quarterly* are in complete agreement upon Mr. Dick as a singularly satisfactory contributor. Joining with them, we consider this latest Dick precisely *our* kind of story: gently witty, observant and pointed, with a striking new idea attractively blending science and fantasy.

For "The Little Movement" Boucher said:

It's a healthy fact that the science-fantasy field is constantly producing new authors with fresh and individual attitudes. Besides the stories of the Old Masters, and quite on a level with them, you've been seeing in the past year or two the works of Kris Neville, Chad Oliver, Mildred Clingerman, Zenna Henderson, J. T. M'Intosh—new writers of a stature to guarantee the future high quality of the field. One of the most striking of these, in our opinion, is Philip K. Dick, who made his debut only a few months ago. In "The Little Movement," the first of his many contributions to *F&SF*, Mr. Dick combines a startling idea (which no introduction should even hint at) with a modern simplicity and directness of writing guaranteed to produce nightmares which no Gothic elaboration could rival.

For "Expendable," Boucher said:

Philip Dick is at his best when dredging up the *wrongness* that lies just below the placid exterior of our everyday living. And, as he marshals his array of terrifying facts he makes it very clear that their wrongness is in our eyes alone. The overall picture of our existence makes excellent sense . . . to those interested parties whose primary concern is not with man.

It is obvious that Boucher held Dick in high esteem. That the feeling was reciprocated is indicated by the coda of Dick's *Preserving Machine* foreword:

Tony Boucher—what is the field going to do without him? It was his encouragement that got me to try submitting my stories; I had never imagined that they might sell. Consider this collection as dedicated to Tony and everything he represented. We shall never see another of his like. *Te amo,* Tony. Forever.

In fact those three stories are all works of merit, although not all equally so. "The Preserving Machine" is a fantasy (as are all of the three) and reflects Dick's concern for and knowledge of classical music. There are references to Mozart, Beethoven, Schubert, Brahms, Wagner, Bach and Stravinsky. This was written during the period when Dick worked in a record store. The story is a most amusing conceit—the conversion of a Mozart quintet to a bird, a Beethoven composition to a beetle, and so on—but is not much more than that, an amusing conceit.

"The Little Movement," despite Boucher's enthusiastic endorsement, is not really so original or striking an idea. The child's fantasy of his toys as alive and either benevolent or malevolent must be a nearly universal one. But the story epitomizes a notion of Dick's. In the Sonoma interview, he expressed it thusly:

Dick: "I ran into a lot of opposition on my fantasies because my early fantasy stories were essentially psychological stories. They were heavily into anxieties such as animals or children would feel, in which the thing that was feared actually came into existence and was treated objectively. And I just stopped writing those because people would say, 'Well, there's really no such thing as ———' The sentences would begin that way.

"So finally I just gave up and wrote straight science fiction. I abandoned the fantasy format because what I meant by a fantasy was evidently not what other people meant by fantasy. My idea of a fantasy was where the archetypal elements become objectified and you have an exteriorization of what are inner contents.

"And I remember, I had a term I used. *Inner Projection Stories.* Stories where internal psychological contents were projected onto the outer world and became three-dimensional and real and concrete. And Scott (Meredith), my agent, wrote me incredibly long letters saying that there was no such thing. There was the inner world of dreams and fantasies and the unconscious, and there was the objective outer world, and the two never mixed.

"So I gave up. But then later when I had established myself more securely in the field I began to go and do it in such books as *The Three Stigmata of Palmer Eldritch.* I reverted to what I wanted to do and had the nightmare inner content objectified in the outer world so I slowly began to reintroduce those elements into my writing."

And still later in the Sonoma interview, Dick said: "Now we have the collective unconscious of a number of people being projected and forming a *tulpa* object. I've read some interesting material on that—Jung was a *major* influence on me."

Of these three stories, "Expendable" may well be the most striking and suggestive of Dick's later themes. As in Arthur Machen's *The Terror* (1917) we see a plot by the humble creatures of the Earth to destroy Man. But Dick elaborates the idea by setting up two competing forces of beasts (actually, insects), one inimical to Man, the other friendly.

Further, where Machen uses the notion to build a story of bafflement and fear, Dick makes "Expendable" a wry exercise *a la* Stephen Vincent Benet or John Collier. And the ending is most typically Dickian: the protagonist, about to be devoured by malevolent insects, is resigned, diffident, even apologetic. And the whole exercise is astonishingly *funny!*

"Impostor" was the only story that Philip Dick ever sold to John Wood Campbell, Jr., the many-years editor of *Astounding/Analog* magazine and high *doyen* of science fiction. Campbell's opinion of Dick was apparently none too high, nor Dick's of Campbell, as expressed in the Sonoma interview:

Dick: "Campbell just called my stories nuts. He said they were crazy. He bought one story, 'The Impostor,' but he told me that psi had to be a premise. Psi is a necessary premise for a science fiction story. And I had a very strong prejudice against psionics in a science fiction story. I thought it was a form of the occult and should not be allowed to invade science fiction. I've changed my mind since. But at that time I thought of it like witchcraft, as superstition. (But now) I think the powers actually exist. I think they're real."

Although only two of the stories in *A Handful of Darkness* were published in magazines edited by H.L. Gold—""Colony" in *Galaxy Science Fiction* for June, 1953 and "Upon the Dull Earth" in *Beyond Fantasy Fiction* #9, 1954—these were only two of a larger number purchased by Gold. In the Sonoma interview Dick said:

Dick: "Horace Gold and I wrote back and forth quite a bit. I later had a terrible fight—it was in '54—with Horace Gold. Because Gold would change parts of your story and add whole new scenes and new characters without telling you and publish them, and you would suddenly discover that you had collaborated with Horace Gold. I just got to the point where I couldn't stand it any more, and I told him that I would not submit to him as long as he was going to take out scenes and put in other scenes. And I did not resubmit to *Galaxy* until he ceased to be editor.

"That was my main market at the time, so I took a tremendous financial risk in doing that. But then I was going into novels. That was one of the reasons why I *had* to go into the novel form. And then I started hassling with Donald Wollheim so I didn't gain a thing."

The two "Gold" stories in A *Handful of Darkness* are probably the most significant in the book. As Boucher had pointed out, the early Dick was a protean author, capable of providing any editor with the kind of story required for a given periodical. Gold's concerns were wry satire, social relevance, and wit. These characteristics, along with a sometimes solipsistic questioning of the nature of reality and our epistemological grasp of reality, have marked all of Dick's major successes.

The extent to which Gold positively influenced Dick, as against that to which their interests and outlooks merely coincided, is conjectural, but the similarities are not.

The actual scientific—or pseudo-scientific—theme of "Colony" is far from original with Dick. It had been treated, with minor variations, by Isaac Asimov ("Misbegotten Missionary," *Galaxy,* November, 1950), John W. Campbell ("Who Goes There?" *Astounding,* August, 1938), and Donald A. Wollheim ("Mimic," *Avon Fantasy Reader* #3, 1947). What makes Dick's treatment distinctive is the paranoia-inspiring (or paranoia-inspired!) imagery of the towel attacking its user, the gloves killing their wearer, the floor eating the feet that stand upon it, and finally the escape-ship devouring all of its passengers! If our most trusted artifacts are ready to gobble us up at any moment, what ease can we find in the world?

"Upon the Dull Earth" is a far more somber tale than "Colony." It deals with profound questions of morality, couched in a bizarre mixture of traditional Christian belief and pure Arthur Conan Doyle type spiritualism. Yet even in this very serious, frightening, and depressing story there are present light Dickian touches of the commonplace and concrete. Thus, Mrs. Everett's steel-rimmed eyeglasses, and the brand-named Silex coffee maker. Such touches were typical in Gold's magazines, and were and still are typical of Dick's fiction.

Two more fantasies are included. "The Cookie Lady" (from *Fantasy Fiction* for June, 1953, edited by Lester del Rey) is a fairly routine supernatural horror story; a vampire tale, in effect, in which the vampire steals her victim's youth rather than his blood. But while the story appears slight on first reading, further consideration reveals a poignancy and moral ambiguity, provoking a sympathy for the vampire equal to—perhaps greater than—one's sympathy for her victim. And "The Builder" (from *Amazing Stories,* December-January, 1953-54) is a decidedly slight gimmick story of the sort typically written by beginners.

Despite this slightness of the story, Dick speaks well in the Sonoma interview of Howard Browne, his editor at *Amazing:* "Howard Browne was a lot of help to me. He was a very good editor. He defined the kind of story that he felt I could best write, and he was quite correct."

Five of the remaining stories can be regarded as minor efforts typical of the science fiction magazines of the day. "Planet for Transients" *(Fantastic Universe)* projects a radioactive earth of the future, in which mutations are the norm and "normal" man is the alien. "The Impossible Planet" *(Imagination)* is thematically related to "Planet for Transients," taking place in the more distant future, by which time the earth is a semi-legendary ruin. (American readers will be amused by the footnote added for the Rich and Cowan edition, explaining the meaning of *E Pluribus Unum* on American coins.)

"Prominent Author" *(If)* and "The Indefatigable Frog" *(Fantastic Story Magazine)* are two more gimmick stories, one dealing with a circularity in time, the other with Zeno's Paradox. Both are readable and amusing, but trivial. And "Progeny" *(If)* is a not-very-successful tearjerker founded upon the obvious difference in attitudes between generations.

Much more of interest is found in "Exhibit Piece" and "The Turning Wheel." The former story *(If,* August, 1954) is one of Dick's earliest treatments of the problems of solipsism and the nature of reality. Specifically, his hero divides his life between a "real" future, and a museum exhibit of 1950s culture—and in time loses the ability to discern reality from construct: "Look, Grunberg. Either this is an exhibit on R level of the History Agency, or I'm a middle-class businessman with an escape fantasy."

Was Lao-tze a philosopher who dreamed he was a butterfly, or a butterfly who dreamed he was a philosopher?

The use of precisely this sort of questioning is of course a thoroughly familiar Dickian strategy, occurring over and over in virtually all of his successful works including *Ubik, The Three Stigmata* and many others, and climaxing in the final resolution of *A Scanner Darkly*.

Philip K. Dick graces the cover of a book about his posthumous adventures (drawing by George Barr)

"The Turning Wheel" *(Science Fiction Stories* #2, 1954, Robert W. Lowndes, editor) is one of the most dense and rewarding of all Dick's stories. In it he projects an odd future, both beautiful and ugly; a realignment of the races (Indian/Mongolian/Bantu /Caucasian), an interesting caste system with Bards at the apex and "Technos" at the bottom; a few jokes tossed in for good measure (note the farmer's daughter and the travelling salesman); and even a dig at L. Ron Hubbard ("Elron Hu"), who by 1954 had abandoned his own career as a science fiction writer in order to promote Dianetics and Scientology.

It was the interplay of Eastern and Western philosophies that, coupled with Dick's profound moral concerns, human sensitivities, and obsession with the multiple aspects of reality (or the aspects of multiple realities) that led him to *The Man in the High Castle* and his first significant recognition as a writer of importance.

FINDING CHASE AND DELACROIX

The first mystery story I ever wrote appeared in *The Orinsaga,* a mimeographed newspaper published more or less daily at Camp Orinsekwa for Boys, located in Niverville, New York. I cannot tell you the volume or issue number in which my story appeared. The date would have been some time in July or August of nineteen forty-something.

When I tried an internet search recently for Camp Orinsekwa I found a few passing references to it, including the fact that an Orinsekwa Road still exists, but the camp itself has long since disappeared from the face of the earth. I think that's a pity. The rolling hills and glittering lakes of that place, the social hall with its wooden stage and amateur theatricals, the camp's cramped newspaper office, its rowboats and sailboats and athletic fields were a summer paradise for a city boy like me, especially one whose home and school life were very far from idyllic.

The disposition of Camp Orinsekwa's archives is a mystery. Perhaps a file of *Orinsagas* reposes somewhere in a library or among a onetime camper's personal effects.

If so, and if some scholarly soul could find that piece of mine, I would be grateful to receive a copy. I don't remember the title of the story or its plot. I do remember my detective's name: Nick Train. This was either a remarkably prescient combination of multilingual pun and *noir* imagery, or a lovely piece of dumb luck on my part. Probably the latter.

But even if I can't tell you what the story was about, I can tell you what *kind* of story it was. It was a brain-teaser. Brain-teasers were a popular form of short-shorts in those days. A typical one would go something like this:

> Three travelers share a ride from the railroad depot to their hotel. One is left-handed, one is wearing a bowler, and one has a smudge on his cheek. Which traveler tips the cab-driver?

Based on the clues given in the story, the reader was supposed to solve the puzzle. Brain teasers were published regularly in mass-circulation slick magazines and collected into inexpensive books. I must have read hundreds of the things and I never got one of them right.

Book cover for Quintet: The Cases of Chase and Delacroix
(cover by Deborah L. Miller)

Some years after I created Nick Train and wrote that now-lost story, the principal of my high school, one Harold Morrison Smith, delivered his pre-commencement lecture to my senior class. He spoke at length about our school's distinguished alumni and their contributions to the well-being of the world, admonishing all of us seventeen- and eighteen-year-olds to go forth and emulate them. I was particularly taken with his comments regarding Willard Huntington Wright.

Dean Smith—he preferred that academic-sounding title to the more generic "principal"—recounted Wright's career as an art historian and as the author of a serious novel about a young man's coming of age, as well as several volumes of nonfiction; as a distinguished editor and associate of H. L. Mencken and George Jean Nathan, and as a scholar whose scathing criticism of the *Encyclo-*

pedia Britannica had led to the creation of the rival *Encyclopedia Americana.*

In later years I learned that this last claim was only half true. Wright had indeed written a controversial book lambasting the *Britannica,* but the *Americana* was already in existence. Its first edition dated from 1829.

Wright also—

At this point the Dean's voice dropped nearly to a whisper. One might almost think that he was ashamed of the words to follow, but was compelled in the name of intellectual honesty to speak them.

—wrote several popular mystery stories under the name S. S. Van Dine.

Even as a teenager I knew I was going to be a writer, and Dean Harold Morrison Smith's reference to a member of this revered fraternity's having attended my school awakened my imagination. Willard Wright might have taken classes in the same rooms where I struggled with chemistry, battled futilely with algebra, and reveled in sweeping tales from history and classic works of literature. For all I knew, he might once have occupied the very desk where I found myself during Dean Smith's lecture, we two kindred spirits separated only by the passing years. I searched for a telltale *WHW* among the age-blackened initials carved in my desktop by generations of departed students, but all in vain.

Ours was an exclusively male institution, and its distinguished alumni other than Willard Wright included a B-movie leading man, some mid-level academics and minor captains of industry, a muscular lineman for the Philadelphia Eagles, and several old grads who had served with distinction in World Wars One and Two.

But—a writer? A mystery writer at that?

Even so, for a good many years my interest in Willard Wright remained dormant. Then in 1992 John Loughery published the first full-scale biography of Wright and I learned that Dean Smith's onetime hero was in fact anything but the noble, scholarly chap he'd been made out to be.

The man was a churl. Willard Huntington Wright was a fascinating but utterly despicable swine.

If you doubt my word, track down Loughery's book. It shouldn't be hard to find, but if all else fails you can sit in my living room and read my copy. Give me a call next time you're in the neighborhood and we can crack the seal on a bottle of some ancient vintage and shoot the breeze for a while. Then I'll leave you alone with this excellent biography. Learn the details for yourself.

Spurred by Loughery's biography, I tracked down copies of Wright's Philo Vance novels and read several of them. To be candid, they are crushingly boring. But as Van Dine, Wright had hit upon a wonderful formula. He wrote about an amateur sleuth, well connected in urban society, who could step in and apply his powers of pure deduction to unravel the most baffling of mysteries. It seemed to me that this formula might be revived to good effect, at least for a brief homage. Still, I didn't do anything about this for a number of years. The stars would have to be right.

My opportunity came in the year 2000, when British anthologist Mike Ashley asked me for a locked-room mystery. That was when I created my amateur super-sleuth, Akhenaton Beelzebub Chase, a.k.a. Abel Chase or simply "ABC," and his lovely, talented assistant, Claire Delacroix.

It seemed to me that the eccentric genius as amateur sleuth was very much an anachronism. Rather than try and drag Chase and Delacroix into the present day, I set my story in the early 1930s. I'd never attempted a locked room or impossible crime story before, and I found it great fun to work one out. The story was well received but I had no intention at that time of returning to my characters and their milieu.

But they stayed with me, and in due course I had reason to revisit them. In 2003 I was informed that I was to receive the Lifetime Achievement Award of the Left Coast Crime Convention, to be held in Monterey, California, in February of the following year. The convention committee decided to issue a mini-anthology in conjunction with its festivities. The editor, Vallery Feldman, asked me for a story. I felt that a Chase and Delacroix case would be apt, and in due course it appeared in the anthology, *Left Coast Crimes*.

Then Lou Anders, the editor of *Argosy* magazine, invited me to submit a story to the latest incarnation of the legendary first pulp magazine ever published. Thus, the third Chase-and-Delacroix. Please note, by the way, that the sequence of writing, the sequence of publication, and the sequence of fictional events are not necessarily synchronous!

By this time I found that Abel Chase and Claire Delacroix were taking on lives of their own. I had created them as fairly minimal characters, but the more I wrote about them, the more I thought and dreamed about them, the more they revealed to me of themselves. What transpired in their inner lives? What had their respective childhoods been like? What were their interests and attitudes and beliefs?

Why, any number of readers have asked me, does she put up with that arrogant twerp?

Eventually I wrote two more Chase-and-Delacroix stories, which appear for the first time in *Quintet: The Cases of Chase and Delacroix*. But even then, the job was not finished. I thought it was, but I was mistaken. Now that Chase and Delacroix had taken on lives of their own, some of the minor characters in the stories began to do the same. The later stories already written had started to move away from the eccentric genius model and more toward the hardboiled world of the pulps. Burt van Hopkins, not even present in the earliest stories, makes a brief appearance later on and becomes a major character in *The Case of the Bilious Bookman*.

I realized that he had a background of his own worth investigating, which led to *The Case of the Martian Colossus*. This story takes place several years *before* the first Chase and Delacroix story and was in fact as much a surprise to me as it will be to anyone else. I felt that it belonged in the present collection, and my editor-*cum*-publisher, Douglas Greene, agreed.

And if you've wondered why there are six stories in a book called *Quintet*, that's the reason.

Is the saga of Chase and Delacroix now over? Will there ever be more stories about them? Perhaps even a novel?

In all honesty, I do not know. I spoke earlier of creating these characters, but in truth I've long since realized that I don't create my stories or the women and men in them. I just poke around in the morning newspaper, observe my fellow shoppers at the supermarket, chat with friends as I exercise at the gym, open my mind to what dreams my come, and find what I can find.

Maybe I'll bring back Chase and Delacroix.

Maybe I'll bring back Nick Train.

[Update, 2013: To my great surprise, the novel that emerged from this process did not involve Chase and Delacroix after all, but none other than Nick Train. It was the inaugural publication of Henry Franke's Dark Sun Press. It's titled Rookie Blues.—*RAL]*

SCIENCE FICTION HAWKS AND DOVES: WHOSE FUTURE WILL YOU BUY?
(*Ramparts* magazine)

The many thousands of readers and several hundred writers who inhabit the chrome-plated world of science fiction have found themselves, in recent years, in a puzzling situation. Accustomed to decades of scorn ("What, you really read that crazy Buck Rogers stuff?") they now suddenly discover that their steadfast faith has been rewarded.

Science fiction novels and anthologies burgeon in the bookshops, *The Wall Street Journal* recently reporting that in the last five years, the number of science fiction novels published annually in the United States tripled from fewer than 60 to over 175. Science fiction films and TV productions receive larger budgets and a more respectful treatment than the potboilers of the past. The predictions of television in every home, radar, jet airliners, nuclear driven submarines and power plants, medical (and mind-altering) drugs, organ transplants and prostheses, cryogenics, monorails, electronic brains, and—holy of holies!—space ships carrying men safely to the surface of the moon and back to earth while scientific probes visit Mars and Venus—all of this is now the reality. Frederik Pohl, a leading science fiction author and editor (and in recent years a highly respected "futurist" capable of extracting large fees from major corporations in exchange for telling them what tomorrow—and the day after tomorrow—hold) has gone so far as to suggest that science fiction is the literature of reality, while the commonly held "realistic" fiction is in fact a species of fantasy.

But this triumph has had a bitter aftertaste. The trouble with the "science fiction world" in which we live is that technology, instead of bringing Utopia, has brought us to the edge of self-destruction. Instead of building a shining civilization, we are caught up in a menacing rearguard action against forces which make the very survival of civilization or of organic life itself beyond a relatively short period of years, a matter for serious debate.

And as might be expected, the heightening awareness of this state of affairs has led to great discomfort in the science fiction community. It has led, in fact, to a schism between those who maintain science fiction's traditional values and others with a very different outlook. It is more than a generation gap; it is a serious philosophical confrontation mirroring that in the larger society.

A member of the traditionalist camp will, of course, hold attitudes on many different issues; there is no party line which traditionalists support point-for-point. But there is a certain congruence of beliefs. Perhaps the prime characteristic is the overall optimism regarding the *status quo* and the course of human development, an optimism placing heavy emphasis on the beneficent role of the machine. One may see as godfather to this group Jules Verne, himself an optimist whose faith seldom faltered, who upheld the established political, national, racial, and economic interests of France and of the growing bourgeoisie of which he was part.

Those science fiction writers who are in revolt against this position are suspicious of technology, to say the least, and pessimistic about the foreseeable future. If there is a spirit hovering over the critical attitude this group has toward existing institutions, it would be that of H.G. Wells, along with Verne one of the fathers of science fiction and himself increasingly pessimistic about the future of mankind. From the start of his career to its end. Wells, a socialist and an internationalist, was deeply apprehensive about the misapplication of technology, and used his writing to popularize his apprehension.

From the very early *The Time Machine* (1895) to *The Shape of Things to Come* (1933) and beyond, Wells' outlook was gloomy: in *Time Machine* he foresaw a division of humanity into a brutal and degenerate species controlling an effete, dispirited remnant of social man; in *Things to Come*, he chronicled the emergence of a joyless authoritarianism.

What Verne and Wells have to do with science fiction in the 1970s is not at all a mere matter of literary history. Verne held Wells and all he stood for in cordial despite, and the heirs of their respective traditions are still locked in struggle; a quick survey of the racks in any paperback bookshop provides ample evidence that the cleavage (albeit with some notable exceptions in the form of "hybrids") is deeper and broader than ever.

Science fiction is a very old class of literature, but its unique identity dates only from the founding of *Amazing Stories* magazine by Hugo Gernsback in 1926. While science fiction stories had appeared—alongside westerns, mysteries and other adventures—in the earlier pulp magazines, Gernsback gave science fiction its characteristic identification as fiction wedded to pulp magazines. Pulp fiction had certain distinctive characteristics. It was distinctly optimistic ("escapist"), extremely colorful ("lurid"), employed caricatures and stereotypes instead of characters (*vide* Doc Savage, Kimball Kinnison, Captain Future, etc.), and it was thoroughly dedicated to rapid and violent action amidst exotic settings (i.e., dealt in external rather than internal values).

Classic pulp fiction—with its emphasis on the externality of things—was "Vernian" whether it happened to be about spacemen, pirates, cowboys or detectives. The prose style was subordinate to the gimmickry and plot. Subtlety, formal experimentation, obscurantist effect, and virtually any other deviation from the concrete and declarative is alien and contrary to the pulp spirit. It is this spirit, as much as the romance with technology, to which the dissident school of contemporary science fiction has opposed itself. The innovators, in addition to criticizing accepted norms of social organization, experiment frequently with the prose form, thereby trying to build a "literature of the future" out of its crude *lumpenprole* past, or at least to bring science fiction up to the standards of general literature which passed it by decades ago.

An illuminating moment in the schism between the science fiction establishment and its foes came about in 1967 and 1968, when the science fiction community, like the rest of American society, engaged in loud debate over the Vietnam war. Starting at the Milford Conference in August 1967 (an annual science fiction writers' workshop) the proposal was made that science fiction writers express themselves on the issue of the war. The mechanism to be employed was left open: it might be a resolution of the Science Fiction Writers of America, or some other device. Those favoring such a move argued that science fiction, dealing with the shape of social evolution, must address itself to such an issue. Those opposed argued that science fiction writers' conferences and organizations should be concerned only with professional matters.

The final result was not one but two statements, which appeared as paid advertisements in 1968 issues of *The Magazine of Fantasy and Science Fiction* and *Galaxy Science Fiction*.

An examination of the signers of the two statements is illuminating as to the state of science fiction, a state which has continued to evolve since 1967-68 but which has not been *essentially* altered since then.

The "war" ad carried 72 signatures including those of Poul Anderson, Leigh Brackett, John W. Campbell, Hal Clement, L. Sprague de Camp, Edmond Hamilton, Robert A. Heinlein, Joe L. Hensley, R.A. Lafferty, Sam Moskowitz, Larry Niven and Jack Williamson. The "peace" ad carried 82 signatures including those of Isaac Asimov, Peter S. Beagle, James Blish, Anthony Boucher, Ray Bradbury, Terry Carr, Samuel R. Delany, Lester del Rey, Philip K. Dick, Thomas M. Disch, Harlan Ellison, Philip José Farmer, Harry Harrison, Damon Knight, Ursula K. Le Guin, Judith Merril, Joanna Russ, Robert Silverberg, Kate Wilhelm and Donald A. Wollheim.

The "peace" ad carried more names than the "war" ad even though it was signed exclusively by professionals while the other was padded with the signatures of fans. What is more significant is the fact that *every* author or editor who signed the "war" ad was a traditionalist. Whatever else divides these traditionalists, they are united by their engineering mentality and its preference for violent, repressive solutions to the political problems posed in its novels. These authors seem convinced that the application of the right materials and the right forces will solve any problem. It is obvious in their fiction.

The late John W. Campbell was a clear example of this mentality. A former engineering student at MIT, Campbell rose to prominence as a science fiction writer in the 1930s. He created a number of impressive mood pieces and some intriguing intellectual puzzle stories, (One of the latter, "Who Goes There?" was adapted for the screen as *The Thing;* it is one of the classic 1950s science-fiction-as-paranoia films, antedating the more widely remembered *Invasion of the Body Snatchers* by half a decade).

But Campbell hit his stride in a series of superscientific, technologically oriented novels like *The Black Star Passes* (1930) and *The Mightiest Machine* (1934). In these stories human values are absent, technology is glorified, force and destruction are implicit in the solution of all problems, While Campbell was the editor of *Astounding Science Fiction* magazine (from 1937 until his death in July 1971, although the magazine had by then been renamed *Analog),* he "discovered" and guided the development of many of the leading authors of the late 1940s and '50s, contributed much to the development of science fiction, and boosted the circulation of his magazine to close to 100,000 copies, triple that of its nearest competitors.

Unfortunately, with the passing of time, Campbell fell increasingly prey to assorted crackpot and rightist notions. In 1947 he introduced to his readers L. Ron Hubbard's *Dianetics,* "the new science of the mind." The literature and procedures of Dianetics reveals it to be little other than a simplified version of orthodox Freudian theory—but restated in engineering-like terms, and offered with absolute guarantees of success. Later Campbell promoted the Hieronymus Machine—a device for concentrating psychic energy—and the Dean Drive, a sort of perpetual motion device for powering spaceships. Still later Campbell's editorials "proved" that slavery was a desirable institution, that nonwhites are inherently inferior to whites, that the whole ecology/environmentalist movement was hysterical silliness, and that the four students killed at Kent State brought it on themselves and deserved what they got.

One of the classic functions of Wellsian science fiction is to act as a warning sign: *Here there be tygers!* Fictions which perform this function are dystopias, of which Orwell's *1984* and Huxley's *Brave New World* are among the best examples. This kind of science fiction asks, more specifically, What happens when urban decay is carried to a logical end? (This question is explored in Harry Harrison's *Make Room! Make Room!* and is examined, with slightly different results, by the English writer John Brunner in *The Jagged Orbit* and *Stand on Zanzibar.)*

But Vernian science fiction, "engineer's fiction." by virtue of its dedication to control, to predictability, to the finite, closed-end solution, finds itself incapable of tolerating a fictional situation lacking clear parameters. The engineer succeeds in dealing with machines; trouble arises for the engineering mind with the entrance of human factors.

It is no accident that science fiction traditionalists have usually either limited themselves to trivial technological stories (like those of Edmond Hamilton), or to brutal barbarian-world epics (like those of Lin Carter). There are those who attempt to write serious sociological science fiction, like the celebrated Robert A, Heinlein, but it tends to be a type of crypto-fascist propagandizing.

"Discovered" by Campbell via a story contest in *Astounding,* Heinlein was graduated from Annapolis in 1932 and, using his engineering background to good effect, quickly established himself as a leading producer of science fiction stories for *Astounding* and its now-defunct companion *Unknown Worlds.* His production increased from two stories in 1939 to seven in 1940, thirteen in

1941. After Pearl Harbor he returned to naval service as a civilian engineer (he worked for a time with de Camp and Asimov); following the war he resumed writing and proceeded from success to success. He became probably the leading science fiction writer of the 1940s.

The typical Heinlein story was for many years a carryover of the pulp tradition: a well-meaning and inoffensive young man is confronted by a villainous old fellow and/or a conspiracy; the two struggle—the villain fighting dirty, the hero clean—until the hero wins out, gets the girl, collects the fortune, and lives happily ever after. Examples are *The Devil Makes the Law* (1940) and *Citizen of the Galaxy* (1957).

This kind of simplistic morality makes for good adventure, but as a serious work it resembles a Barry Goldwater fantasy, (Heinlein was a vigorous Goldwater supporter in 1964; he was also a pioneer Bircher but resigned from the society because of its domination by crackpots rather than genuine reactionaries). As he became increasingly concerned over humanity's distressing pluralism, Heinlein's writing became increasingly bitter.

Starship Troopers (1959) projects a society in which only veterans of military service are permitted to vote. Beyond this notion, however, the real message of the book is that the universe is populated with alien intelligences inherently inimical to humanity: that the exploration of other worlds *must* be a matter of war to the death. This story caused a furor in the science fiction community; both James Blish and Gordon Dickson wrote rather good novels in rebuttal; Heinlein also won the Hugo, the annual award of the science fiction fans, for the best novel of the year.

In 1961, with *Stranger in a Strange Land,* Heinlein— never dreaming that he would become a cult hero for hippies—entered a strange territory himself. The book is a weird and confused jumble of mysticism, brotherly preachiness, and attempts at sexual liberation. (David Crosby used Heinlein's term "water brothers" in his song "Triad.") The book's notion of "discorporation" of enemies was cited by Charles Manson as the inspiration of his own bloody exploits.

Heinlein made his statement on the subjects of power, sex and race in *Farnham's Freehold* (1964). Written during the fallout shelter craze, its hero is a rugged, virile John Wayne type who is thrown into the future by a Soviet nuclear attack.

Along with him go his alcoholic wife, his daughter, his weakling son, the son's fiancée and their Negro houseboy, who is frequently referred to as "a gentleman" (which means that he turns his back in cramped quarters rather than see a naked white woman). We learn that a combine of third world races has picked up the remains of the US/USSR debacle and established a pretty good world order based loosely on classic Moslem culture. We only gradually realize that surviving whites are divided into two categories—house slaves with the males being "tempered" (castrated)—and females kept in harems between service as "bedwarmers" for their masters—and the breeding stock who, we find out much later, serve ultimately as food for the colored masters.

Two years later *The Moon is a Harsh Mistress* appeared; it is, essentially, the story of the war of independence of lunar colonists against the Earth. It clearly depicts Heinlein's notion of an ideal society: a kind of rightist-anarchist state operating virtually without a government.

Social Darwinism and economic determinism take care of everything; the strong and the competent survive, the weak and the foolish perish. For the minimal government preserved, Heinlein's hero and a few cronies set up a mock constitutional convention where all of the word-benders, hair-splitters and democratic rhetoricians can debate to their hearts' content while a little cabal of self-appointed elitists quietly go off and run the world.

Heinlein's latest book, *I Will Fear No Evil* (1970), is slow-moving and almost plotless, but reveals the author's attitude toward the problem of urban development (big-city decay) and his feelings about women's proper role.

The story portrays a crusty old billionaire who undergoes a brain transplant, finds himself turned into a beautiful young woman and enjoys his/her new gender-role, finally dying in childbirth. Throughout the book we see Heinlein striving for liberation and failing to attain it. The protagonist is clearly entranced with the prospect of sampling psychedelics yet instead drinks alcohol for the explicit purpose of "getting tiddly." (This is intriguing, for as early as *The Puppet Masters* (1951) Heinlein permitted his hero and heroine to use a clear analog of "speed" in order to crowd a month-long honeymoon into 24 hours.)

In the cities of *I Will Fear No Evil,* the rich and powerful travel in armored cars, live in walled bastions surrounded by armed bodyguards, and venture beyond these safe confines at mortal peril, for the proles live unpoliced lives of degeneracy and filth. Well, let 'em: if they weren't naturally shiftless they'd be rich!

R.(afael) A.(loysius) Lafferty represents an interesting contrast to Heinlein. A man surely "more Catholic than the Pope," he informs his stories with such passionate religion that they emerge from the page as a series of pious shrieks. Lafferty's religion is deeply rooted in the hope of heaven, and a logical chain can be discerned in them, of this nature: Heaven is a far better place than Earth, and we can reach heaven only by dying (in a state of grace); therefore there is nothing more desirable than to die (in a state of grace).

Lafferty's novels such as *Fourth Mansions* (1969) and many of his short stories are cleverly constructed, brilliantly narrated, and do offer a way out of the dilemma of technology: we need only abandon our wicked worldliness, return to the sheltering arms of Holy Mother Church, and we and our descendants may die securely ever after, in a sort of perpetual Fourteenth Century, world without end, amen.

Fortunately the dead hand of thirty years ago is not the only one that rests on the typewriter keyboard. Many science fiction writers—especially, younger ones—currently exhibit a concern and insight that leads them to make significant and useful statements in their works, statements concerning both the nature of individual life and relationships, and the structure of society.

These same writers often, if not unanimously, are striving with considerable success to broaden and update the lexicon of acceptable techniques, transcending the elementary narrative approach inherited from science fiction's pulp era.

A major influence in this area is the English author J.(ames) G. Ballard. In a series of novels such as *The Crystal World* (1966) and in many short stories, Ballard introduced a device to science fiction not unknown in other realms of literature but new here. Whereas most fiction is comparable to the motion picture, in that "something happens" (one scene), following which "something else happens" (second scene) and so on . . . Ballard's works are more nearly comparable to large-canvas paintings, upon which the artist first sketches his subject, then begins to add detail and color, working on, adding greater depth of impact and feeling, but never *changing* to another scene/event.

In this sense, it might be said that *nothing* happens in a Ballard story: in conventional fiction a serious indictment; in traditional pulp writing a capital crime; but by insight, by powerful symbolism, by sheer strength of his statement, Ballard has forced his works upon a largely resisting science fiction field, and won acceptance and praise from the segment of the professional and readership groups sufficiently open to understand his art.

In Ballard's wake, and with the encouragement of such editors as Michael Moorcock, Judith Merril, and later Harlan Ellison, a new generation of English and American science fiction writers have attempted a more serious art for social comment. A listing of these writers, assuredly subject to debate and addition, must reasonably include Brian Aldiss, John Brunner, Moorcock himself, and in America, Philip K. Dick (a contemporary and fellow pioneer of Ballard's), Thomas M. Disch, Samuel R. Delany, and (in his later works) Robert Silverberg.

The serious fiction of these authors does not contain many (if any) utopias. Somehow the era of grand socially-engineered schemes for universal happiness expressed in fiction is not now: it was the age of Edward Bellamy. It had been the age of Verne; but Wells was unable to sustain it; Huxley set a minor-key tone and Orwell placed the face of death on fictional utopias.

The Gernsback-pulp scene, drawing inspiration from Verne, did attempt to portray glittering futures, but somehow failed, leaving the field of all serious, future-oriented fiction to other tasks. And because science fiction of serious intent has in recent years devoted itself to the tasks of identifying *questions* and fulminating multiple answers, there is plenty to keep it busy.

That the conclusions reached are usually pessimistic is not necessarily evidence that no assistance is offered in building a decent and viable future society. As analyst, satirist, critic and prophet, the writer of science fiction offers just as valuable aid through questioning and warning of dangers as he would by holding out glowing hopes of salvation.

There is no one person of Heinlein's stature writing this kind of science fiction, although a number of writers might vie for such a position: Dick, Frank Herbert (author of *Dune),* possibly Silverberg. But very likely the finest intellect in science fiction today is Thomas Disch.

Disch's best book to date, *Camp Concentration* (1968), deals with the struggle-of-the-spirit of a war-resister, imprisoned in a military detention camp, held powerless and isolated from the outer world, striving to maintain a meaningful existence; from a position of dispassionate reporter, Disch's hero Sacchetti grows to the realization that life in a state of grace is not a matter of passive piety, but of conscience-driven commitment. In this novel Disch addresses what is surely a central issue for millions of persons today, who are aware of rottenness in society but undecided as to whether they shall act for reconstruction or simply withdraw from those parts of society most immediately offensive and "do their own thing."

Also of this party is Donald A. Wollheim, whose critical study of science fiction, *The Universe Makers* (1971), provides excellent insights into the conflicts and potential of this literary form. A radical since the 1930s, Wollheim has the broadness of view to see science fiction as a social phenomenon and an instrument of social criticism, although he understands that the political left has often not agreed. In a recent letter he said, "I was in the 1930s a premature anti-fascist and in favor of socialism . . . the real Communist Party people we met all disapproved strongly of science fiction and of our 'wasting our time' with escapists.")

Wollheim's book is distinctly personal and opinionated; in viewing science fiction as a social instrument, he rejects the Ballard-Aldiss-Moorcock group for excessive pessimism and prefers traditional narrative techniques to experiments, but he sees the thousands upon thousands of science fiction novels and stories as elements in a gigantic macro-history of the universe, in the ultimate chapter of which conscious intelligence will have established itself in a gigantic web, spanning the universe, and (at least in a metaphorical sense) achieving, creating, *becoming* God.

Seeing science fiction as a tool for criticism and construction, Wollheim ends his book by saying:

"We are not going to end with a bang.
"We are not going to end with a whimper.
"We are not going to end.
"That's all."

SPEECHES

WESTERCON, SAN FRANCISCO, CALIFORNIA, 1979: VERY NEAR TO MY HEART

My very good friend Jerry Jacks was Chairman (not yet the politically correct but linguistically absurd, "Chair") of the 1979 West Coast Science Fiction Convention, or Westercon. I remember strolling on the Marina Green in San Francisco with Jerry and my Beloved Spouse a year before. Jerry drew Pat aside for a brief private conference. Then he invited me to be Guest of Honor at the convention. Of course, I accepted.

The duties of a GoH at one of these shindigs are minimal and the perks are very nice. One is expected to circulate and gladhand the fans, sign autographs, and participate in one or more panel discussions. And the biggie, of course: you must deliver the official Guest of Honor speech.

The latter is usually delivered at an evening banquet, but this year the format was modified to replace the traditional evening event with a Sunday brunch. The convention was held in the splendid pre-quake confines of the Sheraton-Palace Hotel in a wonderful courtyard surmounted by a spectacular stained-glass roof. Since there were no transportation expenses involved, the committee had arranged to put my family—three kids, Pat, myself—in a suite at the hotel.

The convention went well. Attendance was high, programming was successful, and I had prepared a speech that I thought might get some attention beyond the usual pleasantries of the day. Someone had set up a video camera and I was interviewed briefly by the great John Stanley, a reporter for the San Francisco *Chronicle* and local TV movie host.

The meal began. As usual on such occasions I had lost my appetite. I'm sure the meal was delicious but I sat terrified as I awaited my turn at the microphone. Finally I stood, my script on the lectern, clutching my wife's hand for all I was worth.

"It's customary to start guest of honor speeches with a word of thanks and a few lines to the general effect of, Isn't science fiction wonderful," I started my guest of honor speech. I continued in the traditional manner for a few minutes, then launched into what I *really* had to say. I won't steal my own thunder by summarizing the speech. Instead, here it is—courtesy of my friend Andy Porter, who obtained my original manuscript after the fact, and has preserved it all these years.

VERY NEAR TO MY HEART
(Guest of Honor speech, Westercon 32, 1979,
San Francisco)

It's customary in guest-of-honor speeches to start with a word of thanks and a few lines to the general effect of, Isn't science fiction wonderful. I'll bow to that tradition.

The first book that I ever read was a Big Little Book by the late Russ Winterbotham. It came out in 1941, when I was six years old, and it was science fiction, and I loved it. I didn't *know* it was science fiction because I'd never heard of science fiction, but that's what it was.

Within ten years the rush of post-World War II magazines had started. I read *Galaxy* and *F&SF* and *Other Worlds* from the first issue of each. And through the fan columns in magazines like *Amazing* and *Startling Stories* I learned that there was such a thing as fandom, and that was as wonderful a discovery, I think, as my discovery of science fiction itself had been.

I was your typical junior-high-school aged fan. Overweight, nearsighted, thoroughly inept at the social graces, too smart by half for my own good, and just *awful* with girls. Science fiction and fandom gave me a refuge from a pretty bad situation. They offered an alternative *set of values* from the rather tough, macho, anti-intellectual standards of my supposed peer-group. They placed value on learning, on rationality, and on co-operation.

They were really a Godsend.

I was strictly what we used to call a "postal" fan all through high school and college. It was only when I spent two years in the Middle West, courtesy of the US army, that I actually hooked up with the Indiana Science Fiction Association. Out of that group emerged at least five pros—Robert Coulson, Juanita Coulson, Eugene deWeese, Beverley deWeese, and myself. I think that's quite a few for a small, local club. Most of the time we had only about six or seven members. In fact, I think I "always" wanted to be a science fiction writer. At least, ever since I moved past the usual childhood ambitions of being a fireman or a fighter pilot—remember, I was a child during the Second World War—eager to get out there and shoot down enemy airplanes.

And this is where I think I've been very lucky.

Most of us have youthful dreams of the things we want to do when we grow up. The things we *really* want to do. Become a rock and roll star. A roller derby demon. President of the United States. A brain surgeon. Pope. I have one friend who still wants to be Pope—and he's Jewish, at that!

But most of us—I'd say *at least* ninety-nine percent—wind up working as factory hands, or insurance sales reps, or junior-high English teachers, serving as faculty advisor to the student literary magazine and pretending to ourselves that it's *Colliers* or *The American Mercury* or even *Thrilling Wonder Stories*.

Of course there's nothing *wrong* with people doing these jobs. The world needs factory hands—at least I suppose it does. And everybody has to earn a living one way or another. But it's kind of tragic when somebody doesn't get to follow his or her star. Sometimes there's just no opportunity. Sometimes the economic pressures are too great to bear. Sometimes we give it a try and discover to our chagrin that we simply don't have the talent to become a professional lion-trainer.

I know that it's easy to succumb to those pressures. I spent twelve years in the computer industry before I became a full-time free-lance, and when I quit my job the computer industry lost the services of a guaranteed third-rate program analyst and manual writer. I want to thank the people who made it possible for me to get out of the computer business. Those include all of my editors and publishers, especially Larry Shaw, who bought my first novel. All of the booksellers who put the things out there where people can buy them. And certainly all the readers who are really the reason that literature exists.

I want to thank everyone who sacrificed and who encouraged me to keep slogging through years of rejection slips. Not that I've seen my last one of those. But the late James Blish refused to accept, "I can't make it," from me, no matter how many times I tried and failed. My three children, who missed allowances and new clothing, and who made do on spaghetti and skimpy rations because Dad was too stubborn, or too lazy, or too proud to throw in the towel and go get a steady job.

And especially, I want to thank one who has stuck with me for more than twenty years, who has endured atrocious behavior on my part, and done menial labor for miserable wages ... so I wouldn't have to leave my typewriter.

Thank you, Pat.

Now through all of this, one of the things I have most enjoyed in my association with science fiction, is this, our community. Of course the literature itself is significant, and I won't minimize its value. But quite aside from that, our community is quite unlike any other that I know of. We are not like the people who invest their passions in baseball, or bestsellers, or ballet.

The basis of our community is not that of a fan/pro dualism, but a sort of brotherhood and sisterhood of people who are interested in science fiction. Some of us are writers, some are editors, illustrators, readers, collectors, dealers. It is not a two-sided relationship, but more that of a group of people, however diverse, who all share a dedication, of whatever degree, to a common interest.

This came about naturally in science fiction. The early fans—I'm talking about the science fiction fans of the 1930s, but this is true to a certain extent even of the old Lovecraft-Long-Kleinert-Greene fandom of the 1910-1920 era—the early fans of the 1930s were largely the pros of a short time later. There was Charlie Hornig, plucked from the ranks of fandom to edit *Wonder Stories*. There was Ray Palmer, writing for the pulps in his teens and editing *Amazing* not long after. There were Don Wollheim, Elsie Balter Wollheim, Fred Pohl, Julie Schwartz—who was literary agent for both Lovecraft and Stanley Weinbaum before he could drink beer legally in New York ... Judy Merril, Virginia Kidd and more.

At the early science fiction conventions, circa 1940, you couldn't tell the fans from the pros because the fans *were* the pros. To a large extent that's still true, and the uninterrupted flow of fans who become professional writers, editors, illustrators, publishers, and critics, continues to amaze me.

This is the science fiction community that I have known and loved for the past thirty years, and I'm afraid it's a sign of incipient middle age—or worse—when I see those institutions changing, and instead of keeping up with the change I get all grouchy and reactionary.

But I do see those institutions veering, and it *is* making me, I'm afraid, all grouchy and reactionary.

I think the major change started to come into our community in the 1960s. At first it could be seen only in the peripheral fandoms created by the special-interest groups that spun off from general science fiction fandom. The first of these was comics fandom. The next was the special *Star Trek* fandom that later expanded to take in other media-oriented groups like the *Star Wars* fans, *Close Encounters* fans, *Logan's Runners*, *Battlestar Galactica*, *Alien*, etc.

These special fandoms and their institutions share a number of characteristics with one another that they do not share with the more traditional, community-based science fiction fandom.

First, they are not spontaneous, they are artificially created.

Second, they are not community-based upwellings of energy and joy, but are externally-controlled.

Third, they are heavily oriented to media, particularly visual media: spectacular, powerful, but usually trivial in content and intellectually shallow.

Fourth, they are dominated by the well-known Hollywood mentality. They are heavy on hoopla and glitter. They are very concerned with money, are often well-heeled and able to spend money, and certainly are designed to make money. And they are molded to the configurations of a rigidly stratified caste system. That's *caste* with an E on the end.

Let me tell you a little bit of my experience with this kind of operation.

The first convention of the sort that I attended wasn't totally dominated by this kind of thinking. It was put on, in fact, by a very good-natured local group. But it was a group that had evolved out of *Star Trek* fandom, had had experience only with *Star Trek* type conventions, and naturally followed their example.

I was invited to their grand event, stood in the registration line, and received my badge. It was just like everybody else's membership badge, except it had a little green circle on it. In short order I discovered that green circles were for officially designated privileged characters. Pros, top echelon members of the convention committee, folks like that. They didn't make very much difference in the way one was treated, but I discovered that there were minor—well, what sociologists call *rituals of deference* attached to having a green circle on your badge.

I attended some program item where the room was very crowded, and I saw a person leave a seat near the front of the room. I figured he was departing for the rest of the hour and slid into his chair. In ten minutes he came back, looked at me in distress, and indicated that he wanted his seat back.

I started to leave. He *was* in the right, of course.

At this point, the poor fellow spotted my horrid *green circle* and fled! Great Klono! What would have happened to him if he'd actually thrown an officially designated privileged character out of his seat!

Well, that was my first exposure to Privilege, and I did not like it.

My second was at a *Star Trek* convention. I had been invited to attend and to participate in a panel discussion. I didn't know much about *Star Trek*, I told the committee-person who had invited me, and didn't think I really would have much to say to that audience.

Oh, no, I was assured. This was a *science fiction* panel. The members were all science fiction people, not just *Trek* personalities. So I consented—somewhat reluctantly.

Shortly before the convention, I discovered that the panelists were being paid. I'd never heard of such a thing. Well, *some* of the panelists were being paid. The person regarded as having the Biggest Name was to receive $500. One or two lesser lights were to receive $200 apiece. And a couple more of us were expected to perform *gratis*.

Now I found myself doubly offended. I really didn't like the elitist notion that the panelists were being paid, at what I was still very naively thinking of as some sort of community gathering; and I was personally insulted that I was considered "big" enough to appear there with, well, let's call them Jules Wollstonecraft Wells and Clare Kinnison . . . but they were getting paid and I wasn't.

So I quickly changed my plans and didn't participate.

My third encounter with this kind of outfit, came at a supposed "charity event" sponsored by a *Star Trek* group. Since this was for charity, I was willing to perform—notice the change coming over my vocabulary—at this function, *gratis*.

I arrived at the appointed site and was met by a cordial member of the committee, and was given my membership badge. There was nothing subtle this time. No green circle. Instead there was a little shiny gold star pasted on my badge, just like I used to get for good spelling in second grade.

I was led to a backstage area, ushered into a VIP lounge generously stocked with lavish cold cuts and expensive booze, and introduced to my personal gopher, a very pleasant young person who hovered so close that at one point I wondered if I would be permitted to visit the rest-room unaccompanied.

I met a number of real Hollywood stars, had an altogether pleasant time, and learned how such personages are treated.

Speech: Westercon San Francisco CA 1979

Well, for starters, I was wrong about everybody-donates-to-charity. The Hollywood attractions *were* paid, and very generously so. They were met at the airport by limousines, chauffeured to their hotel, surrounded by security squads, driven to the hall where their eager fans awaited them, snuck in through a back door, presented onstage, hustled backstage again to stoke up and tank up at the VIP room, and eventually limo'd back to their hotel and/or airline.

Everything was spelled out by contract. Mr. Luminary agrees, in exchange for a fee of X dollars, payable in advance, to make *blank* many appearances of *blank* many minutes duration apiece. He will appear in costume... in street clothing... in formal wear. He will deliver a prepared talk of *blank* minutes length, will/will not respond to questions from the audience, will/will not be available for *blank* many periods of so-many minutes apiece, to shake hands and sign autographs for the fans.

All of this leads to a whole new form of social organization. In place of the familiar community of fans, writers, editors, collectors and so on, we have a fairly clear-cut, two-tiered system.

The upper tier, or privileged classes, are further stratified into:

Stars (that is, the actors; Trekkies don't realize that William Shatner is an actor who once portrayed a space-captain; to them, he *is* a space captain)...

Associates (this includes producers, directors, writers, technicians, etc.) On one occasion an executive producer's *secretary* was a Special Guest. Not wishing to cast aspersions on the profession of secretary, but what did she have to say? "Oh, working for Mr. Big was the most wonderful experience. I got to meet so many Stars! Well, let me tell you what Ms. Sexpot is *really* like, off the screen!"

Committee People (who get to rub elbows with Stars and the Associates of Stars, thereby obtaining a sort of status by osmosis). Also associated with this class of lesser privileged characters are the security squads, gophers, and lesser functionaries who don't quite get to rub the illustrious elbows, but are allowed to stand nearby and warm themselves in the Presence...

Well. In the lower echelon of this new order are the—why, you and I would call them fans, or convention members. To the Hollywood mind they are customers, or audience, also known as hayseeds, rubes, or marks. They buy the tickets to support their betters in luxury and comfort. Their function is to pay their money; in return for this they are permitted to seat themselves and see the show.

Somehow it works. Of course, it isn't community. It isn't family. It's business. Show business.

Unfortunately, I can see some of this stuff—some of these attitudes and practices—creeping over into *our* community. Specifically, into our conventions. Signs of this were visible last year at the Worldcon in Phoenix.

For instance, there was Class A (reserved), and Class B (general) seating at the Hugo ceremony. There were blue badges for the peons, and red badges for the officially designated privileged characters—the pros, key committee members, and recognized Big Name Fans. At one point during the program I mentioned that I found these practices objectionable. Specifically, I mentioned the red badges and the blue badges. I felt as if I were back in the army, where officers had one color parking stickers for their cars and enlisted troops another for theirs.

Well, one of my colleagues on the panel challenged me. "Lupoff," he said—words to this effect, anyway—"Lupoff, you've got your head fifteen years in the past. You can't run a convention for six thousand fans the way you could run a convention for six hundred.

"These badges aren't for *our* benefit. They're for *their* benefit. These poor kids traveled thousands of miles to see us, and these red badges are to make us visible for them!"

He had a point, but I still don't like the VIP system. Maybe I picked up a radical, egalitarian streak as a small child in the Great Depression, but I don't like a caste-based society.

Besides, it leads to this kind of thing... One well-traveled writer has made it known that he just won't attend *any* convention, unless he's paid to do so, or unless he's named Guest-of-Honor.

Word of this, and of others being paid to attend conventions, spreads and those *not* paid start to feel mistreated. I had a letter recently from an East Coast science fiction writer, one of the finest literary minds and one of the most splendid persons in the science fiction world.

I'd written and urged that, if at all possible, the person attend this Westercon. Back came a letter saying, "Am I just being paranoid, or are there now two classes of pros, the ones like—X—who get paid to attend conventions, and the ones like me, who get played for suckers?"

It's divisive. It's discriminatory. It's exploitative.

And the ones who are being exploited are—you, the fans.

What can the science fiction community do about this? Well, we can't stop Space Gems Conglomerate Limited Incorporated from putting on a giant star-studded show, soaking the suckers for everything the traffic will bear, and getting rich off the proceeds. Let 'em have their conventions. And if you want to attend, as a paying customer, and if you think you're going to get your money's worth, there's nothing wrong with that either. I'll tell you a secret. If any of these bozos make me an offer I can't refuse, I won't refuse. I'll cash their check. Willingly.

But for decency's sake, let's try and keep them out—and keep their poisonous, insidious ways out—of our own, our real, our traditional-type, community based, science fiction conventions. Let's keep having our family reunions from time to time, and if the family is getting kind of big, that's fine too.

I said "*Let's* do this," and "*our* conventions," but I don't think that I can do much about it. The established pros can't. They're too busy and it's somehow a little bit unseemly for a science fiction author to put on a science fiction convention. I've spoken of this science fiction community as a sort of seamless garment, but even so it does have a body, and sleeves, and maybe a cowl or hood; the parts are one but they're not interchangeable.

The *fans* run the conventions, and I hope that you fans will keep control of your conventions. Whatever you do, don't let them fall under the sway of the big-buck, it's-all-show-biz, caste-system-oriented Hollywood sharpies. Or it's all over now, baby blue.

~ ~ ~ ~ ~

One more little bit. I've taken a lot of time. I've kind of broken the rules by speaking beyond the usual pleasantries and reminiscences and talking about some real stuff that is very near to my heart.

But I want to take just a couple more minutes and examine, briefly, what those Hollywood types think of science fiction as a cultural form, and of the science fiction community that you and I are all members of.

First of all, it's obvious to Hollywood that there's money to be made in science fiction. *2001* in the movies and *Star Trek* on TV were the early indicators of that.

Secondly, fandom—or, the rubes—can be a nice little source of revenue themselves, if not for the big-buck producers then for a crew of smaller fry who cluster around them.

Thirdly, fandom can be useful in other ways. The skillful manipulation of fandom in the famous *Star Trek* letter-writing campaign was an outstanding example of successful exploitation.

Fourthly, fandom can't *always* be manipulated. The total flop of the attempted *Battlestar Galactica* letter campaign proved *that*.

Clearly, Hollywood is interested in science fiction because we're a good potential source of money-making stuff. But don't kid yourself that they give a damn about us. This is mainly the pros' problem, not the fans', but it might be of interest to you anyhow.

Let's take, for example, Brother George Lucas. I've never met Brother Lucas but he's obviously smart and energetic, and I understand that he's a nice fellow into the bargain. All of this I concede. He also made one hell of a movie.

He brewed up a mixture, so-many percent Doc Smith, so much Jack Williamson, a generous portion of Heinlein juvie, a little dash of Frank Herbert, a touch of the Wizard of Oz and a whiff of Laurel and Hardy, and *voila!*—*Star Wars*. A billion-dollar, that's billion-with-a-B, dollar, property.

However, no credit and no payment to Messrs. Smith, Williamson, Heinlein, etc.

Don't you find that objectionable? I do. I really do.

But it's legal. You know the old maxim. Take from many sources and it's research.

Well, along comes Brother Dan O'Bannon. I've never met Brother O'Bannon, either, but he's also reputedly a prince of a chap and I'm sure, in fact, that he is. He wrote the screenplay for a movie called *Alien*, allegedly based on a story by himself and one Ronald Shusett. A splendid movie, too.

It's a delightful adaptation of *The Voyage of the Space Beagle*, also published as *Mission; Interplanetary*, by A.E. van Vogt. Specifically, *Alien* comes from two episodes in Van's book, "Black Destroyer" and "Discord in Scarlet," that appeared in the old *Astounding Science Fiction* fully forty years ago. It's all there, fans, every bit of it, all the way down to poor Mr. Executive Officer Kane and his really excruciating tummy-ache.

Take from one source and it's plagiarism, friend.

Now these Hollywood people aren't really *evil* people. They didn't set out to rip off Jack Williamson or Frank Herbert or A.E.

van Vogt. That's just their little old Hollywood way of doing things.

They think of themselves as business entrepreneurs. Even as creative artists.

But they have no concept—just no concept—of what the creative process *really* is. They're brilliant technicians but they think a photograph is superior to a painting because it has greater precision and finer detail. They do not understand what A.E. van Vogt went through, or what he accomplished.

So they just take and use.

Just take and use.

It's just a product, isn't it?

Isn't it?

Or is it?

Does it mean anything more? I think it does, and you must think so, too, or you wouldn't be here. If it were just a product, you wouldn't be here at this convention. You wouldn't attend a Lifebuoy Soap convention, and it's fine soap. But it's just a product.

Well, I've wandered a little. I was talking about this science fiction community that we have, and it seems to me that the guardianship of this community is first and foremost in the hands of the fans. Of you.

You've created a splendid thing, and I would rather see it destroyed outright—much as I'd regret that—than to see it snatched from you and perverted to the purposes of privilege and profit.

LATER

The speech went over well. There had been a little grumbling and uncomfortable stirring about at certain points, but nobody stood up and marched out in protest, at least that I could detect. Afterwards I received a number of congratulatory handshakes and favorable comments on the speech. I remember in particular Bob Silverberg's. "You really held their feet to the fire," he said. That pleased me a lot.

I don't recall what I did the rest of that afternoon, but a few hours later Pat and our three kids—then aged seventeen, fourteen, and ten—and I trooped into the elegant main dining room of the Sheraton-Palace. As we stood in the entryway waiting to be seated, a prominent science fiction writer rose from his seat nearby.

Maybe I shouldn't mention this fellow's name. *Hmmm.* On the other hand, maybe I should. Oh, what the heck, we need to take responsibility for our actions, don't we. So:

As we stood in the entryway waiting to be seated, Jerry Pournelle rose from his seat nearby. He lurched toward my family and myself, planted himself in front of me, drew back his arm, clenched his fist, and delivered a haymaker aimed at my jaw.

Fortunately he was very drunk at the time and the punch missed me by at least a foot. Throwing himself off-balance, Pournelle would probably have landed face-down on the carpet if it hadn't been for his long-suffering wife, Roberta. She had jumped to her feet and run after her husband, arriving just in time to catch him in midair and half-carry, half-guide him back to their table.

Then she returned and started to apologize to me. But in fact the person I most pitied in the incident was Roberta.

It's been forty-three years since that all took place. Jerry Pournelle has never seen fit to utter a syllable of apology. What a guy! But maybe he isn't just being churlish. Anybody as stinking drunk as he was that day might very well have no recollection of his conduct.

LIFETIME AWARD ACCEPTANCE SPEECH: A STORY AND A MESSAGE
Left Coast Crime Convention
Monterey, California, February 2004

I'M GOING TO TELL you a story and then I'm going to deliver a message. The story is for everyone in this room. I think you'll enjoy hearing it. After all, telling stories is my profession and with all due modesty I think I'm pretty good at it.

As for the message, that's for one person. Trouble is, I don't know who that person is. But it's somebody in this room. And whoever you are, when I get to the message, you'll know it's for you.

First, that story. It starts in 1957. June of 1957. I was a soldier at the time, a very young soldier. I was assigned to an army post in Indiana. I heard that an event very much like this one was going to take place in an adjoining state, so I wangled a weekend pass and made my way to the motel on the outskirts of Cincinnati, Ohio where the convention was set to occur.

I said that it was very much like this Left Coast Crime Convention, but it was a great deal smaller, and it was very informal. The dealer's room consisted of the trunk of a huge old Dodge sedan owned by a bookman known to one and all as Big-Hearted Howard DeVore. The people at the convention spent most of the weekend leaping in and out of the motel's swimming pool. There were poker games each night and considerable alcohol was consumed.

The closest thing to a formal program rook place on the final evening of the convention. Everyone traveled to a nearby Italian restaurant where we shared a communal dinner. After the last strand of spaghetti was consumed and the last plate of spumoni had disappeared, two fellows stood up in front of the room. You may have heard of them. One was Wilson Tucker, a mystery and science fiction writer whose most famous novel was *The Chinese Doll*.

The other was Robert Bloch. At that time Bloch was best known for a 1943 short story, "Yours Truly, Jack the Ripper." But even as we assembled in that Italian restaurant in Ohio, a story was unfolding in Bloch's home state of Wisconsin. A seemingly normal, even bland, citizen named Ed Gein was creating his ideal mate by variously murdering women and robbing graves and assembling body parts in his home. Gein was arrested in November, 1957, and eventually became the model for Norman Bates in Bloch's novel *Psycho*.

Tucker and Bloch had been lifelong friends. Each had a wicked sense of humor. And that night in the restaurant in Cincinnati, they stood in front of the room and entertained the conventioneers with a nonstop flow of banter, wisecracks, insult humor, and over-the-top dramatic readings of scenes from each other's books.

They brought down the house.

I will confess that I had a mixed reaction to their act. On the one hand, I thoroughly appreciated the show. Their performance was smart, funny, and practiced. Also, I had read the works of both and I enjoyed those works and admired their authors. I felt honored just to be in the same room with them.

On the other hand, I experienced that mixture of admiration and jealousy that we call envy. There they were, two famous writers, standing in front of the room, basking in the spotlight, winning the applause of the entire convention. And there I was, an anonymous reader, sitting in the shadows in the back of the room, wishing that I could be the one standing in the spotlight, getting the attention and winning the applause.

The next day I headed back to my post in Indiana and reported for duty. But I had the good fortune to have access to a typewriter and in my off-duty hours I tried writing a story. I actually finished it and sent it off to one of the magazines that I liked to read, and back came a rejection slip.

Followed a series of efforts and rejections, and after a while I gave up. But several years later I decided to give it another try. I was out of the army now, an ambitious young businessman with a wife and a career. And I wound up with another series of rejection slips. And I gave up again.

Third try is magic, or so I've heard. And again, after the passage of several years, I started writing stories once more, and one day—lo! and behold—I opened an envelope from a publisher and instead of a rejections slip I found a letter of acceptance. And after a while, there was another. And another.

Soon I was writing novels and short stories and signing autographs instead of collecting them, and tonight . . .

... tonight I had dinner with Sharan Newman and Gillian Roberts and Walter Mosley and hizzoner the Mayor of this Fair City of Monterey. And the lovely people running this convention have done me the honor of presenting me with their Lifetime Achievement Award.

I had made my way from the back of the room to the front of the room. From the distant shadows to the spotlight. And I can tell you right now—it's great! And it only took me forty-seven years.

And that's my story.

Now for the message that I promised you. There's somebody in this room right now who's feeling the same feelings and thinking the same thoughts that I felt and thought in that Italian restaurant in Cincinnati in 1957. Some young man or woman—or not-so-young man or woman—who's thinking, "I wish I were up there in front of this room, basking in the spotlight, instead of sitting in the back of the room, hidden in the shadows."

Okay, that's the person for whom I have the message. Whoever you are, I want you stay in this hotel and enjoy the rest of the convention. Then when you get home I want you to boot up your computer, open a file, and start writing your story. If you sell it, that's great. If you don't sell it, go ahead and write another story. And another one, and another.

Eventually, instead of rejection slips you will receive a letter of acceptance, and then a lot more such letters. And eventually you will find yourself at a convention and you will be the one standing in the front of the room, basking in the spotlight and enjoying the applause.

Now you've heard my story and you've heard my message, and I thank you again for this wonderful award and for your attention during my speech.

THEM DAZE

SHAMELESS SELF-PROMOTION
2006

A few years ago I came across a copy of *Being Red,* the autobiography of Howard Fast. Fast was a fascinating character as well as a talented writer. He served in the United States Army during World War II, or maybe he was a civilian "attached" to the Army. It wasn't quite clear to me, and I'm feeling too lazy at moment to look it up. In any case, he did have some amazing adventures in the service of Uncle Sammy, and recounts them in detail alternately suspenseful and hilarious in the book.

I recommend it very highly.

After the war he wrote regularly for the Communist newspaper *The Daily Worker,* turned out a number of fine novels including *Spartacus* and *Citizen Tom Paine,* and wrote a fair number of pretty good science fiction stories. He was not above selling those stories to periodicals like *Amazing Stories, Fantastic Universe,* and (mainly) *The Magazine of Fantasy and Science Fiction,* although, alas, he shied away from calling them science fiction when they were collected in book form.

In the course of his autobiography, Fast mentions his attitude toward schoolwork. By the time he reached high school, he records, he had decided what profession he would pursue and had pretty well formed his interests and attitudes. Thus, he worked hard and performed brilliantly in composition and literature courses, as well as in such subjects as history. Courses which did not interest him, and which he expected never to use, he simply ignored. These included algebra, geometry, chemistry, and physics. He slept during class and he ignored homework assignments.

As a consequence, he wound up with a report card consisting entirely of A's and F's. Nothing in between.

When I reached the end of this section of Fast's autobiography I laid down the book, put my head in my hands, and heaved a great, despairing sigh. Why hadn't I thought of that fifty or sixty years ago? What kind of educational system do we have and how did it get that way?

Maybe some history-minded reader will answer these questions. As for me, I think I might have the answers, but they're more a matter of inference and conjecture than of fact. I think our educational system is essentially the system we inherited from the English, and it originated in the first quarter the eighteenth century, just about the time the Industrial Revolution was getting into high gear. While farmers and artisans were being herded into smoky new cities and set to work in factories and mines, and new fortunes were being built by capitalist entrepreneurs, the children of the upper classes and the inheritors of "old money" were being taught the values of a disappearing way of life.

The educational system was especially designed to prepare the sons of the British gentry to become the next generation of country squires. As such they would assemble in the evening over a pipe and a glass of port and discuss such matters as gentlemen of culture ought to find of interest.

I don't think the store of human knowledge had grown so great or spread so wide by then that an educated individual had to pick and choose. One could more or less "know everything." You were expected to know Latin and Greek and maybe even a smattering of Hebrew, as well as French and German. You would learn Euclidean geometry and some "natural philosophy"—a mixture of chemistry, physics, and biology. You would be able to quote classical literature in the original languages and to translate your citations into English.

Most of the sons of the gentry had private tutors until they were of age for further studies at Cambridge or Oxford.

As for young females, their education was somewhat different, and did include at least a few of the practical arts such as weaving and sewing.

What I think happened was this. The English system of education, which was never suited for more than a very narrow stratum of society, was imported to the American colonies. This provided the basis for American education in the colonial and post-colonial eras, and we've never got over it. Maybe I should mention, *en passant,* that there was also a good deal of religious indoctrination included in the curriculum. We've been trying for the past couple of hundred years to get that out, and we seem not only not to be winning that struggle but actually to be losing ground, these days.

To which I can only say, *Oy, gevalt!*

When I was in high school the preprinted report card forms we received still listed Greek and Rhetoric, although neither was taught in our school any longer. But I suffered through courses for which I had no aptitude and in which I had no interest: algebra, geometry, trigonometry, chemistry, physics. Hey, not to put these fields down and certainly not to denigrate people who specialize in them. I am endlessly grateful to the great scientists and engineers who have made my life longer and better than would have been the case had I been born a few centuries ago.

Still, those fields are not *my* fields. Like Howard Fast, I am interested in and use literature, composition, history. Heck, I even cook a little! But I never did figure out what a Wheatstone Bridge was. The Bronx Whitestone Bridge, yes.

It took me a long time to get around to doing what I wanted to do with my life, instead of what I thought I "ought" to do. Maybe it was my upbringing or maybe it was a generational thing. I don't want to start over-generalizing again. Been there and done that! But it seemed to me, when I was a teenager, that the path was pretty clearly marked.

Finish high school, go to college, spend a couple of years in the Army, get a job with a large corporation, work my way up the ladder . . . jeez, there I was at the age of 17 and no adventures left. Straight from adolescence to retirement with only a few decades of soul-deadening labor in between. Was that what life was all about? Why didn't somebody tell me about sex, drugs, and rock 'n' roll?

For the next eighteen years I followed the ordained path, not because I chose to but because it never dawned on me to do otherwise. Before you mutter to yourself, *Oh, the poor dodo,* let me pose a question: Do you wake up in the morning and ask yourself, "Shall I walk around on my hands today with my feet in the air, or on my feet with my head uppermost?" Of course not. It isn't a question. You just do it.

Oh, there were a few times when I felt like chucking the whole thing and going off to become a writer, but practical considerations (and maybe a case of cold feet) always held me back.

Finally, in 1970, I decided to take the plunge. And in the three-and-a-half decades since then, I think I've had a much better time puttering around this planet. Not that there have been no rough spots. And I *know* I'd be in better financial shape if I'd stayed in the corporate world. But it would have been a hell of a life. And I mean that in a *bad* way.

So comes a moment a few years ago—August, 2001, in fact—and I'm attending a little convention in Providence, Rhode Island. Visiting the huckster room I stop off at the Fedogan & Bremer table. F&B is a Minneapolis-based company that published a collection of my stories called *Before 12:01 and After* way back in the 1990's. There ain't no Fedogan, BTW, and there ain't no Bremer, neither. The company is run mainly by a pair of onetime University of Minnesota buddies, Phillip Rahman and Dennis Weiler, along with a kludge of fans, pals, and hangers-on. They've turned out some nifty books.

At the table this day I saw Scott Wyatt, a Minnesota wild man, motorcyclist and poet, and a member of the F&B family. Scott says, "You've been writing Lovecraft-type stories for a while now. Do you think you have enough to make a book? If so, we'd like to publish it."

I answered in my usual authoritative manner: "Dunno. I'll check when I get home."

Which I did, and it turned out that I did have enough such stories, and we wound up with the electronic equivalent of a handshake deal for the book.

But F&B didn't push me to deliver a manuscript and I didn't push them to send me a contract and the whole project just kind of drifted along for several years. Finally I got my act together and wrote to them suggesting that we get moving on the book.

Back comes an email from Dennis Weiler. Alas, as happens so often with small publishing companies, they've run into some personnel problems and some financial reverses. The company is still there and still getting out books, but on a v-e-r-y stretched-out schedule. They really like the idea of my book but they don't know when they can possibly get to it, certainly no time soon, and if I would like to pull it and find another home for the book, they will surely not object.

In fact, I got the distinct impression that they would be relieved.

So I went outside and kicked a rock around the block, then came home and worked up a little proposal for the collection and sent it to half a dozen publishers. I think this is too much of a "niche" book for any major commercial house, so I concentrated on specialty publishers.

Back came, let's see . . . I think there was one rejection, one this-sounds-intriguing-but-we're-overstocked-right-now-try-us-in-six-months, and three acceptances. One company didn't answer at all, which I also took for a *no*.

Of the three *yeses* (is there such a word?) one appealed a lot more than the others. The editor wrote to me personally. He has a day job. This *is* a small press. He's a lit prof, has followed my work for years, and uses some of my short stories in his honors composition classes. Hey, nice! Also, he says, I have too many suitable stories to fit into one book. If I would be willing, he'd like to make it a three-decker.

Well, of course I hesitated and sighed, but eventually I gave in. The company is called Elder Signs Press and it's located in Lake Orion, Michigan. And I always thought that Sauk City, Wisconsin was an obscure address! Once we were up and rolling ESP announced the first book on their website. There was to be a limited hardcover edition plus a larger trade paperback edition. The hardcovers sold out in less than twenty-four hours, just from the website, although I'm sure that some of the buyers were bookstores or dealers who plan to resell their copies.

The book actually appeared at the end of 2005 and the paperback version is still in print.

Each of the three books has a mix of stories—some never-before-published, some published in magazines or anthologies but not previously collected, and a few recycled from my earlier collections. The most fun has been a trio of novelettes set in San Francisco in the winter of 1905-1906. The stories feature a Jewish psychic detective named Abraham ben Zaccheus and his "Watson," an Irishman named John O'Leary.

These stories will be the backbone of the second book, *Visions*. Peter Beagle is writing an introduction for the book (as Fred Chappell did for *Terrors*). I handed Peter a printout of the stories in the book, and after he'd read them he said that the Abraham-and-John stories were his favorites. "Abraham ben Zaccheus reminded me of Avram Davidson," Peter told me.

"That's funny," I said, "Abraham *is* Avram Davidson."

"Oh," said Peter Beagle. "Ah, oh, I see."

If you're interested in the professional exploits of this old fan, you can pick up *Terrors* now. I hope your local bookstore carries it. If not, I'm sure they could get it for you. You can also buy it from an internet marketer, or from a dealer (via abebooks.com), or best of all from Elder Signs Press. Just google 'em and you'll find their website. Tell 'em Lupoff sent you.

I've got one more story to write for *Visions*. The book should be out before the end of 2006. And *Dreams* should be along in 2007.

[2103 update: Well, Edler Signs Press ran into the usual problems, too. I should have anticipated as much. But the second and third books in the set were taken over by a little outfit called My-

thos Books, which brought out limited—very limited!—hardcover editions, and then went belly up. Are we having fun yet? The books were then taken over by a fine outfit called Hippocampus Press, and as far as I know they are still in print from Hippocampus. I hope you will want to read these books, and I hope you will be able to find copies of them. I wish you luck! –RAL]

CUT TO THE FLAG
1966

Lyndon Johnson was President of the United States and I was editor of the Poughkeepsie, New York, edition of *The IBM News*. I was bored with my work and frustrated with my ambitions. My boss called me into his office and asked if I thought I could handle an additional assignment, writing a movie. Of course I jumped at the chance.

Understand, this wasn't going to be *Gone with the Wind* or *All about Eve* or even *Frankenstein Meets the Wolfman*. It was more likely to be *Progress in Development of Silicon-based Circuit Design Elements of 1966*. Even so, it sounded challenging and involving and you can bet I wouldn't turn it down.

I trotted over to the film department and reported in. The manager there was a fellow named Ed Casazza. We chatted briefly, found each other simpatico, and Ed announced that I would be borrowed for one film. It was to be an annual progress report of our product development lab, an organization of some four to five thousand programmers, engineers, managers, documenters and product testers.

Ed took me around the department and introduced me to my new co-workers: Joe Boehmer (cameraman and film editor), Jack Rush (lighting and sound technician), Jerry Lemieux (writer/director), and Kathy Romash (secretary). You can see that we were a small group, non-union, and everybody got to do everything, more or less.

My first few days were devoted to scouting around different hardware and software development groups, gathering material for my film. Once I'd got my information together I sat down to rough out a movie script. The format was pretty simple. In fact, having done a little work writing comic book continuity, I discovered that the format was almost identical.

Each section of the film was broken down into scenes and scenes into shots. I would describe the visuals of each shot, then write the lines for my "actors" (engineers, programmers, managers) or voice-overs, then time out each shot.

Fifteen seconds of device development manager talking directly to camera, explaining purpose of new gizmo.

Twenty-five seconds of engineer setting up the gizmo to go through its paces.

Thirty seconds of the gizmo doing its stuff.

Once I had the script ready to go I set up appointments with each department and location we were going to shoot in. And on the appointed morning we would show up, Joe Boehmer and Jack Rush and myself. We'd set up, get our "actors" to run through their parts, and roll film. We usually did several takes of each shot. As Joe liked to say, "Film is the cheapest thing we have."

Joe had been born and raised in Austria. He was the middle of three brothers. During the First World War, he told me, all of the children from his village had been evacuated to a nearby castle. Living there while battles raged was exciting but there were drawbacks as well, the chief one being that they had very little to eat. By the end of the war in 1918 the growth of the oldest children was permanently stunted. The middle kids, like Joe, were able to catch up a little after the war ended and food became more plentiful. The youngest kids wound up being the biggest.

When he came of age Joe became a cinematographer and still photographer. He married a journalist. Joe and Hilda were motorcycle enthusiasts. In the late 1920s they had his-and-hers motorcycles shipped from Europe to South Africa. They climbed aboard and headed north. They rode together the length of the continent. Joe snapped pictures throughout their trip and Hilda made notes. Once their expedition was completed Hilda wrote a book about it and it was published, illustrated with still photos by Joe. Thirty-odd years later Joe showed me a copy. The test was in German so I couldn't read it, but the photographs were remarkable. Many scenes were taken in villages whose inhabitants had never seen a white person before, no less a motorcycle. The title, as translated, was *Capetown to Cairo by Motorcycle*.

Back in Vienna, Joe and Hilda pursued their careers. Joe was working as a newsreel photographer. Hilda was writing. They were also active in politics. They were "SD's"—Social Democrats. As the 1930s got under way, Joe told me, they could see where things were headed. Joe and Hilda were Catholics but, moving in intellectual and artistic circles as they did, and being involved in Austrian left-wing politics, they had a great many Jewish friends.

After a while they decided that they'd have to get out of the country so they went to the American consulate in Vienna and got their names on the list for immigration visas to the US. As the weeks and months passed they moved up the list, and eventually they reached the top. I was surprised when Joe told me that the visas were transferable. Shades of *Casablanca*. As Joe and Hilda felt relatively safe, they gave their visas to Jewish friends, went back to the consulate and put their names back on the bottom of the list. I don't know how often they did this, but I have the impression it was three or four times.

By now Hitler had come to power in Germany, and then on March 12, 1938, he announced *Anschluss*—the union of Germany and Austria. In effect, Austria ceased to exist as a separate nation and became part of Germany. Every former Austrian was now a German citizen.

Thirty years later, Joe told me about that day. "I was filming Hitler's arrival in Vienna." He paused, then announced proudly, "I ruined every frame!"

But then Joe and Hilda really had to get out of Europe, and they managed to get visas and come to America. They rented a comfortable apartment in Manhattan and found jobs. Three years later the United States was at war with Germany. Joe and Hilda were living in New York and they were, overnight, enemy aliens.

What to do?

They sublet their apartment to friends and made their way to the Canadian border. They managed somehow to get across, and boarded a ship bound for Havana. Shortly, Joe told me, by crossing the right palms with the right amount of silver, they had become Cuban citizens. They then hastened to the American consulate and applied for immigrant visas to the US, as Cubans.

Once the paperwork was accomplished they sailed back to New York and applied for citizenship as Cuban immigrants. They even got their old apartment back.

But now we were in Poughkeepsie and the year was 1966. My little group made its way from set-up to set-up, shooting our film. Once everything was in the can, sent off to the lab for developing, and back in our so-called studio, we sat down to edit the film.

Joe Boehmer was doing double duty, editing the film he had shot for me—just as I was doing double duty as writer and director. Joe set up the first shot on the Movieola—a marvelous old-school device used for editing film—and ran the footage. Hey, it looked good to me.

But Joe turned to me with a pained expresion on his face and asked, "Where are the heads and tails?"

I was baffled. "What heads and tails?"

"When you want a shot to run fifteen seconds on screen, you don't shoot fifteen seconds. You call for thirty-five seconds, ten seconds of heads and ten seconds of tails, so we can adjust up and down, throw away a few extra frames, cut everything together smoothly."

I'd never heard of such a thing. It looked as if I'd made a disaster instead of making a movie.

Joe said, "All right, each time that happens we'll just cut to the flag."

It became a standing joke. Whenever there was a problem with continuity, "Cut to the flag." Somehow Joe salvaged that film for me. I don't know how he could do it, but if he could shoot Hitler's arrival in Vienna and ruin every frame and get away with it, he could certainly shoot circuit boards and hard-working programmers for me at IBM.

In fact everything worked out so well, I was transferred permanently to the film group and my assistant at *The IBM News* took over my job there. Ed Casazza had been transferred to another IBM location and he was replaced by a former pulp science fiction writer named Fox B. Holden. Our mutual boss, a level up, was a bright young ex-hockey player and amateur poet named Craig Harkins. Joe Boehmer was getting close to retirement age but he was still my cameraman.

We had a chance to make a film about a development project that our engineers were working on under a navy contract. The navy wanted to know if we could concoct a system that would allow navy pilots to land jets on aircraft carriers at night or in such bad weather that the carrier was essentially invisible from the air.

Our engineers were working on a system of holographic photography. They hoped to make a holographic image of each carrier in the fleet. The appropriate holograph would be mounted in the aircraft and linked to the carrier by radar. The pilot would see a three-dimensional image of the carrier which would change in real time based on data from the radar link between the aircraft and the carrier.

The engineers had got as far as an actual working mock-up of this so-called "heads-up system" in the lab, and they wanted to know if we could make a motion picture of it in action.

Joe and I showed up and an engineer gave us a demonstration of the system. A device representing a navy jet moved along a guide rail. From the viewpoint of the pilot, the jet approached the carrier, the holographic image changing until the aircraft had landed on the deck.

"Can you film that?" the engineer asked.

Joe Boehmer whipped out his trusty light meter. I wondered, was it the same one he'd used the day Hitler arrived in Vienna? He pointed it at the hologram and said, "I get nothing. No reading at all."

But rather than pack it in we decided to shoot at several exposures. We sent the film off to the lab and waited for it to come back. When it did we discovered that we had a gorgeous monochrome image. We had filmed virtual reality. True, we hadn't captured the 3D effect, but I'm sure that would eventually become possible. But in the meanwhile, we had made what I believe was the world's first "VR" motion picture.

Not long after that, Joe Boehmer retired. I was in Kansas City for a conference of industrial filmmakers. I'd learned a lot from Joe Boehmer, starting with my embarrassing lesson about heads and tails. I'd learned a lot from our manager, Ed Casazza, too. Ed's philosophy included "editing in the camera," so that chopping and pasting and editorial sleight-of-hand could be held to the minimum.

Ed also preached, "I want movement. Keep the subject moving. If you can't keep the subject moving, then keep the camera moving. But they're called motion pictures for a reason."

And Ed liked dialog. Get some people on-screen and get 'em talking. I suspect this all sounds obvious, especially if you've seen a film like *My Dinner with Andre*. But the world of industrial films can turn out some serious snooze-inducers.

Ed Casazza kept entering my films in industrial film competitions and they kept winning prizes. I couldn't figure out why because I didn't think they were really very good. Then one day he called me into his office and told me—didn't ask me—that I had to fly out to California to attend WESCON. Not the science fiction Westercon. This was WESCON, the Western Electronics Show and Conference. They'd had a competition for industrial films and my latest opus had won first prize.

In case you're wondering, it had the dazzling title *TSS67*. "TSS" stood for "Time Sharing System," the eo-version of what we call today multi-tasking. It ran on IBM System/360 Model 67, so now you know everything you need to know and then some.

Okay, I flew out to SFO, made my way to the Cow Palace, and sat in on screenings of all the winners and runners-up in the film competition. Now I saw why my films kept winning. They were motion pictures. The subjects moved. When the subjects didn't move, the camera moved. At least, that's the way my films worked. The ones we beat didn't move. Stationary people. Buildings. No dialog. Voice over. Nothing happening. They might as well have been slide shows with recorded narration.

Thank you, Ed Casazza.

Eventually Ed was transferred to another IBM location and was replaced by a super-bright fast-riser named Craig Harkins.

A while after Craig took over, I was sent to attend a conference of industrial filmmakers in Kansas City. I checked into my hotel, ate my dinner, and got a good night's sleep. The next morning I was walking down the corridor when Craig approached me. He looked very glum. I asked what was the matter. Craig said, "Boris Karloff died."

Ah, well. One of the greats.

"But I have some good news, too," Craig said, brightening. "I was just out in Southern California and I've hired a young cameraman to replace Joe Boehmer." A good idea, that, as Joe was very close to IBM's mandatory retirement age.

I gave Craig my best *Go on, I'm listening* look.

"He's just finishing film school there. He's really talented. His name is Atta el-Naccash. He's Egyptian."

There was a moment of uncomfortable silence.

Then Craig said, "And you're Jewish."

And the 1967 war was not that far in the past.

Yup.

Well, I returned to Poughkeepsie. Atta reported in. Craig introduced us and we shook hands. We also made eye contact and reached an instant tacit agreement. It went like this: *"Here we are, a couple of Middle Eastern Semites in a department where we're surrounded by WASPS. We'll show them who's got the talent!"*

There was one codicil to that pact. *"We will not discuss the politics of the Middle East."*

Atta and I kept that pact until one Sunday night in the bar of the Holiday Inn in Rochester, Minnesota. It was January and the wind was howling and the snow was up to here. We were supposed to meet a special project manager and the following morning proceed to the nearby IBM facility to rescue a botched film project. We had a phone call. Our manager had been visiting family in Indiana and got into a fender-bender on the highway. No injury. He'd meet us Monday morning and we'd go to work.

But it was Sunday night and there wasn't a hell of a lot to do, so Atta and I had a drink at the bar, and then we had another drink and before you could say Yassir Arafat, we'd somehow decided to breach the no-politics codicil of our personal peace treaty. What happened next will have to wait because this is getting too long and I am getting too tired to keep going.

BREAK OUT MY CAPE AND TIGHTS, HONEY, I'M FIGHTING CRIME TONIGHT!
2013

I enjoyed Arnie Katz's essay about flop superheroes. But I don't think you ever saw a few of my favorites. Uh, I use that word in a very special way. And I might have a few comments on some of your favorites.

The Black Hood, for instance, was the lead feature in a pulp magazine. I've never actually laid eyes (no less hands) on a copy, but I've seen pictures of the pulp, and it's definitely the same guy. As I recall, he wore a standard set of yellow tights plus—right!—a black hood. If anybody out there has a copy of a Black Hood pulp, please do get in touch with me.

You mention the Shield, who was a World War Two patriotic superhero. His costume looked as if it was stitched together from roll-ends at a flag factory. He was, of course, a low-budget imitation Captain America. And in the 1950s still another Captain America clone was created by Jack Kirby, who had created the original Cap. This time he was called Fighting American (and had a "Bucky" analog called Speedboy).

The Wizard, as far as I can recall, was the only comic book superhero who actually lost a battle with the bad guys and was killed. His brother was so incensed that he fashioned himself a set of lovely green tights with a knotted executioner's rope for a belt, dubbed himself The Hangman, and set out to resume his deceased brother's war against crime.

There was Dr. Midnight, who wore a truly ugly superhero suit complete with helmet and goggles, and a little toy stage (yes!) on his abdomen. There was a proscenium arch and when he pulled the curtains back the motto "Fair Play" was exposed to the many eager readers. There must have been two or three of them, anyway.

Hydroman could turn himself into water and rush through the pipes. Imagine this guy flowing up through a toilet and punching a crook on the ass!

Mirrorman had a similar power; he could step into any mirror and step out of any other mirror.

The Bouncer was an avatar of the earth god Antaeus. His power, achieved through contact with Mother Earth, was—right, he could bounce. Of course he would be totally helpless in any city where he had to walk on pavement or macadam, or enter a building.

Captain Future bore no resemblance to the great pulp science fiction hero of that name. He was a regular strong crime fighter who wore a red T-shirt with a lightning bolt on the chest and a pair of very silly tight blue shorts.

Alfred Bester created a superhero of sorts, named Genius Jones. He wore a set of purple tights and his power—I kid you not!—was that he was a lexicographer.

There were innumerable Captains. I wondered why that particular military grade was chosen, until no less a personage than the late Otto Binder suggested that it wasn't really a military grade. They were captains in the sense of ship's captains. Or maybe the captains of athletic teams. Still, as I recall, there was at least one attempt to up the ante: Major Victory. Not a smashing success.

There were a fair number of superheroes inspired by animals. Joe Kubert's rendering of Hawkman were gorgeous. My little grandson Ethan has asked me repeatedly why Hawkman didn't wear a shirt. I explained that he was poor and only owned one shirt and it was in the laundry. Hawkgirl, of course, did wear a shirt. Modesty, please!

Since Batman was so successful, there was soon a Catman. There was also a Catwoman. I don't know how many other animal superheroes there were, but my favorite was the Green Turtle. Of course there was Green Arrow (never very interesting) and the Green Lantern (a great character, created by my friend Marty Nodel). There was also the Green Lama, a pulp character created by science fiction and mystery writer Kendall Foster Crossen. The comic book version was illustrated by the great Mac Raboy, who did truly beautiful work. As I recall, a backup feature in the same comic book was Corporal Hitler, Jr., scripted by H.L. Gold. And speaking of colors, there was the Blue Beetle and there was the Red Tornado and there was also, as I recall, the Purple Zombie.

Jerry Siegel and Joe Shuster, having created Superman, went on to create a number of less successful superheroes. There was Funnyman, a crime-fighting clown. And The Owl, a really impressive looking guy who wore purple tights and an owl mask, but this one didn't quite take off, either.

Am I fantasizing, or was there a superhero called the Jaguar, who had a moustache? Only superhero I can recall with such hirsute adornment. When he underwent his magical transformation his moustache disappeared. Who would ever guess? And there was The Fly, whose only nemesis was a particular brand of bug poison. Which he had to avoid like, uh, poison.

But my all-time favorite silly superheroes were Samson and Davy. Strong man and boy sidekick. Who could ask for anything more? They were, of course, inspired by the Biblical figures that I learned about in Sunday school.

Hey, man, the above is just off the top of my head. With a little research the list could much, much, much longer.

But all of this talk of comic books makes me think of a recent comment by my pal Frank Robinson. He argued, I think very plausibly, that reading a pulp magazine required a certain application of the intellect. However rudimentary the story telling, it was still necessary for the reader to decode those little black squiggles and turn them into words, then into stories. But a comic book "reader," Frank pointed out, only had to look at pictures.

Frank's comment evoked the following response from my humble self:

This happened when I was—not really sure, but I would guess, about ten years old.

I was sitting in an ice cream parlor in a small town in New Jersey eating a banana split. I was a fat kid with thick eyeglasses. I had no social skills and I was too smart for my own good—a perfect potential science fiction fan, which is exactly what I became a few years later. I saw two kids from my school sitting side-by-side in a booth, looking at a comic book. Believe it or not, I remember the comic and the story they were reading because I had read the same story. It was a Supersnipe story. (Supersnipe was a kid who had stitched together a superhero suit for himself and tried to have adventures; always, of course, getting into trouble.)

In one scene Supersnipe gets captured by some crooks who tie him up in a sack. After a while he manages to escape.

The two kids reading the comic were scoping out the story from the pictures. They were too lazy to read the speech balloons and narrative panels.

One of them, describing the story aloud, said, "Supersnipe unfurls his cape!"

I thought to myself, *No, he doesn't. I know that panel. That's the cloth sack and he's escaping from it. If you'd just read the words you'd know that!*

Isn't it odd that I remember that whole incident so clearly? It took place nearly seventy years ago!

~ ~ ~ ~ ~

When my friend John Pelan saw the above little essay he offered a couple of pointed comments. Regarding the Wizard and the Hangman, he pointed out, "Actually it was the Comet who was the Hangman's (deceased) elder brother."

Ah, yes, it comes back to me now. The Comet wore a peculiar lens that stretched across both his eyes. When he flipped it up, like a baseball player flipping *down* his shades in order to see a pop fly against the sun, a weird black cloud would come *fooshing* out of his eyes so the bad guys couldn't see anything.

As for Dr. Midnight, I seem to have conflated at least two superheroes. John says, "As ugly as Doc's costume may have been it didn't (thankfully) open to reveal anything. The chap that was the champion of fair play was Mr. Terrific (also a rather ugly costume). Apropos of nothing, in all the dozens, nay hundreds, of Golden Age strips that have been reprinted, I don't think anyone has ever bothered reprinting a Mr. Terrific strip. Considering how miserable some of the so-called Golden Age strips were, how bad must Mr. Terrific have been that DC has never reprinted a single page of his exploits?"

John goes on for a while from there. I love corresponding with this guy. Sometimes I think he knows everything—or everything that I *don't* know, which is really fun!

And having been corrected in regard to the Wizard and the Comet and Dr. Midnight and Mr. Terrific, I actually sat down and did a little research of my own and learned that the Shield was not at all a knock-off of Captain America. If anything, it was the other way around! The Shield, written by Harry Shorten and drawn by Irv Novick, debuted in *Pep Comics* for January, 1940—some 14 months *before* the first appearance of Simon & Kirby's Captain America.

Live and learn! My own lesson for the day is, *Be careful about writing too soon. Do the research first!*

BOOKS, BOOKS, AND MORE BOOKS!

H. BEAM PIPER

Word of H. Beam Piper's death by self-inflicted gunshot rushed through the science fiction community like a shock wave. The date of his death was unclear—probably November 6, 1964, although he was alone at the time of his suicide, no one heard the shot, and Piper's body was not found for several days. He was sixty years of age, a popular author of science fiction short stories and novels. His works appeared most often in *Astounding Science Fiction,* where he frequently won the "Analytical Laboratory" readers' poll, thereby earning added prestige as well as bonus payments from the publisher.

Talented and successful, a novelist with a growing following and one of the most popular contributors to the best-known and most respected magazine in the field, why would Piper take his own life? Not only did he rank high among science fiction authors, he had also sold a well-received murder mystery, using as background his personal hobby of collecting antique firearms and bladed weapons. Further, he had a stable day job. In the course of introducing a Piper story in his 1951 anthology *World of Wonder,* Fletcher Pratt said,

> *Mr. Piper is an engineer on the Pennsylvania Railroad—not the train driving kind, but the type who stays in a shop and operates a slide rule.*

Piper was a perpetual paradox. He seemed to like the writing and fan communities, frequently traveling from his home in Pennsylvania to New York or other cities to attend science fiction conventions or meetings of the Mystery Writers of America or the Hydra Club, an informal association of science fiction professionals. As such, the Hydra Club functioned as a forerunner of the Science Fiction Writers of America.

Yet Piper kept his personal world separate from his literary life. Few if any in the science fiction community knew much about Piper. Even the Pratt introduction was only half true. An article in a 1953 issue of *Pennsy,* the Pennsylvania Railroad employee magazine, refers to Piper not as an engineer but as a watchman, and goes on to describe him thusly:

> *Mr. Piper, a tall, slim man with sharply chiseled features and a sinister black mustache, could pass for a villain in his own mystery novel. He spends the somber midnight hours patrolling through the Altoona shops, watching out for trespassers and possible fires.*
>
> *At 7 A.M. he goes home to the third-floor apartment he shares with his aged mother, and gets into pajamas and drinks a glass of black Jamaican rum—"not Porto Rico, I'm very bigoted on the subject of rum" he says.*
>
> *"Then I light up my pipe with Serene tobacco—been smoking that brand the last thirty years—and either go over what I wrote or plan out what I'll write that afternoon. I usually go to bed about 8:30 A.M."*

So much for Piper's day job as an engineer. He worked as a night watchman when he wasn't busy writing. Had he lied to Fletcher Pratt, or was Pratt engaged in some harmless puffery in the *World of Wonder* biography? It is unlikely that we'll ever know.

John F. Carr's biography of Piper, published by the academically oriented McFarland & Company, goes a long way toward clearing up the mystery of who H. Beam Piper really was. Carr knew Piper personally and knows his works thoroughly. He has edited and assembled collections of Piper's short fiction and has written sequels to Piper's novels.

For the biography he utilized many sources, relying chiefly on three. These are "Piper," an unpublished, apparently book-length manuscript, by Piper's friend Mike Knerr; "The Early Letters," an unpublished compilation of correspondence between Piper and his friend Ferdinand "Ferd" Coleman; and Piper's own diary, now at the Pennsylvania State University Library in Altoona. In addition, Carr cites letters exchanged between Piper and his editor at *Astounding,* John W. Campbell, Jr., and between Piper and his wife, Eliabeth Hirst Piper. Carr also conducted interviews with John J.

McGuire, Piper's onetime collaborator, and McGuire's widow, daughter, and son.

So thoroughly researched a biography should give the reader a good understanding of its subject, and Carr's effort succeeds to a substantial degree. In life, Piper held most of the world, surely the people who read his books, at arm's length. In death, he is better known to us. Thanks to Carr's work, Piper emerges as a tragic, emotionally wounded figure, less powerful and certainly less imposing that his works might have suggested, and certainly a man who deserved better of the world, and who might have obtained it if he had not held the world at a distance, as he did.

As for Carr's attempt to locate Piper, to define and to analyze him, the task was obviously a daunting one. For instance, Carr devotes several pages of his book to trying to find out what the "H" stood for in H. Beam Piper. Was it Henry, Horace, Homer, Harry, Hezekiah? In the end, after citing several inconsistent sources, Carr apparently settles on Henry. The fact is that Piper's grave marker says "Henry." That's good enough for Carr, and the present reviewer is not going to disagree.

And since Piper always went by "Beam," signing his correspondence thusly and expecting friends to call him by that name, it doesn't matter very much.

Piper was an only child. His mother was forty when she gave birth to him. His father apparently died when Piper was young. Carr cites various sources and commentaries regarding the elder Piper, but the gentleman seems to fade out of the story rather than making a definite exit. Maybe Carr gives a date of death for the senior Piper, but if so, the present reviewer has been unable to find it in the book, despite Carr's extensive and invaluable index.. Piper's mother, on the other hand, lived with her son for the rest of her life, dying in 1954 at the age of 90.

Apparently Piper was a poor student. He never completed high school, but pursued independent studies, primarily in the field of history. He made himself an expert in those areas of history—late medieval France, and America, especially in the Civil War era—and an authority on antique weapons. He lectured on his subjects at local institutions, and once he moved to France late in his life, his collection became a semi-permanent exhibit at a museum in Pennsylvania.

According to Carr, Piper read the usual science fiction and fantasy writers in his youth—H. G. Wells, Edgar Rice Burroughs, Bram Stoker, A. Merritt—and began, at an early age, to send stories to pulps ranging from *Argosy All-Story* to *Black Mask*. He was a perfectionist and his writing methods were painfully laborious. Quotations from his letters and diary indicate that he spent long periods preparing each story, jotting down notes, working out characters and structure. Once he began writing he would throw away his work—he called it "manufacturing wastepaper"—and start over repeatedly. In some cases he would work on a story or a novel for years, making false starts, abandoning them, setting the story aside to work on others, then resuming work.

He was a free thinker and distinctly a libertarian. He was militantly opposed to organized religion, despised Prohibition, railed against blue laws and exhibited conventional sexual tendencies despite his lengthy bachelorhood.

He did not break through with his first sale until 1947, when he was in his mid-forties. His work was received enthusiastically from then onward, but he never made much money as a writer. He abandoned his job with the railroad when a staff reduction took place. Piper might have saved his job at the time, but he felt that he was being treated badly and quit cold. He was a heavy drinker and smoker. He fancied himself something of a dandy, certainly a rarity for a resident of a grubby railroad town like Altoona, Pennsylvania, and spent inordinate amounts of money on custom-tailored suits.

A caring an affectionate man, he became the unofficially adopted uncle of the children of his few close friends. He had several romantic entanglements in his life, sharing modest quarters with his aging mother. By his middle fifties he was considered a confirmed bachelor, only to surprise his friends and colleagues by marrying Betty Hirst, a divorcee who worked for a student travel service in Manhattan. At first he commuted between Altoona and New York to spend time with his new wife. When she was transferred to her company's Paris branch, Piper accompanied her. Carr reports that Piper hated living in Paris, a surprising turn of events in view of his interest in French history.

In any case, Piper returned alone to the United States. He moved from Altoona to nearby Williamsport, Pennsylvania. To the typical science fiction reader it would appear that Piper's career was rolling from triumph to triumph. He produced his most popular novels, *Little Fuzzy* and *Space Viking*, he continued to appear in *Astounding* and made other short story sales, and he sold motion picture rights to *Little Fuzzy*.

But despite his apparent success his income was shockingly poor, and with his wife, Betty, living in France, her steady salary was no longer the stabilizing influence for Piper that it had been while he lived with her in Paris. His checks from publishers came irregularly, and when they did he would typically use the money to catch up on back rent, invest in a new wardrobe, stock up on rum and tobacco—and find himself broke again. On one occasion, described heart-wrenchingly in a diary entry, Piper succeeded in shooting a pigeon and deep-frying it for his dinner. He was literally starving to death.

He could have appealed to friends and colleagues for assistance, but his pride prevented him from doing this. If he had asked Betty for help, she would almost certainly have air-mailed a check or wired funds to him. Despite their separation, there clearly remained a strong emotional bond between the two. But Piper obviously considered himself the "competent man" of his own fiction, an archetype of Spartan self-sufficiency promoted by Campbell and featured in stories by many of Campbell's pet writers including Robert A. Heinlein and Piper himself.

When Piper's literary agent, onetime pulp editor Kenneth White, died unexpectedly, Piper's already poor business affairs took a turn for the worse. Another agent assumed responsibility for Piper's account. Piper at this time had an arrangement with his magazine and book editors—primarily Campbell at *Astounding*—actually, *Analog* since 1960—and Donald A. Wollheim at Ace Books—whereby Piper's long stories would be published in *Analog* as serials or broken into series of novelettes. They would then be reassembled for book publication by Ace.

The new agent, unaware of this standing pattern, arranged for the premature book publication of Piper's current series. Campbell then cancelled his end of the deal. Piper was devastated. He spread painter's tarpaulins through his apartment, put the muzzle of a revolver in his mouth, and pulled the trigger. The tarps made it much easier for others to clean up the mess.

In the forty-four years since Piper's death most of his works have gone out of print and memories of him have largely faded. One exception is Little Fuzzy, an alien whose enduring popularity might surprise Piper, whose general preference was for a tougher, hard-edged kind of story. However, Piper's copyrights have largely lapsed. As a consequence, most of his works are available for free download from Project Gutenberg or other websites. At the same time, hard copy editions of at least some of them are once more available from Ace Books and Wildside Press. He remains worth reading. He should have lived longer and written more.

It would be pleasant to report that Carr's biography of Piper is a splendid book in its own right. In a way it is. The information is here. The elusive H. Beam Piper does come through, vividly and movingly. But the biography has very serious flaws. Carr relies too heavily on quoted correspondence. Much of, especially in the first third of the book, is crushingly dull. Once Piper makes his first sale to *Astounding* and his career is finally, belatedly launched, the book becomes interesting, even exciting. But it's very hard to follow Carr's chronology. All too often he gives dates by month and day but seldom by year. The result is frequent and frustrating flipping of the pages.

Some remarkable assertions are made. For instance, Carr makes the following statement:

> *Campbell confided to a few associates that very few fans actually sent in Analytical Laboratory votes for their favorite stories, so Campbell picked the winners himself, and used it as a means to raise the word rate for those authors whose work he most valued.*

Carr attributes this statement to Mike Ashley, citing Ashley's 1981 index to *Astounding* and *Analog*. This is a very serious charge. If true, it would represent a serious ethical breach on Campbell's part, and might possibly provide grounds for some ugly lawsuits.

In fact, that's very unlikely to happen. Campbell has been dead for nearly forty years and the writers who might have been cheated by Campbell's vote-fixing are either deceased or very aged. Still, and with due respect to both Mr. Carr and Mr. Ashley, who is a fine scholar and a scrupulously honest individual, the reader is entitled to some sort of explication, documentation, or supporting evidence. To quote Ashley's statement and simply leave it there is unfair to Campbell and the reader alike.

In fact, Campbell comes off poorly in Carr's book. Carr reports that Campbell insisted on Piper's changing one story to avoid offending union workers. On another occasion Campbell rejected a Piper story because in it Piper failed to kow-tow to "psionics," Campbell's hobby horse *du jour* at the time.

The AnLab vote fixing, the "union" incident, and the psionics rejection all reflect badly on Campbell. In fact, while he was for many years Piper's champion and chief market, the relationship between the two was spotty at best, and Carr quotes some very angry remarks about Campbell by Piper.

Carr also seems to have trouble identifying characters. Early on, he mentions that John J. McGuire was Piper's only collaborator. When McGuire is reintroduced, Carr tells us again that he was Piper's only collaborator. Later in the book he tells us a third time that McGuire was Piper's only collaborator. Really, enough is enough.

On the other hand, Carr mentions Piper's "finishing off" a Hydra Club meeting in New York by heading for a nearby pub with Randall Garrett and Larry Shaw. Garrett is mentioned a number of times in Carr's book, but this is the sole reference to Shaw. No identification is given. In fact, Larry Shaw was a onetime fan, a minor but talented science fiction writer, and an important magazine and book editor for many years. In the science fiction field he edited *Infinity Science Fiction, Science Fiction Adventures* (in one of its incarnations), *Worlds of If,* and lines of books for Lancer, Regency, and Dell. Great, if you already knew who Larry Shaw was. Otherwise, why mention his name but furnish no other identification?

Similarly, there are references to Charles (or "Charlie") and Marsha Brown. In fact, Charles Brown is identified, minimally, in a list of information sources for the book, but a more complete introduction at a relevant point in the text would have been useful. Surely readers of *Locus* will recognize the founding editor and publisher of this periodical, and many will recall his onetime spouse. But it is hardly appropriate to assume that readers of *H. Beam Piper: A Biography* will know Mr. Shaw, Mr. Brown, and the onetime Mrs. Brown.

Another serious flaw in the book is its typographical design. Page size is roughly 7" x 10"—compared to the more common 6" x 8.5". The large format shows off a portrait by Alan Gutierrez of Piper on the laminated cover to excellent effect,. But the large page size makes for an uncommonly long line of type. The book is set in two sizes of type. Carr's main narrative is in a very small typeface. Between the small type and abnormally long line, the mere act of reading becomes a chore. Lengthy quotations from correspondence or other sources are set in even smaller type. Reading them without the assistance of a magnifying glass is sheer torture.

DOUG DORST MAKES HIS DEBUT

Indulge me, please, if I open this review with a brief personal note. I was invited to *Locus* World Headquarters a few weeks ago to pick up a certain book for review. While I was present and in a vulnerable mood my genial host pressed another book upon me. It was *Alive in Necropolis,* by Doug Dorst. It's a longish novel—well over 400 pages—by an author I'd never heard of. The jacket illustration is murky. It takes a close look to realize that it represents a night scene of a police officer pointing a flashlight at a tombstone. At first I'd thought it was an undersea scene of divers searching a wreck. This did not bode well for the book.

It required considerable arm-twisting to get me to take this one home, but once I opened it I was—pardon the superlative—blown away by an utterly brilliant performance. This is the best book I have read in the past year. No *maybe*, no *might be*, no *candidate for the title of* . . . . It is simply, *the best.*

And who the heck is Doug Dorst?

Information furnished by the publisher is not extensive. The author is described as a graduate of the Iowa Writers' Workshop and a former Wallace Stegner Fellow at Stanford University. He also holds a degree in law from the University of California, Berkeley. A longtime San Franciscan, he is now a professor at St. Edward's University in Austin, Texas. His website also mentions that he was a three-time champion on the TV game show *Jeopardy.* He's written short stories—a collection of them is forthcoming—and is also a sometime playwright.

Alive in Necropolis is his first novel.

Okay, enough of that. What's this book *about?*

For starters, it's a ghost story. The necropolis of the title (if you can't figure that out you could look it up) is Colma, California, a city located a few miles to the south of San Francisco. Ever since the famous Gold Rush, San Francisco real estate has been at a premium. San Francisco covers roughly seven miles square, located at the northern tip of a peninsula, and as people poured in and started erecting homes and stores and industrial buildings the local Powers that Be decided that too much valuable real estate was being used for cemeteries. As early as 1849 and as recently as the 1940s, developers were buying up burial grounds and relocating graves outside the city limits.

At last count, Colma had 16 cemeteries holding the remains of 1,500,000 humans and an unspecified number of pets including diva Tina Turner's dog. There are also approximately 1,500 non-dead residents of the city. My limited mathematical prowess suggests that the dead outnumber the living in Colma by 1,000 to one. The motto of the Colma Historical Society is, "It's great to be alive in Colma."

Many prominent figures from the worlds of sports, politics, business, and entertainment lie interred in Colma. If you want to visit the gravesite of Joe DiMaggio, baseball's famous Yankee Clipper—it's in Colma. If you want to visit the gravesite of Western gunfighter Wyatt Earp—it's in Colma. If you want to visit the gravesite of rock impresario Bill Graham—it's in Colma.

Lillie Hitchcock Coit, the world's greatest firefighter groupie and financier of San Francisco's legendary Coit Tower; Joshua Abraham Norton, the self-proclaimed Emperor of the United States of America and Protector of Mexico; Lincoln Beachey, the great aviator and stunt pilot whose monoplane lost its wings and buried itself thirty feet deep in the mud of San Francisco Bay (with Beachey himself securely belted into the cockpit); Phineas Gage, the railroad worker who survived an explosion in which an iron rod pierced his head from chin to cranium . . . all lie at rest in Colma.

Or do they? In Dorst's novel they all walk, fight with the ghosts of violent mobsters, and carry on a bizarre *totentanz* night after night. Dorst has worked out a metaphysics of death that's new to me, although other writers may have used it before. The shades that hang around the cemeteries of Colma enjoy a spectral life of their own, never aging and apparently never suffering illness or—what to call it?—a natural "death after death." They can, however, be "killed" by other specters, or even "commit suicide" after a fashion. What happens to them then? Deponent knoweth not.

It is sometimes possible for the living to see and hear the dead, and vice versa, although any cop who claims he's been seeing ghosts puts his credibility on the line. To say the least! This is only one of the dilemmas Dorst's police officers—who will be the major characters of the novel—face.

Enter Michael Mercer and Nick Toronto, two members of the Colma Police Department. Toronto, a veteran cop, is approaching middle age. Mercer is a rookie. They're on patrol together. Dorst handles the familiar cop-buddy tropes with skill.

These guys are not just cops. Each of them is a fully developed character with his own needs, his own desires, his own neuroses. Mercer in particular, the main focus of the novel, struggles with a full array of issues that have little or nothing to do with chasing crooks. He has serious issues with his father, he has a difficult sort of foster-son-foster-mom relationship with the older widow of a fellow Colma cop, and he is deeply involved with a middle-aged nurse who works at a local hospital. And with her cat. At the same time, Mercer's neighbor, the widow, has fallen under the spell of a TV evangelist who is draining her inheritance to support his own alleged good works.

Toronto, on the other hand, has an ex-wife and a young, sexy girlfriend, a professional acrobat employed by a traveling circus. Their relationship is wobbly to say the least, and is complicated by the fact that Toronto has a serious drinking problem. In fact, most of the characters in the book have serious drinking problems, save for the younger set, who tend to favor more exotic (and illicit) chemical recreation.

The possibilities are endless, and there is peril here to lapse into bathos or farce. Dorst manages to maintain a precarious balance between the two.

Checking out one of the Colma cemeteries for vandals, the two cops come across a teenage boy, partially nude, bound, and left to die of exposure. They manage to rescue him and Mercer takes it upon himself to find out who abused the kid. It turns out that the youngster is the son of a millionaire film producer. He's brilliant and talented. His parents push him to excel at all endeavors, including classical music. He practices on a priceless family heirloom. He rebels against his upscale upbringing by hanging out with a crowd of adolescent slackers.

When Mercer tries to get information from the youngster, the kid insists that he can remember nothing of the night he was abandoned in the graveyard. Maybe he's covering up for his slacker pals, or maybe he was dosed with the infamous date rape drug and truthfully has no recollection of the night's events. The more his parents try to force him to conform to their values and lifestyle, the more he is drawn to the slacker adolescent milieu of his increasingly dangerous playmates.

If this all sounds like a prescription for disaster—I mean, literary disaster—there is every reason to expect a first novelist to plunge into a maelstrom of characters and themes, relationships and plots and subplots, and never quite emerge. Somehow Dorst manages to keep things in order. His prose is sensitive, powerful, and lucid. There were moments, I will confess, when I was brought near to tears by this book. I feel as if I know these cops and their world, the women and men and teenagers who inhabit it.

By the end of the novel Dorst does not tie everything up in a neat package. There is no climactic blazing gun battle, no glorious wedding, no pinning on of medals. As in real life there is a mixture of joy and pain, triumph and failure. There is a tincture of tragedy in anyone's happiness and at least a grain of hope in the lot of every loser. That's the way reality works. For better or for worse—no, for better *and* for worse—tomorrow is another day.

Alive in Necropolis contains occasional bits of what Harlan Ellison has referred to as " 'Look, Ma, I'm Writing' Writing." And while Dorst maintains an almost hypnotically rhythmic pace through most of the book, there are a few brief segments in which he seems to be losing his way. At these points the novel starts to sag. But each time that it looks as if the tightrope walker is about to plunge to the tanbark he manages to regain his balance and resume his graceful progress to the far platform.

The attention to character and relationships is the touchstone of mainstream fiction at its best, and the novel of character is mainstream fiction at its best. But *Alive in Necropolis* is also a gothic tale, a cop buddy story, a story of manners, an occasionally comic novel, and an example of regional fiction that ranges from Pacifica to Sonoma, with some excellent local color in San Francisco's Mission District, a neighborhood with a long history and energetic culture that is not often treated by novelists. If you live in the San Francisco Bay Area you will recognize landmark after landmark; if you've never been here, you couldn't ask for a better travelogue.

Thank you, thank you, *Locus,* for getting me to read this book. And when that promised collection of Doug Dorst's shorter fiction comes up for review—keep me in mind, will ya!

I, CURMUDGEON

Okay, so I sound like an old curmudgeon grumbling about these kids nowadays and how they have no respect for their elders and the world is going to hell in a handbasket. So do me something.

My pal Jack Rems who owns the brilliant Dark Carnival bookstore near my home handed me a copy of *The Ten-Cent Plague* by David Hajdu (pronounced Hay-Dew) with the comment that it would interest me. It did indeed look intriguing. Great jacket art by Charles Burns. Shows a kid in pajamas reading a copy of *Weird Mysteries* with other comic books strewn on his bed.

There's a picture of President Dwight David Eisenhower on the wall, along with a close-up of a beagle and a family portrait. The kid, the room, and the wall pix are all in black and white but the comic books are in glowing, lurid color. *The Perfect Crime, Fear, Zombie Romance, Crime Terror.*

Definitely interesting. But I didn't quite feel like ponying up twenty-six bucks so reluctantly handed the book back to my pal. And when I got home, as Fate would have it, there was a package on my doorstep and when I opened it, out popped a review copy of *The Ten-Cent Plague*. Clearly, I was meant to read this book.

If there had been any doubt in my mind, it was removed when I wandered in front of the TV and turned on my favorite porn channel. Just kidding. I turned on C-SPAN, looking for something really exciting, and there was David Hajdu sitting onstage in front of an auditorium full of people, being interviewed about *The Ten-Cent Plague.*

So okay, I'll read it, I'll read it.

And I did.

There's a subtitle, "The Great Comic-Book Scare and How it Changed America." The blurb writer at Farrar, Straus and Giroux starts the book's flap copy on a different note, talking about a "lost world of the imagination—the world of comic books." But then the blurb goes on to point to the censorious reaction to the comics that led to their downfall as a major publishing medium.

And if you've looked lately, you'll notice that comic books, at least in their great, traditional form, are now little more than a minor cultural fossil. They were indeed kicked around a lot in the 1950s, the chief villains being the infamous Dr. Fredric Wertham and that ol' coonskin-cap wearing Democratic Senator from Tennessee, Estes Kefauver.

The book itself—enough about the dust jacket, right?—starts on a familiar note. Professor Hajdu (he's on the faculty of the Graduate School of Journalism at Columbia University) tells the story of the origin of comics-as-we-know-them. He gets this right, and I commend him for it. It's common cant that the comics originated in single-panel newspaper cartoons which eventually evolved into multi-panel narratives; hence, the familiar newspaper comic strip.

So-called "albums," compilations of newspaper comics, appeared early in the Twentieth Century. By the 1930s kids could buy comic books in the classic format, and the supplanting of reprinted comic strips by original material is a familiar story. In fact, this story has been told a good many times. One excellent version is the book *Men of Tomorrow,* by Gerard Jones.

All of which leaves one wondering why Hajdu bothered to write his book and why anyone else, at least anyone else who knows the story, should read it.

One thing that Hajdu gets brilliantly right is the fact that comic books had two parents, not one. They took their *form* from the newspaper strip but their content came primarily from pulp magazines. Almost every familiar comic book trope has a direct antecedent in the pulps: gangsters, science fiction, westerns, horror, romance, aviation, jungle adventures, fantasy, war, sports stories, pirates . . . am I leaving anything out?

I don't know of any funny animals pulps, that's true. Maybe some maven will jump up at this point and wave a copy of *Fuzzy Barnyard Buddies Quarterly* from 1931, and I will stand corrected.

Hajdu makes the case that comic books were popular with young readers because they were created by youthful writers and artists. He's certainly right about those youthful creators. Most early comic books—I'm talking about the late 1930s and the 1940s now—were indeed written and drawn by young men (and a few young women) in their teens and twenties. But I don't think this was the nature of their appeal to the kids of the era.

This is where Old Curmudgeon rises from his rocker and shakes his walking stick at the whipper-snapper David Hajdu. I was one of those kids. I started reading comic books *circa* 1940, when I was five years old, and positively doted on the things for the next dozen years or so. Weaned myself of them just about the time I started college. And in those years, especially the earlier years, I didn't know and didn't care who wrote or drew the comic books I loved.

The last years of my comic-book addiction coincided with the grand flowering of the EC line—*Weird Science, Tales from the Crypt, Frontline Combat,* and the original, outrageous *Mad.* Older kids, teenagers who got off on the EC's, did know about the writers and editors and artists. Bill Gaines, Al Feldstein, Jack Davis, Frank Frazetta, Roy Krenkel, Al Williamson, Reed Crandall, Johnny Severin, Will Elder, Jack Kamen. A decade and a half later when I was editing for Canaveral Press in New York I got to work with Frazetta, Krenkel, Williamson, and Crandall.

Ah, them was the days, sonny, them was the good old days.

Why did I so love comics? Because they were colorful, they were exciting, they offered me wild, violent power fantasies and soaring flights of the imagination. Most kids feel powerless and rebellious as they come into their true identities. What a great fantasy to imagine yourself Billy Batson or Freddie Freeman or Mary Batson. Just by uttering a magic word you could be transformed into a superhero who could fly, you could perform incredible feats of strength, artillery shells would bounce harmlessly off your chest. Wow!

You could be the Human Torch and hurl balls of fire at your enemies. You could be Prince Namor, the Sub-Mariner, and rule an exotic kingdom beneath the sea. You could be Green Lantern, charge up your power ring, recite a mighty oath, and perform all sorts of astonishing feats. You could be Prince Ibis the Invincible and vanquish your foes with the aid of your magical Ibistick. And there was sexy Princess Taia at your side all the while!

Hajdu doesn't write very much about superheroes, by the way. I think he's missing a bet here, unless he has another book up his sleeve, for I think that the superhero is the heart and soul of the comic book. He does, however, go into the Superman myth at some length. He buys into the notion—he did not originate it— that the Superman story is a metaphor for the story of immigrants to America, particularly the story of Eastern European Jews. And it's true that many of the key creative persons in the comic book world were immigrants or the sons of immigrants, most of them Eastern European Jews.

These greenhorns would arrive in America wearing their funny old world costumes, following their funny old world customs and speaking funny old world languages. As soon as possible either they or their children would learn English, adopt American ways, don American clothing, and in many cases take new American names.

And here's little Kal-el, sent by his parents Jor-el and Lara from Krypton, a planet about to be destroyed. The infant arrives in a literal new world, is adopted by Americans, and receives a new American name. *Clark Kent!* How WASP can you get?

As he grows up he adopts a secret identity so no one will know he's really a strange visitor from another planet. He devotes his life to righting wrongs and protecting the downtrodden. All the while he blends into the society that surrounds him. Blue suit, day job, horn-rim spectacles.

Yeah.

The trouble with this theory is that it's a lot of bunkum. The Superman Myth is at least as old as the Book of Exodus. The baby Kal-el, raised by the Kents of Smallville, is really the young Moses, found floating in the bulrushes by Pharaoh's daughter and raised as a prince of Egypt. He and his brother Aaron do some funny tricks in Pharaoh's court. That was a nifty stunt, turning a stick into a snake! It takes a few nasty plagues to get the Children of Israel out of bondage. Then there was that whole business of the sun standing still, the Red Sea parting for Moses and the Jews and then rushing back to destroy Pharaoh's army.

Great pulp!

If you want a more recent antecedent, try that glorious old pulp magazine *Blue Book* and the works of that great old pulpster Philip Wylie (1902-1971). Along with his sometime editor and sometime collaborator Edwin Balmer, Wylie wrote *When Worlds Collide* (1933) and *After Worlds Collide* (1934). The story of Krypton and the escape of an infant to Earth is right there, with two differences. In Wylie's books it's Earth that's being destroyed and Bronson Alpha to which survivors head. And of course there's a sort of giant Space Ark full of people and animals making the trip rather than just one baby.

Okay, okay, maybe a familiar theme, maybe Wylie and Balmer and Siegel and Shuster all cribbed from the Bible. But wait, there's more. In 1930 Wylie wrote a novel called *Gladiator* that has some bearing here, as well. His title character is the protégé of a super-scientist who sets out to create a super-man. And does. It's a terrific book, by the way.

Transplant Wylie's Superman—er, super-man—into the Worlds Collide scenario and—*voila!*— there we are. With no need for sociobabble about Hebrews hiding under the bedclothes.

Oh, by the way, Wylie wrote a book called *The Savage Gentleman* (1932) that is credited with being the inspiration of the pulp character Doc Savage. And Wylie wrote *The Murderer Invisible* (1931) that may or may not have had something to do with the creation of The Shadow.

As for Kal-el's adoptive name, Clark Kent—Doc Savage's full name was Clark Savage, Jr., and the Shadow's *real* secret identity wasn't Lamont Cranston at all, it was Kent Allard. You could look it up.

Okay, I've beaten this thing to death. We old codgers get garrulous. Hand me back my cane, it flew across the room there, sonny, when I started waving my arms around a little while ago.

Hrmph!

Back to that young upstart David Hajdu. The real substance of his book has to do with the efforts to blame comic books for everything from juvenile delinquency to illiteracy, poor eyesight, and childhood obesity. Most critics have dated the anti-comics movement to the early 1950s but Hajdu, a very admirable researcher, finds and documents earlier efforts. Pompous fuddy-duddies were condemning comic books as early as 1942 and newspaper comics practically from the creation of the form.

Hajdu is a great researcher, conducting interviews with survivors of the comics industry going back to the 1940s and '50s, and locating recorded interviews with others more recently deceased. He does a fine job in this regard.

And the picture he paints of the era is even uglier than I remember, having lived through the Wertham-Kefauver pogrom as a dedicated comic book fanatic. Hajdu documents mass comic book burnings in Middle America undistinguishable from book bonfires in Nazi Germany.

American children were dragooned into taking anti-comics pledges in ceremonies reminiscent of Hitler Youth rallies. Dozens if not hundreds of artists, writers, editors, and publishers lost their careers. Some lost their lives. It was a scene straight out of the infamous House Committee on Un-American Activities and its anti-Communist blacklists of the same period.

By the time Wertham and his co-witch-hunters were finished, the comic book industry was virtually destroyed. That was the great meltdown of the early 1950s and the end of comic books'

Golden Age. Of course there came a revival a decade later and the blossoming of the so-called Silver Age. And then comic books died a natural death.

Or did they?

In fact they did not. The archetypes and classic plot devices merely migrated to other media. As the pulps had contributed their themes and the newspaper comic strips had given their format to the creation of the comic book, so the comic book has passed those themes and tropes and icons on to motion pictures, to television, and to video games. The comics are booming as never before. You just have to know where to look for them, and that is not your corner newsstand.

Most intriguingly, comic book superheroes have begun to provide thematic fodder for an increasing number of serious novelists. Hardly a week goes by, as I scan incoming review books, without a novel about superheroes landing on my desk. I mean the books, not the superheroes.

Some of them are pretty feeble attempts but others have real literary merit. I'll take credit for anticipating this trend, if not for kick-starting it, with my own 1976 novel, *The Triune Man*. And, hey, there's a new edition of that book with an introduction by my son Ken that I hope you will rush out and buy.

If your local bookstore doesn't carry the thing, threaten the proprietor with great bodily harm. Or simply order it from the publisher at www.ramblehouse.com .

[2013 update: Some times you're happy to be wrong, and this is one of those times for me. The past couple of years have seen a brilliant reflowering of comic books in all genres. Long disappeared characters have returned to print; new creations abound. There's even a surprising recognition by young readers of the creations of the past. My eight-year-old grandson Ethan has taken permanent possession of my two-disk DVD set of The Adventures of Captain Marvel *even as he waves his Luke Skywalker light saber and his Harry Potter wand. It's a grand era for fantasy!—RAL]*

POE

Breathes there a science fiction enthusiast who hasn't at least heard of the Moon Hoax? And didn't Edgar Allan Poe have something to do with that? Or was Poe the schemer behind the Balloon Hoax? Or . . .

What the heck was that all about?

Matthew Goodman is a tireless researcher. In *The Sun and the Moon* he sorts it all out, gives his readers context, history, and interpretation as well as biographical sketches of the many larger-than-life characters who were involved in the affair. Or affairs.

Yes, Poe was one of the actors. Phineas T. Barnum was another. Joice Heth, James Gordon Bennett, Horace Greeley, Benjamin Day, Dr. Thomas Dick, Sir John Herschel, and Richard Adams Locke all played their parts. Locke was the chief perpetrator of the Moon Hoax. Remember that name. Remember his initials. They seem strangely familiar to your reviewer.

The *Sun* of the book's title has nothing to do with that big yellowish disk you see each morning. It's a reference to a daily newspaper published in New York between 1833 and 1950, at which time it was acquired by a new publisher and after a series of mergers finally disappeared in 1957. The title was revived for a new daily in 2002, but the new *Sun* failed to attract sufficient readers and advertisers to sustain itself and once more the *Sun* set.

Goodman's book is divided into two major sections. The first has little to do with the Moon Hoax or any other hoax. It's the story of newspaper publishing in New York in the early decades of the Nineteenth Century. As Goodman describes the situation, in the early years of this period the city's papers were literally broadsheets, devoted mainly to commerce—the arrival and departure of wind-powered cargo ships carrying trade goods and raw materials across the Atlantic. These papers sold for six pennies per copy—expensive by the standards of the day—and were typically spread out on table tops for study by businessmen.

Benjamin Day, a printer by profession, had decided to create a newspaper, primarily in order to promote his own printing business. The first issue of his paper, *The Sun,* was dated Tuesday,

September 3, 1833. It was printed in a smaller, more convenient format than the broadsheets and it sold for one penny. Instead of concentrating on commercial news, *The Sun* took a populist approach, featuring stories of crime, sex, entertainment, and sports. It was an immediate hit, defying predictions of certain failure. It was soon the largest-selling paper in New York—eventually, in the world—and its original purpose as a promotional device for Day's printing shop was forgotten.

The great Edgar Allan Poe (portrait by Gavin O'Keefe)

The second section of Goodman's book lives up to the volume's subtitle: *The Remarkable True Account of Hoaxers, Showmen, Dueling Journalists, and Lunar Man-Bats in Nineteenth-Century New York.* The chief protagonist of these wild doings was one Richard Adams Locke, born 1800 in England, immigrated to the United States in 1826. Goodman's obsessive research provides us with information on several generations of Locke's family, probably more than we really needed to know. During the long trans-Atlantic crossing, Locke read an old copy of the *Edinburgh New Philosophical Journal.* In it he found a brief article titled "The Moon and its Inhabitants," describing the observations of two German astronomers, Franz Von Paula Gruithuisen and Wilhelm Olbers, who claimed to have seen evidence of life on the moon.

Today these assertions seem laughable, but in Gruithuisen and Olbers's day they were not so. Telescopes were fairly crude instruments and it was easy to "see" what one hoped and expected to see. After all, half a century later Giovanni Schiaparelli "saw" his famous *canali* on Mars. And after its discovery in 1976, the rocky "face" on Mars has led some observers to detect at least one huge city. The face is a striking formation, although with millions of rocks on Mars it should not be surprising that such an object would occur, like the image of the Virgin Mary on a potato chip—but a city? Really?

Locke was impressed by what he had read and—pardon me!—locked it away in his memory, to be retrieved in 1833 and put to good use. In the meanwhile, making his way in New York, Locke found work as a journalist. He worked for one of the broadsheet "merchant papers" but also moonlighted for Benjamin Day's rising *Sun*. He achieved his first big success with his series of articles about the trial of one "Matthias the Prophet," the charismatic leader of a religious cult. Matthias had been accused of a variety of offenses, including the financial and sexual exploitation of his female followers.

The reports Locke wrote for the New York *Courier and Enquirer* were suitably restrained. Those that he filed (anonymously) for *The Sun* were not so. Circulation of the little paper soared, and when Matthias's trial ended Benjamin Day gathered Locke's reports into a booklet that became a best-seller. Day then paid Locke a bonus, which helped the struggling writer to support his family.

There now dawned upon Day—sorry!—a great way to boost circulation and Locke had found the key—I'm sorry, I can't help this!—to earning a decent living. They needed a new, sensational series that Locke would write and Day would publish in *The Sun* and then reissue as a pamphlet.

Locke remembered the paper he'd read in the *Edinburgh New Philosophical Journal* in 1826. He was also aware that the English astronomer John Herschel had recently established an observatory in South Africa and was busily at work cataloging the objects in the Southern sky, a task which his father, William Herschel, had previously performed for the Northern sky. Locke proceeded to fabricate a series of dispatches, allegedly copied from material published in the *Edinburgh Journal of Science* by John Herschel's assistant, Dr. Andrew Grant.

Grant never existed, Goodwin writes, but was purely the creation of Locke's imagination. "Grant's" dispatches were never written, no less published in Edinburgh, but Locke turned them into a series of articles for *The Sun,* where they ran under the heading, "Great Astronomical Discoveries." They were wildly popular. The circulation of *The Sun* rose higher and higher. Crowds gathered outside the newspaper's office each day, eager to get their copies hot off the press. Other newspapers began reprinting the stories from *The Sun*, first in New York, where even the staid six penny "merchant papers" joined in the frenzy, then across the still-young nation, and finally overseas.

The "Grant" dispatches—Locke's name was not initially associated with them—described a new, high-powered telescope that John Herschel had developed. Using this to scan the surface of the moon, Herschel discovered mountains, seas, forests, and beasts. Some of the latter resembled familiar earthly animals. Others were strange and exotic. Among the latter were a species of beaver-like creatures that walked upright, built primitive dwellings and used fire.

Next came the greatest discovery of all: a race of lunar creatures closely resembling humans, only furnished by Nature with great, bat-like wings that permitted them to fly and that folded neatly and conveniently against their backs when not in use. These man-bats or *Vespertilio homos* lived in a scattering of communities. They wore no clothing. They were gentle and affectionate to one another and they even performed acts in public which *The Sun* omitted to describe lest its readers be shocked. They were great architects and had constructed huge, enigmatic triangular structures which "Grant" inferred were actually temples.

When the series concluded in *The Sun* the installments were gathered into a pamphlet which became a best-seller. Also successful was a lithograph of the moon's inhabitants.

While the series was greeted with some skepticism from the outset, most readers apparently believed every word of it. After all, there were the reports, in black and white. The prestigious name John Herschel was associated with the claims. And, remarkably, many Christian philosophers and clergymen supported the claims.

Astronomy was opening the heavens. The old notions of the Earth's central position and unique importance in the universe were dying or dead. Thomas Dick and others preached and wrote that God would surely not create the multiplicity of worlds that He had made, and populate only one of them, leaving the others as barren orbs. Surely there were living beings, probably intelligent and civilized beings, inhabiting what were known as "the plurality of worlds."

The notion that all the planets of our solar system are more-or-less earthlike and inhabited was widely held. Even the sun—not

The Sun—might be inhabited. The glowing object we see was not a great ball of burning gas. Rather, it wass a hollow globe of hot, luminous clouds. Inside was a cooler region, and at the center is an inhabited planet.

Your reviewer's little science-fictionist's heart went pitter-patter when he read this passage. He is staking his claim to this image. Be warned. The *No trespassing* signs are posted!

In fact, *sans* the element of theology injected by Thomas Dick, the plurality theory remained common currency for more than a century. It is, in fact, the shared imagery of science fiction writers from Edgar Rice Burroughs and Otis Adelbert Kline to Edward Elmer Smith, Leigh Brackett, Ray Bradbury, and Edmond Hamilton.

In the meanwhile, Edgar Allan Poe had published his long story, "Hans Pfaall—A Tale." Poe's story bore certain resemblances to Locke's (or "Grant's") dispatches. The chief difference was that Phaall actually traveled to the moon in a balloon. Poe grumbled that the "Grant" dispatches were plagiarized from "Hans Pfaall." He achieved little traction with his claim, but did follow it with a hoax story of his own, concerning a new model balloon that could cross the Atlantic Ocean in three days. Alas, poor Edgar failed to achieve anything close to the excitement of Richard Adams Locke's Moon Hoax.

Other hoaxes provided mass entertainment—if not enlightenment—in the era. One of these concerned an aged black woman named Joice Heth, allegedly 161 years old. None other than the famous Phineas T. Barnum promoted her one-woman show in which she sang hymns, answered questions, and told stories of cuddling and playing with her "little Georgie" Washington when she was his nursemaid. Following Joice Heth's death, Barnum, never one to miss a chance, sold tickets to her autopsy, which determined that she was in her eighties.

While the Moon Hoax was first published anonymously, it did not take very long for Locke to be identified as the true author of the "Grant" dispatches. Initially, Locke tried to pass off the reports as true. After some years he changed his story and admitted that the reports were a hoax designed to sell copies of *The Sun*. Still later he changed his story again, and claimed that the Moon Hoax was a parody designed to show up the ridiculousness of the Christian doctrine of the plurality of worlds

The idea of the Moon Hoax lives on. More than a century later, people who never heard of Benjamin Day, Richard Adams Locke,

Thomas Dick, or Andrew Grant, were exposed to the claim that the Apollo moon landings starting in 1969 were all a fraud, staged on a movie set and televised to the world for political purposes. A new Moon Hoax, the doubters alleged, had been perpetrated on the public, and had been every bit as successful as the original Moon Hoax of 1833.

CAPTAIN FUTURE AND THE FUTUREMEN

We remember where we were and what we were doing when we learned of world-changing events. If you're old enough you surely remember the Japanese attack on Pearl Harbor. Sunday morning, December 7, 1941. I was a small child. The bulletin came over the radio in the kitchen where my brother and I were sharing a meal. Young as I was, I had only a vague idea of what war meant, and of course there was no television then to bring its images into our home. But I knew it was important, and I knew it was terrible, and I ran to get crayons and construction paper and start making flags of the United States and other warring powers.

I remember the invasion of Normandy, D-Day, June 6, 1944 . . . the death of President Roosevelt in 1945 . . . the assassination of President Kennedy in 1963 . . . Neil Armstrong's first footsteps on the moon on July 20, 1969.

Small children of today will tell their own grandchildren and great-grandchildren seventy-five years from now, where they were when Barack Obama was inaugurated as President of the United States.

The same is true of more personal, life-changing events. I recall vividly the day I was commissioned an officer in the United States Army . . . my wedding day . . . the birth of each of my children . . . and grandchildren.

I remember June 25, 1964, the day my daughter was born. I was an editor at Canaveral Press in those days. I'd had lunch with two colleagues, Donald Wollheim and Terry Carr, both of Ace Books. I phoned my wife to see how she was feeling. She told me I'd better meet her at Lenox Hill Hospital. When I got there, Patricia was well advanced in labor. An hour later, Katherine Eve entered the world.

That evening I was at home with Kathy's nearly-three-year-old brother. The babysitter had left, Kenneth was asleep, and I sat down to while away a few hours. I was collecting pulp magazines in those days, and had recently come into possession of a complete set of *Captain Future* pulps—sseventeen issues published between 1940 and 1944. I'd been too young to read those magazines when they were new, and by now, as a sophisticated young businessman, I was too old for them. Or so I thought.

Still, I picked up the first issue of the magazine and examined it. The title and subtitle read, *CAPTAIN FUTURE Wizard of Science.* There was a blurb for "CAPT. FUTURE AND THE SPACE EMPEROR A Complete Book-Length Novel of Planet Conquest by EDMOND HAMILTON." The cover painting (by George Rozen) was colorful enough. It showed a heroic spaceman in a red suit and bubble helmet firing a pistol from which a series of varicolored disks seemed to emerge. A huge robot loomed over the spaceman and a weird looking dead-white fellow fired orange flames from a gun.

The price was fifteen cents.

Was Edmond Hamilton ever this young?

Okay, fair enough. Edmond Hamilton was a well known science fiction writer. In fact by 1940 he was a veteran, one of the pioneers of space opera along with Edward Elmer "Doc" Smith and Jack Williamson. Hamilton was known as "The World Wrecker," no less.

Space opera was a literary form that I looked down on. I opened the magazine to a brief introductory blurb that tempted the reader with promises of "the most colorful planeteer in the Solar System" and an "all-star parade of the most unusual characters in the realm of fantasy." The opening spread of the lead novel included another tempting blurb and a grand illustration of "Wesso," showing the great hero in an alien city, a horde of weird humanoid beings, a dark, shadowy figure, and—surprise!—the lovely heroine, bound and helpless.

Looking through the rest of the run, I found the later cover paintings by Earle Bergey every bit as colorful and enticing as Rozen's effort on that first issue.

All right!

I started to read and, to my own surprise, I was hooked. Maybe it was the surroundings, maybe I wasn't nearly as adult and sophisticated a reader as I thought I was, or maybe it was just the right story at the right moment, but over the next few days I read through the entire run of *Captain Future* magazines. I didn't get to the later Captain Future adventures chronicled in *Startling Stories* as late as 1951. How much the sweeter!

Once I'd realized what a treasure trove these stories were, I tried to obtain rights to publish them in book form at Canaveral Press, where I was moonlighting at the time as an editor. Unfortunately, that didn't work out—one of the great regrets of my career.

In 1967 I wrote my own first science fiction novel. By the time of that year's World Science Fiction Convention in New York the book was hovering on the brink of publication, and I was swaggering around the convention hotel brandishing a dummy copy in its brilliant Jack Gaughan cover. I was acting as if I had just won the Pulitzer Prize for Literature.

The disease is known as *novelitis primus,* and any time you see a sufferer approaching, one hand clutching a copy of his debut novel and the other reaching for your shoulder, make tracks in the opposite direction at maximum speed.

Recognizing a couple of my fellow professionals, I strode up to Edmond Hamilton and Leigh Brackett, two living legends in the field, introduced myself and brandished the dummy copy of *One Million Centuries.*

In all honesty, if Ed and Leigh had given me a quick brush-off it would have been nothing more nor less than I deserved. But they didn't. They asked some polite questions and welcomed me into the fraternity of published science fiction authors. That was another moment I will always remember.

In the years that followed, Captain Future and my failed attempt to bring the saga back into print never completely left my mind. The books did come back a few years later, after a fashion, in a series of Popular Library paperbacks, but the packaging was spotty and fewer than half of them were included in the reissue series.

Ed Hamilton died on February 1, 1977. I had not seen him or Leigh Brackett for several years, but in October of that year, Pat and I attended a science fiction convention in Santa Rosa, California. Shortly after arriving we stopped in the coffee shop for a snack and recognized a woman sitting at the counter, eating a sandwich. It was Leigh Brackett!

We approached and asked why she was eating all alone.

She said, "I don't know why I'm here. Nobody knows me and nobody cares."

We managed to coax her into joining us at our table. A moment later a passer-by stopped, did a double take, and exclaimed, "Leigh Brackett!"

That was Marion Zimmer Bradley.

We invited Marion to join our group, and over the next hour fans and pros aggregated around us until Leigh was surrounded by a horde of admirers.

I didn't know at the time that Leigh was already fatally ill. She died less than six months later. That day in Santa Rosa was another I will never forget.

But now, What about these Captain future novels? Do they really have merit? Or is my fondness for them just an artifact of my long-ago innocence?

When I learned that Stephen Haffner was planning to publish *The Collected Captain Future,* I was thrilled. And when Stephen asked me to introduce the first volume, I was flattered—but also, I admit, intimidated. Imagine a movie fan being asked to introduce an Academy Award winning star, a music fan being asked to introduce the world's greatest violinist, a small-town mayor being asked to introduce the President of the United States.

Oh, wait, that last one is a little bit too close for comfort, isn't it?

Well, you get the idea.

I haven't seen sales figures on the *Captain Future* magazine and I don't know whether the issues of *Startling Stories* featuring Captain Future episodes sold significantly better than other issues of that magazine. It would be fascinating to have this information. Maybe the records survive somewhere, in some corporate archive. I hope so. Obviously, though, the series was popular or it would never have lasted as long as it did.

In any case, I've tried to understand the appeal of these stories. Certainly they are not great literature, nor was there ever any pretense that they were. They are more or less standard pulp fare—

overdrawn characters engaging in fast-paced, action-filled adventures laid against colorful, exotic backgrounds.

Of all the space operas ever written, I think the most outstanding are Ed Hamilton's *Captain Future* series, Edward Elmer Smith's *Lensman* cycle, and Jack Williamson's tales of *The Legion of Space*. All of these meet the criteria listed above, and all of them have thrilled generations of readers. But each has an additional ingredient that in my opinion adds the crowning touch to their appeal. Each of them is about a *team*. The reader feels that he or she is not merely an observer of the grand adventure, but is part of it.

Thus, the Captain Future stories are not just about Curtis Newton. They're also about Grag, Otho, Simon Wright, Joan Randall, Ezra Gurney, and even the two inhuman companions' extraterrestrial pets. The reader gets to know Captain Future's lunar headquarters and the little spaceship *Comet*. We get to feel at home there, to look forward to the next visit with our interplanetary friends, just as we do when we turn to a Sherlock Holmes mystery, as much to settle into the coziness of 221b Baker Street with Dr. Watson and Mrs. Hudson along with the Great Detective, as to watch the Great Detective ply his crime-solving craft.

Of course Edmond Hamilton did not invent the adventure team format. I suppose a true antiquarian would trace the imagery back to Jason and the Argonauts, perhaps even farther, but in recent times it seems to have its roots in the works of Alexandre Dumas. Think of D'Artagnon as the apprentice hero, learning his craft at the behest of the dashing Athos, Porthos, and Aramis! At the end of *The Three Musketeers* he emerges as the full equal and companion of his three mentors.

In fact, Jack Williamson openly attributed his Legion of Space to Dumas's great masterpiece.

Pulp-oriented historians have suggested that Ed Hamilton was inspired by Lester Dent's Doc Savage saga. There is no denying the similarities between Clark Savage, Jr., "the man of bronze," and Curtis Newton, the tall, muscular, magnificently athletic, optimistic and cheerful "man of tomorrow." Doc Savage had his band of assistants—Monk, Ham, Renny, Long Tom, and Johnny—as well as the lovely Patricia, conveniently identified as his cousin so as to preclude a sexual tension that might distress young readers. There were rivalries within the team and quarrels over the superiority of their pets, all echoed in the Captain Future saga.

A minor digression: Some years ago I found myself in an informal writers' group that included mystery novelist Bill Pronzini, science fiction and mystery writer Michael Kurland, and the sainted Avram Davidson. We were trying to figure out how to get rich, and we decided that the best way to achieve our goal would be to create a hugely successful television series. But how to do this?

We deconstructed three immensely popular shows, situated in three different genres: *Bonanza*, *Barney Miller*, and *Star Trek*. We discovered that each featured a team of heroes. In each case the chief protagonist was a serious, intelligent, dynamic individual who could be stern with his associates when necessary but who really loved them like a father. The surrounding characters were selected to manifest varying qualities. One might be gloomy, one was physically dynamic, one was an intellectual, one was played for comic relief. Surely you're familiar with at least one of those series, probably more than one. Make a list of the regular characters and see how they fit the matrix.

For that matter, consider the most successful comedy series in television history, *Seinfeld*. There's Jerry, the calm, responsible father figure. There's Kramer, the physical comic. There's George, the neurotic, self-involved foil. And there's Elaine, sexy but safe—after all, she and Jerry had once had a fling and decided it was better just to be friends.

There's even a recurring sneering villain, played to perfection by Wayne Knight.

"Hello, Jerry."

"Hello, Newman."

~ ~ ~ ~ ~

The solar system of the Captain Future stories was one that science fiction readers and writers of a certain era knew and loved, even if we didn't quite believe in it in 1940, no less in the Twenty-First Century. Ed Hamilton posited a system in which every planet and many of the lesser bodies were inhabitable and inhabited. All nine planets—yes, there were nine in those days, before June 11, 2008, when those villains calling themselves the International Astronomical Union defined a class of objects called *plutoids* and removed Pluto, the "icy prison planet" of the Captain Future series, from the roll of worlds.

Ah, well, farewell ice-bound Planet Nine!

Ed Hamilton's treatment of the denizens of the non-terrestrial worlds might come as a disappointment, even a shock, to readers in this so-enlightened modern era. From the very first Captain Future adventure, *Captain Future and the Space Emperor,* the relationship between Earthmen and—well, in this case, Jovians, but fill in the planet to suit yourself—is very much like the relationship between Europeans and indigenous peoples in every corner of the Earth several hundred years ago. There is at best a kind of condescending, "white man's burden" attitude, and at worst the restless natives are treated as subhuman beasts, suitable to be exploited if not actually enslaved, while they receive the benevolent influence of *homo sapiens'* civilization. Hence, the treatment of "greenies" and others of their alien ilk.

You want to grab those Earth colonists by the shirt front and shake 'em 'til their teeth rattle. "Listen here, this is *their* world, not yours. You barged in uninvited. Now act with respect. Request, do not demand, landing privileges. We are guests here, not masters!" At least, that's what *I* want to do.

But then 1940 was long ago (although the stories take place in the remote future of 1990) and the distant worlds of Captain Future's universe are far, far away.

It may surprise some readers to learn that this notion of the planets as all being abodes of life dates at least to the year 1823 and the publication of a book called *The Christian Philosopher; or, the Connection of Science and Philosophy with Religion,* written by a Scottish schoolteacher named Thomas Dick.

Dr. Dick argued that God would not create an entire huge universe including the numerous planets that circle our sun, and then place intelligent creatures on only one body, the Earth. What a waste! Surely, Dr. Dick decided, all the planets must be more or less Earth-like, and all of them inhabited by creatures capable of appreciating the gift of life and the beauties of Nature provided by their Creator.

Quod erat demonstrandum.

Remove the theological element from Dr. Dick's argument but retain the rest of his thought, and you have—*voila!*—the Captain Future solar system. And, of course, that of Edgar Rice Burroughs and Otis Adelbert Kline and Leigh Brackett and even Ray Bradbury. Mercury was hot and dry—but inhabitable. Mars was cold and dry—but inhabitable. Venus was hot and wet—and covered with steaming swamps teeming with gargantuan life. And so on, all the way out to tiny, ice-bound Pluto.

Alas, alas.

We know better now, or think we do, but it was a lovely dream while it lasted and we can still revisit it by simply opening the pages of *Captain Future's Challenge* or *The Magician of Mars* or *The Comet Kings* or any other Captain Future story by Edmond Hamilton or by Manly Wade Wellman or Joseph Samachson, who pinch-hit for Ed a few times when the grind got too much and Ed needed a rest.

But is that dream a mere fantasy? For decades, our hopes of finding livable environments, no less actual life, on any planet other than our own, seemed to be growing dimmer with each new discovery. But now that we can explore the solar system with robots, if not yet in person, things have taken a surprising turn. Or several such! We think there might be water or water ice on Mars—and methane gas!

Methane gas? Remember your high school chemistry class? Remember good old CH_4? Remember the two chief sources of this gas in Earth's atmosphere, active volcanoes and—*snigger, snigger*—flatulent cows?

Cows—on Mars?

And while the gas giant planets may not offer us anyplace to stand, their moons are very promising. Not mere cold rocks, we now know that they have atmospheres, oceans, and volcanoes. There may be no Jovians—sorry, Cap!—but there just might be Ganymedeans or Callistans waiting to greet the *real* Curtis Newtons and Joan Randalls of some future generation.

And Ed Hamilton—Ed was a busy guy, remember. He didn't write only the Captain Future adventures, but many, many other science fiction stories and novels. Check any standard bibliography and you'll be impressed.

He also wrote for other, non-science fiction pulps, most notably *Weird Tales,* where he was one of the most prolific contributors. His horror stories, collected as *The Vampire Master and Other Tales of Horror,* may creak a little in the twenty-first century, but like so much pulp fiction they are still good fun if seen in the context of their time.

Hamilton had a whole other career writing for comic books. Ironically, while there was once a Captain Future superhero feature, it bears little resemblance to the pulp version. And as far as I can determine, Ed Hamilton did not write it. His work was done mainly for DC's superhero and science fiction comics between 1946 and 1966.

Erroneous reports to the contrary, he was *not* involved in preparing the fifty-three episode, Japanese-produced animated Captain Future television series. Still, reviews of the cartoons have been pretty good, and I for one would love to see at least some sample episodes. As best I can learn, these are available in Japanese, Spanish, French, Italian, and German-language versions on DVD. Just not in English. Isn't that a hit in the head!

Ed Hamilton did return to the ongoing spaceman-hero theme in the late 1960s with the *Starwolf* series. These books combined all the verve and proverbial sense of wonder that science fiction fans enjoy with a more mature mindset and sophisticated narrative voice than was present in Hamilton's earlier work.

He influenced other writers, not surprisingly including his wife, Leigh Brackett. Check out the "reverse evolution" theme in *Captain Future and the Space Emperor,* and then read about *Shanga* in Brackett's Eric John Stark stories.

Oh, there's so much I'd like to say about Captain Future and about Ed Hamilton, but I've blathered on far too long already, and if you haven't given up and simply turned to *Captain Future and the Space Emperor* before now, this is the time to do it.

Climb aboard the *Comet* with Curt Newton, with Grag the giant robot, Otho the dynamic android, Simon Wright the living brain . . . and, of course, with the lovely Joan Randall, secret agent of the Planet Police. Shake hands all around. Make sure that your synthesilk suit is zipped up and your gravity regulator is set for Earth-normal. Don't forget to exchange greetings with that tall fellow grinning happily and gazing out the window at the wonders of alien worlds.

That will be me.

MORE EDMOND HAMILTON COLLECTIONS

It seems to this reviewer that science fiction has been fighting a civil war for as long as there has been a recognized form called science fiction. Longer, in fact, for the very term "science fiction" wasn't invented by Hugo Gernsback until he launched *Science Wonder Stories* and its companion magazines in 1929. Hugo's previous attempt, *Amazing Stories,* dated from 1926, but *Weird Tales* had been publishing stories that were clearly science fiction since 1923, and the general pulps, most notably Frank Munsey's *Argosy,* had been doing it since the 1890s.

For all this time there has been a tug-of-war going on in science fiction, between those writers (and readers) who regard the form as a medium of pure entertainment—grand and colorful adventure tales—and those who see it as something more serious. The two schools look to their founders, Jules Verne and H.G. Wells, for inspiration.

Verne wrote marvelous stories of futuristic submarines, human-carrying projectiles blasting off to the moon, spelunkers discovering cavemen and dinosaurs surviving in the center of the earth.

Wells wrote of similar wonders, but always with a more weighty intent than Verne. His Martians were thinly disguised British imperialists conquering and exploiting indigenous peoples here on earth. His Eloi and Morlocks were exaggerated but recognizable effete capitalists and brutalized proletarian workers. His Invisible Man was any idealist driven to violence, tyranny and madness by his own excess of power.

Edmond Hamilton (1904-1977) came down heartily in the Vernean camp. From his earliest stories, published in *Weird Tales* in 1926, through literally scores of novels and hundreds of short stories, as well as a vast outpouring of comic book scripts, he seldom deviated from his role as a troubadour singing exotic ballads: narratives marked by colorful settings, exaggerated characters, and fast-paced, relentless action, action, action.

A few commentators, most notably the late Sam Moskowitz, have suggested that Hamilton could write more serious stuff, and occasionally did. Moskowitz's favorite citation was Hamilton's mid-career (1952) "What's It Like Out There?"—a grim, downbeat story of interplanetary exploitation and suffering. No question, Hamilton could write serious fiction, but he chose to be an entertainer; he was wildly successful in that role, and I would not in the least fault him for making the choice that he did.

Which brings us to the Haffner Press and Stephen Haffner and the three books at hand. Haffner has been working for years to bring out a library of collected pulp fiction, most notably by Hamilton, his wife and sometime collaborator Leigh Brackett, and his friend and colleague Jack Williamson.

The Metal Giants and Other Stories is intended as the first volume of Hamilton's collected fiction, although Haffner had already published *The Vampire Master and Other Tales of Horror*, by Hamilton, and *Stark and the Star Kings*, by Hamilton and Brackett.

The new book contains thirteen stories originally published between 1926 and 1929, eleven of them in *Weird Tales;* one each, in *Amazing Stories* and *Amazing Stories Quarterly*. If that pedigree sounds strange, note that *Weird Tales* published a great deal of science fiction in its early years. *Weird Tales'* editors in that era referred to these stories as "weird scientifics" as distinguished from the gothic-themed narratives that they called "weird supernaturals." Their themes ranged from lost race and dead civilization stories to undersea monsters to interplanetary warfare to time travel to that grand old stand-by, robots run amuck, to that even grander old stand-by, giant insects.

Praise is due to pulp authority Robert Weinberg for a knowledgeable introduction to this book. There is also a lengthy and marvelously enjoyable appendix in which Haffner reproduces the artwork that accompanied the original publication of Hamilton's stories, readers' comments originally published in the letter sections of the magazines, and facsimiles of letters to Hamilton from Farnsworth Wright, longtime editor of *Weird Tales,* starting with a rejection slip (!) and continuing through the years that followed.

The second volume at hand, *The Star-Stealers,* contains "The Complete Tales of the Interstellar Patrol." Ah, the wonderful Interstellar Patrol! The three great space opera writers, Edmond Hamilton, Jack Williamson, and Edward Elmer Smith, all created teams of heroic adventurers. "Doc" Smith's were the Lensmen, Williamson's were the Legion of Space, and Hamilton's—well, we start but do not end with the Interstellar Patrol.

Hamilton launched this series with "Crashing Suns," published in *Weird Tales* in 1928 but set 100,000 years in the future. The space-faring companions are Hal Kur, Jan Tor, and Mur Dak. There are many references to the Eight Planets—ironically prescient, for Pluto had not yet been discovered and welcomed into the family or planets, only to be expelled decades later by the International Astronomical Federation.

We must remember that Hamilton was using an old model of the solar system, in which all eight worlds were considered to be inhabitable. Okay, Mercury was hot and dry, but so was the Sahara. Mars was cold and dry, but so was the Gobi. Venus was hot and swampy, but so was the Amazon Basin. And so on.

The planets had all been colonized, banded together under a Supreme Council that assembles in the Hall of Planets. A distant sun is headed straight toward our solar system, and unless it can be diverted all life on the eight planets will be annihilated. The Interplanetary Patrol (later to morph into the Interstellar Patrol) undertakes the task of setting things aright, only to discover that the errant sun is being guided by a race of aliens shaped like giant eight-legged beach balls. Their own sun is dying and they want to crash it into ours to generate a fresh supply of heat and light.

The Patrol's spaceships, by the way, are powered by "ether waves," and as the series progresses these ships attain speeds hundreds, thousands, even—do I remember this accurately?—millions of times the speed of light. Hamilton was a trained electrical engineer and should have had some understanding of science. After all, Einstein had published General Relativity in 1905.

But one must not be too critical about these stories. If you can't believe three impossible things before breakfast you can't enjoy classic space opera.

The stories of the Patrol—they jump to 200,000 years in the future in the blink of an eye—follow a familiar pattern. Hamilton keeps raising the odds, from the destruction of planets to solar systems to entire galaxies. The readers certainly noticed this, as indicated in a letter from one Mrs. M. Kliman, of Detroit. She complained, "I know I am going to bring all Weirdom down about my ears, but I am frankly tired of Edmond Hamilton's everlasting Federation of Suns. He uses the same situation in all, namely, the impending doom of the Galaxy. Can't we remedy this in some way?"

Margaret St. Clair, who would enjoy considerable repute for her own stories in later years, agreed. "... the prospect of another story by Edmond Hamilton moves me to hysterical outcry. He makes me want to scream and bite my nails— 'captured thirty-six suns' indeed! His style is nothing but exclamation marks; his idea of drama is something involving a fantastic number of light-speeds; he is, in the words of one of my favorite comic strip characters, flies in my soup. He is science-fiction at its worst . . ."

Letters like these two set off a raging debate in the *Weird Tales* letter column. Mrs. Kliman's complaint was absolutely valid and Ms. St. Clair's accusation, while perhaps exaggerated, was not entirely without merit. But it appears that the majority of readers loved Hamilton's stories, possibly because of the familiar pattern and the hyperintense action rather than despite these characteristic. By the time Hamilton reached the longest of these stories, "Outside the Universe" (July-August-September-October, 1929) the scope had grown to three complete galaxies engaged in a huge space-war involving hundreds of thousands of ether-ships, blasting each other with an assortment of destructive rays.

If I may insert a personal note at this point, let me mention that I read "Outside the Universe" on a long ride courtesy of Amtrak, from Reno, Nevada to Emeryville, California. I was amazed at Hamilton's ability to sustain the action of this story for 163 large pages, and for many hours. By the end of the ride I was as exhausted as if I'd been aboard one of those ether-ships myself.

Hamilton's prose was generally unremarkable; it may seem slightly strained and old-fashioned to today's reader, and often, especially in describing battle scenes, wildly over-the-top. But on occasion he could wax rhapsodic, almost poetic. Consider this paragraph from "Outside the Universe":

> "It was toward our left that the light lay, for to the right and in front and behind us the eye met only blackness, the utter, unimaginable blackness of outer space. Left of us, though, there stretched along the ebon heavens a colossal belt of countless brilliant stars, the gathered stars of our galaxy. A stupendous, disklike mass of stars, it floated there in the black void of space like a little island of light, and hundreds of billions of miles outward from the outermost suns of this island-universe our little squadron flashed through space, parallel to its edge. Looking toward the great galaxy from that distance, its countless thousands of glittering suns seemed merged almost in one mighty flaming mass; yet even among those thousands there burned out distinctly the clearer glory of the greater suns, the blue radiance

of Vega, or the yellow splendor of Antares, or the white fire of great Canopus itself. Here and there among the fiery thousands, too, there glowed the strange, misty luminescence of the galaxy's mighty comets, while at the galaxy's edge directly to our left there flamed among the more loosely scattered stars the great Cancer cluster, a close-packed, ball-like mass of hundreds of shining suns, gathered together there like a great hive of swarming stars."

Wow! That's what we used to call the Sense of Wonder, and for this reader, at least, it still works.

Again, the volume contains an enjoyable introduction, this time by Walter Jon Williams, and an appendix with reproductions of period illustrations, readers' letters (including correspondence from the young Donald A. Wollheim and Henry Kuttner), and letters from Farnsworth Wright to Hamilton. One of Wright's letters contains the following memorable paragraph:

"I was in a sanitarium for four weeks in December, which is why I was unable to send you advance sheets of *The Star Stealers*. I did not try to add any love interest to the story, for your stories would be injured by such a diversion lugged in by the heels; but I merely changed Dal Nar, male, to Dal Nara, female, for cover design purposes, not injuring the story thereby, for it may be taken for granted that men and women will bear equal part of that far-distant day in such exploits. I would have taken even that slight change up with you except for the rush incident to my journey to the sanitarium."

Well, what's a little sex change between editor and author? And what was Editor Wright's medical emergency that prevented him from consulting Author Hamilton about the change? I'm afraid we will never know.

Which brings us to *The Collected Captain Future, Volume One*. In the interest of full disclosure, I must mention that this book contains an introduction by myself, and that I am an unashamed booster for the novels about Curtis Newton, the Wizard of Science, and his intrepid companions Grag the robot, Otho the android, and Simon Wright, the living brain. Plus the beauteous Joan Randall, Marshal Ezra Gurney, and the rest of the gang in these tales of the Futuremen.

A little bit of pulp history: When Hugo Gernsback lost control of his publishing company, and thus of *Amazing Stories,* in 1929, he simply rented another office and started a new string of magazines, the bellwether of which was *Science Wonder Stories.* This evolved into just plain *Wonder Stories,* and when Gernsback sold out to publisher Ned Pines in 1936, the magazine morphed again into *Thrilling Wonder Stories.* The editorial director was Leo Margulies, and under him a rotating staff of editors including Mort Weisinger and Horace Gold ran TWS and several companion titles in the fantastic fiction field.

Three years later Margulies and Company hired Edmond "Earth-wrecker" Hamilton to create a new hero whose interplanetary adventures would be featured in a brand-new periodical. By the end of 1939 the first issue of *Captain Future—Wizard of Science* was on the nation's newsstands, bearing an official publication date of 1940.

The recurring protagonist was of course a well-established feature of fiction magazines, from the days of Poe's Chevalier Dupin and Doyle's Sherlock Holmes and George Edward Challenger, through dime novel heroes like Nick Carter, Baseball Joe, and Dead-eye Dick, to dozens of pulp heroes who appeared in self-titled periodicals or as recurring features in more general magazines. Most prominent, of course, were the Shadow and Doc Savage; pulp scholars can cite scores of others like the Green Lama, the Phantom Detective, the Spider, the Moon Man, Ki-Gor, and so on.

Originally conceived as "Mr. Future," the new character quickly evolved into Captain Future. His band of assistants included Grag the giant robot, lumbering and not very bright; Otho the android, rubbery and hairless and wildly agile; and Simon Wright, the living brain, a brilliant scientist whose body had been destroyed in the course of an earlier adventure. The central cast of the series was rounded out by the lovely Joan Randall and crusty, elderly Marshal Ezra Gurney.

If there had been a single flaw in Hamilton's earlier space operas . . .

Wait a minute, did I actually say that? Okay, let's take it from the top:

If there had been a single flaw in Hamilton's earlier space operas, it was lack of characterization. The heroes of the Interplanetary and later Interstellar Patrols most often came in threes, with first-person narration by their leader, invariably a human being.

His companions might be plant men, insect men, octopus men, metallic cyborgs, or just about anything else you can think of, but once introduced they never exhibited any particular personality, history, interests or emotions other than the need to get the job done, i.e., saving the planet/solar system/galaxy.

In the Captain Future series, Hamilton corrected this shortcoming. With a vengeance. The first novel in the series, *Captain Future and the Space Emperor,* includes a full-fledged origin story featuring the elder Newtons in their lunar laboratory. When the site is raided the scientists are fatally wounded but they manage to save their baby, Curtis, and give him into the care of Grag, Otho, and Simon. These three companions raise the child to manhood, and he proceeds to share adventures with them over a span of seventeen issues of the *Captain Future* magazine plus several more in *Startling Stories.*

Again the solar system is that of an earlier era, with virtually every body inhabitable and inhabited, from broiling Mercury to the icy prison world of Pluto. Ah, yes, Pluto had been discovered by now, and was enjoying its temporary status as a full-fledged planet.

The magazine featured many splendid cover paintings, maps, drawings of action scenes and portraits of the characters. I suspect that the illustrator, "Wesso" (Hans Waldemar Wessolowski), consulted *Silver Screen* or some similar movie fan magazine for inspiration. His version of Curtis Newton was a dead ringer for matinee idol Cary Grant. Joan Randall could have passed for a third sibling to glamorous sisters Constance and Joan Bennett. And Ezra Gurney bore an uncanny resemblance to character actor Charles Winninger.

Captain future didn't quite wear a superhero costume, but his reliable "red synthesilk zipper suit" (sometimes blue) came close.

The stories were of course repetitious, involving scoundrelly villains, nefarious plots, dire perils, breathtaking chases and captures and rescues and escapes. The good guys were good and the bad guys were bad, the settings were exotic and the action was fast-paced. The philosophy, if there was any, was pretty simple.

All right, this is hero pulp, what did you expect, Thomas Mann?

Toward the end of his career, Edmond Hamilton started one more space opera series. There were only three Star Wolf novels but they were brilliant examples of the type. Hamilton's art had matured and the books stand head and shoulders above other, latter-day space operas. But that's another story for another day, dear children. The earlier Hamilton stories may creak here and challenge the reader's credulity there, but with the willing suspension of disbelief they are marvelously enjoyable escapades.

It is certainly possible to overdose on them, and the prospect of reading these three volumes—they total more than 2,000 pages of fiction!—is daunting. My recommendation, then, is to read until weary, then set aside the book at hand and take a change of pace, perhaps with a contemporary murder mystery or a good autobiography—maybe Sarah Palin's—before returning to the exploits of the Interstellar Patrol or the adventures of Captain Future and the Futuremen.

Stephen Haffner is to be commended for the fine job of assembling, packaging, and production that he has done with these collections. At $40 per volume they are obviously pricey, but at 700 pages each, with excellent typography, good paper, fine bindings and attractive jackets, they are well worth the dollars. I will eagerly anticipate the publication of further volumes in the series.

VULTURES

Histories of science fiction in its every manifestation, whether regarded as a social phenomenon, pure art, commercial phenomenon, or a playing field for aficionados, abound. Which leads one to ask, Why bother with another one?

British editor and researcher Philip Harbottle answers that question with *Vultures of the Void: The Legacy,* a compendium of fact, opinion, history, criticism, personality sketches, personal reminiscences, happy achievements, vain regrets, historical photos, cover reproductions, and a clear, unabashed love of science fiction. Reading *Vultures* was for me a sheer pleasure, and at 411 pages not a word too long.

Harbottle starts with his own discovery of science fiction, a common experience to be sure, by way of comic books. Harbottle was born in 1941, when England was taking a pounding by the Luftwaffe and came of age during the postwar years, known as the "mushroom period" in English publishing.

Paper had been in extremely short supply during the war, and government-controlled allocations were eagerly sought after by publishers who found they could sell anything they printed, regardless of quality or taste. After the war, as paper supplies became more plentiful, more and more publishers jumped on the bandwagon of cheap paperback fiction. The preferred genres, not surprisingly, were hardboiled crime novels, westerns, and of course science fiction.

But then flash back to the 1930s. Just as fandom in the United States was being pushed by Hugo Gernsback with his Science Fiction League, British fandom was getting its start through the British Science Fiction Association. And just as enthusiasm over the possibility of space flight was a favorite theme in both the pulp magazines and their fannish followers, in the UK there was a heavy overlap of membership between the BSFA and the fledgling British Interplanetary Society.

This was all before Harbottle's time but both period documentation and interviews fortunately recorded with those pioneers during their own lifetimes provided plenty of raw material for this book.

There were the usual club meetings, pub parties, and fanzine production. Self-documentation has always been a major feature of fandom on both sides of the Atlantic, and on both sides of the ocean fandom was long the spawning ground of future science fiction professionals.

Try to imagine a trio of young science fiction fans hovering over a recalcitrant mimeograph machine, struggling to get it to perform so they could run off the new issue of their fanzine and distribute it to their friends and subscribers. Fingers black with gooey mimeograph ink, paper particles stuck in their hair, spectacles smudged with oil and perspiration. Sounds like a scene out of some period sitcom—or out of the teenage years of Wilson Tucker, Robert Bloch, Harlan Ellison and Robert Silverberg.

But then realize that these three young fans were William F. Temple, Eric Frank Russell, and Arthur C. Clarke. Moments like that abound in Harbottle's book. Time after time I was brought up sharply with a gasp or a chuckle at another marvelous scene.

Imagine Temple, serving in His Majesty's Armed Forces during the war, trying to write a science fiction story only to have his partial manuscript blown to smithereens by an explosive round from a Nazi-fired cannon.

After the war the servicemen came home and the British science fiction community got back into gear. There were suddenly plenty of markets for science fiction manuscripts. Paperback houses and magazines abounded. The typical British paperback of the era was relatively short, not much longer than the shank half of an Ace Double. The pay rates were poor but the standards were low. Just about anyone who could string together 40,000 words into some sort of story line could find a publisher.

Harbottle points out that the same fast-producing authors who turned out hardboiled pseudo-American gangster novels were often assigned by the publishers to write science fiction as well. The results were occasionally hilarious but more often just bad books. The gangster novels also featured excessive brutality and lurid sex scenes. Some of the habits of the writers who produced such books spilled over into their science fiction.

Often the publishers insisted upon the use of "house names," fictitious personae that belonged to the publisher rather than to a particular author. Again, the parallel to practices in the US is remarkable. As Robert Silverberg has remarked on occasion, "When

I was a kid I really admired Ivar Jorgenson. I didn't realize that I'd grow up to be him!"

An interesting parallel occurs at this point. In the United States political outrage at brutality and gore in comic books and on the covers of paperback "sleaze" novels drew the wrath of a Congressional investigation spearheaded by Senator Estes Kefauver. In Britain action occurred on a local level, with "mushroom" publishers being prosecuted, convicted, fined, and in some cases actually jailed. The offending publications were almost entirely violent pseudo-American hardboiled fiction and sexually explicit (or at least suggestive) photographs. While "mushroom" science fiction caused severe damage to British science fiction, the removal of the "mushroom" publications opened the way for a superior brand of story.

As for Harbottle's personal involvement in British science fiction publishing, he became the editor of the short-lived but lovingly produced magazine *Vision of Tomorrow*. The stories of his struggles with printers and distributors are painfully familiar to anyone who has ever worked in the magazine field.

Following the demise of *Vision of Tomorrow*, Harbottle became a literary agent, representing many of the leading science fiction writers in Britain, most notably John Russell Fearn (1908-1960) and E. C. Tubb (1919-2010). Fearn in particular has been a lifelong obsession for Harbottle, who by his own statement spent 58 years collecting every possible book, magazine appearance, manuscript, and bit of ephemera by Fearn, either under his own name or a bewildering array of pseudonyms, the most memorable of them being Volsted Gridban.

Gosh, you could have fooled me!

Harbottle is still at work, dedicating himself to the perpetuation on both sides of the Atlantic of the works of British authors who might otherwise disappear from human ken.

There's no way any reviewer can summarize this massive volume in a few hundred words. The book is a treasure trove of information and total joy to read. I'll leave it right there.

MALCOM JAMESON: WHAT MANNER OF MAN ?

Malcolm Jameson was a late bloomer. No fault of his own. He never intended to be a science fiction writer, or any other kind of writer for that matter. He was a career naval officer.

Born in 1891, as a young man he obtained a commission in the United States Navy. Details of his early life are spotty, and as yet no full-scale biography of Jameson exists. According to John W. Campbell, Jr., writing *In Memoriam* following Jameson's death in 1945, Jameson was instrumental in developing modern naval ordnance.

In an interesting parallel with his younger colleague Robert A. Heinlein (1907-1988), Jameson was forced to abandon his naval career prematurely, due to health problems. Why he turned to science fiction is uncertain, but the stories that he wrote reflect a thorough familiarity with and understanding of the field, causing one to surmise that he stepped into science fiction gracefully and with ease.

His first published story was the oddly-title "Eviction by Isotherm," in *Astounding Science Fiction* for August, 1938. From the outset, Jameson's writing was naturalistic and smooth. A further remarkable synchronicity: Heinlein's first published story, "Life-Line," appeared in the same issue of the same magazine.

Jameson was an immediate success, and his production soared. By my count, he published two stories in 1938, five in 1939, eleven in 1940, fifteen in 1941, and twenty-three in his peak year of 1942. By this time, however, one infers that his health was failing, and his production flagged. He published thirteen stories in 1943, eight in 1944, and five in 1945, the year of his death. One previously unpublished story remained, and appeared in 1946.

The amazingly prolific output of those peak years meant that Jameson had to spread his works over numerous outlets. His stories appeared in *Astounding,* in that periodical's fantasy-oriented companion magazine *Unknown,* in *Weird Tales, Amazing Stories, Thrilling Wonder Stories, Planet Stories, Startling Stories, Astonishing Stories, Super Science Stories,* and even, on one occasion, in the pages of William Hamling's semi-professional magazine, *Stardust*.

The two short novels included in the present volume were both published in *Startling Stories*, a pulp magazine whose sensational covers and sometimes adolescent editorial personality belied a remarkable array of first-rate science fiction. A series of editors ran the magazine. During the era of Jameson's contributions these included Oscar J. Friend and Horace Gold.

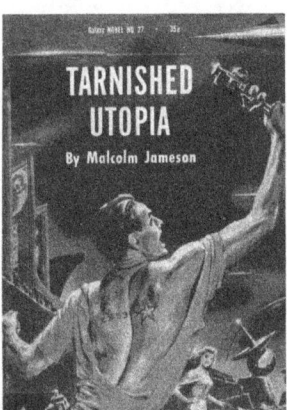
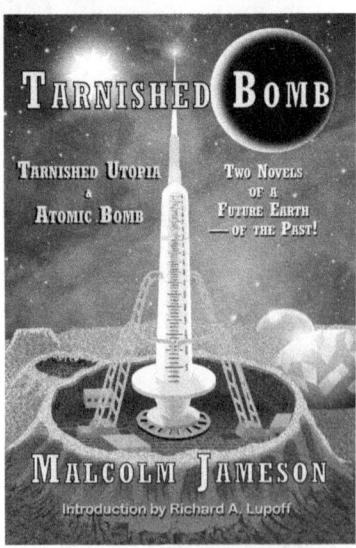

Jameson's first book publication was *Atomic Bomb*, issued by Bond-Charteris Publications in 1945. It is based on Jameson's *Startling Stories* novel *The Giant Atom*, originally published in the issue for winter, 1943. The atomic bomb was very much in the news in 1945, following the destruction of the Japanese cities of Hiroshima and Nagasaki by this weapon, and the surrender of Japan which brought the Second World War to a close. In the Bond-Charteris edition the text is slightly tweaked to give it more currency, but the novel is not seriously altered from the magazine version.

Bond-Charteris was a short-lived publishing company, little more than a private label for Leslie Charteris (Leslie Charles Bowyer-Yin), the creator of the gentleman-rogue-adventurer Simon Templar, better known as the Saint. Some fourteen of the eighteen books issued by the company were either authored by Charteris or were anthologies edited by him. Another was a western novel written by the editor of *Startling Stories*, Oscar J. Friend. And another was Malcolm Jameson's novel.

Jameson's second book, *Tarnished Utopia*, was a Galaxy Science Fiction Novel. A companion series to *Galaxy Science Fiction* magazine, founded and initially edited by Horace Gold, the Galaxy Novels included many outstanding books. The format, like that of the Bond-Charteris books, was similar to that of a digest-sized magazine. Most were reprinted from earlier hardbound editions; a few were original publications including Arthur C. Clarke's *Prelude to Space;* still others were resurrected from the back issues of pulp magazines. This was the case with *Tarnished Utopia,* which had originally appeared in *Startling Stories* for March, 1942.

In later years, Horace Gold spoke of his experience editing the Galaxy Novels. He told me that his budget allowed him to pay a flat fee of $500 per novel, whether it was a reissue of a previously published book, a reprint from a magazine, or an original publication.

It would be superfluous to summarize the plots of the two novels in the present volume, but some comments might not be out of place.

Atomic Bomb starts like a throwback to the classic space operas of Edward Elmer Smith. Jameson presents a genius loner scientist who has designed and built a spaceship single-handed. As the novel opens, the inventor is showing his creation to a lovely young lady, the object of his affection. One immediately sees the parallel to Smith's pioneering *Skylark of Space*. Jameson's Stephen Bennion stands in for Smith's Richard Seaton. Seaton's sweetheart,

Dorothy Vaneman, becomes Katherine Pennell. And Smith's *Skylark* is Jameson's *Katherine*.

But Jameson pulls a surprising switch on any reader who thought he was about to settle in for a good old-fashioned space opera. Bennion's private laboratory is taken over by a corporate raider or "vulture capitalist" of a type with which we are all too familiar in present times. Bennion had been working on a new power source for his spaceship and the greedy corporate managers seek to pursue an abandoned experiment of Bennion's.

The disastrous result is the so-called "giant atom"—an almost perfect prediction of the black hole. The only difference between the giant atom and the modern conception of the black hole is that Jameson's atom emits brilliant light and searing heat while the black hole absorbs light and heat. Still, it grows continuously and threatens to destroy the entire planet Earth and eventually the entire solar system.

Some of the scenes in *Atomic Bomb* are reminiscent of Lester del Rey's story *Nerves* (1942). But one need only think of Chernobyl, Three Mile Island, or Fukushima to see real world analogs of Jameson's creation.

Tarnished Utopia first appeared in *Startling Stories* for March, 1942. Its only book publication prior to the present edition came as a Galaxy Novel in 1956. Closer to conventional science fiction than *The Giant Atom,* this novel harks back to the "long sleep" theme previously utilized by H. G. Wells in *When the Sleeper Wakes,* by Philip Francis Nowlan in *Armageddon 2419 A.D.,* and by Edgar Rice Burroughs in *Beyond Thirty,* which short novel it most closely resembles. Other influences on Jameson are obvious, the most striking one being Stanley G. Weinbaum's Martian "Valley of Dreams" (1934).

Starting with an American aviator escaped from a German prisoner-of-war camp and caught in an Allied bombing raid, Jameson transports his protagonist into a future world in which Asian conquerors rule the earth. Not only this, they have built permanent colonies on the moon and established commercial relationships with the planets of the solar system.

Jameson's protagonist, Allan Winchester, is captured and enslaved by the overlords of the future, and soon seeks to organize and lead a revolution against them. While fairly predictable in plot, the book is surprising in its political content. No information has surfaced to suggest that Jameson was himself a Marxist, yet in the Utopian society which Winchester strives to establish in place of the despotism of the future: *Each did, for the good of all, what he could; each received, according to his nature, his proper needs.*

Not long after this astonishing outburst, Winchester colludes with the Asian ruler, Prince Lohan, to round up and annihilate everyone who might possibly be considered disloyal or a threat to the ruling clique. This is, of course, a clear reference to the infamous Stalinist purges and show trials of the 1930s. One can hardly imagine that Jameson intended Allan Winchester as a stand-in for Stalin's chief prosecutor, Andrei Vyshinsky, and yet the parallel is hard to avoid.

Jameson wrote at least one other novel, *Quicksands of Youthfulness,* serialized in *Astonishing Stories* in the winter of 1940-41. It is to be hoped that the installments of this novel will be gathered and the book will be made available to modern readers. In addition, Jameson's series of novelettes about a future spacefaring hero, *Bullard of the Space Patrol,* were gathered into a "fix-up" novel in 1951. Very popular in its time, a new edition of this book is planned by Surinam Turtle Press.

In addition, a series of collections of Jameson's shorter fiction has been initiated by our sister imprint, Dancing Tuatara Press, under the talented editorship of my friend and colleague, John Pelan.

One is tempted to speculate on Malcolm Jameson's present stature in the world of science fiction had he not died after so short a career. Had he continued to write for another ten to twenty years, it seems entirely possible, even likely, that he would have become as influential and would be remembered with as much respect as Robert A. Heinlein. The reappearance of his many fine works in new editions, one hopes, will lead to his recognition, however belated, as one of the premier talents of his generation.

A brief note on the text. As previously mentioned, both *Tarnished Utopia* and *Atomic Bomb* (originally *The Giant Atom*) first appeared in *Startling Stories* magazine. They were then published as digest-size paperback books. The book editions were slightly revised from the magazine versions. The texts in the present volume are based on the first book editions of these two short novels.

I have tried to remain faithful to the author's intention, altering the text only to correct obvious typographical errors or lapses of memory. While the Galaxy Novels version of *Tarnished Utopia* is reasonably clean typographically, the Bond-Charteris version of *Atomic Bomb* was apparently rushed into print after the bombings of Hiroshima and Nagasaki in 1945 to seize the moment of maximum public interest. Typographical errors abound and punctuation marks must have been inserted with a shotgun. I have tried to clean up this typographical disaster while observing all possible respect to the fine creations of Malcolm Jameson.

HOLMESIANA

Certainly Sherlock Holmes is one of the world's most popular and enduring fictional characters. Since his biographer, John H. Watson, and Dr. Watson's literary agent, Arthur Conan Doyle, saw fit to gift the world with a limited number of stories and novels about the Great Detective, a major school of literature has grown up, its hungry printing presses—and cameras and microphones and circuit boards—nourished by an endless brigade of admirers. Said admirers offer readers a seemingly limitless supply of "secret adventures," "lost cases," "rediscovered manuscripts," even spirit dictations of Sherlock Holmes.

So voluminous is the outpouring of *faux* Holmesiana, there have grown up a variety of subgenres: the boyhood adventures of Sherlock Holmes, the lost years of Sherlock Holmes, the cases of Sherlock's brother Mycroft Holmes, of Dr. Watson, of Mrs. Watson, of Sherlock's archrival Dr. Moriarty, of the ghost of Sherlock Holmes. And then there are the *Sherlock Holmes Meets* adventures. The Great Detective has met Herr Bismarck, Prince Edward, Count Dracula, Cthulhu, Sigmund Freud, the Martians, and most of the population, actual and fictitious, of the Victorian and Edwardian Eras.

In *The Shadow of Reichenbach Falls,* by John R. King, Sherlock Holmes meets Thomas Karnacki. And in case you are unfamiliar with this fellow, let me explain that he was a psychic detective created by William Hope Hodgson (1887-1918). Best known to fantasy fans for his powerfully atmospheric, darkly brooding tales of the sea and of the distant future, Hodgson also wrote a good many pulp adventures in a career ended by his death in the first World War.

The first six Karnacki stories appeared in British magazines between 1910 and 1912. They were collected in a slim book published in 1913. You can obtain a collectible copy of the 1913 edition for a mere $3,000 if you are so inclined.

Enter August Derleth. As chief honcho of Arkham House and its sister imprint, Mycroft and Moran, Derleth published first a huge omnibus of Hodgson's fantasy novels. He then unearthed three Karnacki stories omitted from the 1913 volume and published an expanded edition of *Karnacki the Ghost Finder* in 1948.

Typical of their genre, the Karnacki tales have titles like "The Hog" (probably the most famous of the cycle), "The Thing Invisible," and "The Searcher of the End House."

Back to Reichenbach Falls, the site in Switzerland at which Sherlock Holmes and James Moriarty, locked in mortal embrace, fell to their joint demise in 1891. The event is recorded in Dr. Watson's story "The Final Problem," 1893. Clearly Dr. Doyle was tired of agenting these tales for his friend Watson, and he considered "The Final Problem" to be the end of the Holmes saga. While Dr. Doyle eventually relented, other authors have contributed endlessly to the canon. After Doyle's death his heirs fought tirelessly to control the property and keep poachers from publishing unauthorized pastiches. Eventually the works passed into the public domain, and in recent years the Holmes Derby has become a free-for-all.

John R. King opens with a focus on Karnacki. A wandering vagabond and petty grifter (at least in King's version), Karnacki's peregrinations bring him to Reichenbach in the guise of an American tourist. He meets a lovely young woman and just as it looks as if romance is about to blossom they witness a figure tumble from the heights. They rescue the victim. He is suffering from serious injuries (no surprise) including amnesia. As they struggle to get him to medical assistance, another shadowy figure appears and starts shooting at them.

I don't want to get into endless plot summarization. That's boring and it's also unfair to both the author and any potential reader. Well, just two more tidbits, which I offer because they are as obvious to the reader as a giant pizza dropped onto a trackless snowfield. The amnesiac is none other than Sherlock Holmes and the mysterious gunman is the infamous Professor Moriarty.

The Shadow of Reichenbach Falls is an ambitious and structurally complex novel. King flashes back to Moriarty's youth and provides a biography that I can only compare to the late Norman Mailer's final novel, *The Castle in the Forest,* which featured the young Adolf Hitler as its protagonist.

King throws in every bit of Holmesiana within reach, including a major detour into Sherlock-Holmes-meets-Jack-the-Ripper territory. And this may not be entirely a detour at that, for King skillfully mixes in Moriarty, Holmes, and Leather Apron Jack.

It's unfortunate—almost tragic—that the author of the present book has bitten off so much, for in fact he does not chew it very well. The novel is riddled with flaws of style, research, and vocabulary. The general prose style is contemporary, while the theme and setting cry out for the more mannered prose that we have come to associate with novels set in the Victorian Era, and that is virtually *de rigueur* for Holmesian pastiche. To list just a few of the scores of solecisms that mar the book:

~ A character is described as being "in his fourth decade" and then as "in his forties." But one's fourth decade is one's *thirties*.

~ The word *elicit* is used where the author clearly means *illicit*.

~ A truffle, described by Webster as "a candy made of chocolate, butter and sugar . . . and coated with cocoa," is described by King as a "cherry cordial."

~ The East End of London is described as the "East Side"—a term usually applied to a section of Manhattan.

~ Copenhagen (Denmark) is described as being to the west of Cardiff (Wales); a simple glance at any map of the region will show that the opposite is the case.

~ A character sees a copper wire with a black coating—wait a minute, if there's a black coating how does he know that there's a copper wire inside?

~ The author describes a six-pointed pentangle. Huh?

~ The term "waylaid" is used when the author clearly means "misled."

~ The author describes a character as a "nebbish." Major anachronism, and just one of many in the book. Others include "This is it" for "I am dying," "zap" as a verb, and "rookie" for a beginner.

~ In Paris, King's characters use English money instead of French, and nobody seems to notice anything odd about this.

~ Describing a supernatural manifestation, clearly referring to ectoplasm, the author instead calls it protoplasm. This gaffe occurs at least twice.

It may be unfair to blame the author for all of these errors, and believe me, the above list is a mere sampling. More far-reaching are apparently pointless switches in viewpoint, tense, and narrative voice. A good editor should have taken this manuscript in hand, marked it up mercilessly, and returned it to the author for revision. I've worked with some very good editors over the years and I have felt the sting of such critiques, but the result has been, in every case, a much improved manuscript.

Did Mr. King not have an editor, or was his editor incompetent or so overworked that he or she didn't have the time to pay necessary attention to the manuscript? Your humble reviewer readily admits that he does not know.

The Shadow of Reichenbach Falls reads like a first novel based on a good idea but executed by an inexperienced and immature author. The fact is that John R. King (sometimes writing as J. Robert King) has more than a dozen previous novels in his bibliography. And he is himself an editor at Houghton Mifflin. All of which leaves this reviewer shaking his head in something very much like despair.

A STREET IN MANILA,
AN APARTMENT IN CHICAGO

The last time I saw E. Hoffmann Price we were sitting in the living room of his comfortable, modest house in the hills above Redwood City, California. Redwood City is a pleasant middle-class suburb of San Francisco. I believe this was the last interview that Price ever gave, shortly before his death on June 18, 1988, fifteen days before what would have been his ninetieth birthday.

We had spent much of the afternoon taping an interview for a local radio station. I had two partners with me, making for an overcrowded air sound. Normally only one or two of us would have done the show with Mr. Price, but nobody wanted to miss out on this opportunity.

Mrs. Price, a gracious hostess, served Turkish coffee to the guests. It was, to coin a phrase, so dense that a spoon would stand up in it and so strong that it nearly melted the spoons. I don't think I slept for three nights after drinking a tiny cup of that fierce brew.

The room was furnished with a lifetime of memorabilia. On one shelf stood a row of miniature sculptures, created by Clark Ashton Smith as gifts for his friend Ed Price. A magnificently carved antique wooden throne stood against one wall. Ed Price warned us that no one was allowed to sit there. It was reserved for the Son of Heaven, should he ever deign to visit. Crossed swords—not the display variety, but actual weapons that might once have inflicted fatal wounds—were hung upon another wall.

Price was a great raconteur, and in a long life had known an astonishing who's-who of the pulp world. On one occasion, while driving from California to Louisiana, he had stopped at Cross Plains, Texas, to visit Robert E. Howard. Soon ensconced in New Orleans he had entertained Howard Phillips Lovecraft, serving him a bowl of homemade chili that, in Price's words, "would have raised blisters on a saddle." Even Lovecraft, who prided himself on his fondness for fiercely spiced dishes, admitted that Price's chili was an outstanding brew.

Shortly before my colleagues and I were to leave, Ed Price drew me aside. He was a onetime army man, a West Point graduate and veteran of the First World War. He had traveled all over the world. He knew that I, too, was ex-military, a onetime enlisted man and then again an officer and a gentleman. My two associates had never served in uniform.

Indicating the others with a tilt of his head, Ed spoke to me *sotto voce*. "They've never been in the service, they wouldn't understand. But you and I—listen, if you'd like the address of the best whorehouse in Manila—"

Then he interrupted himself. "*Hmmm*, come to think of it, the last time I was there was 1915."

That's the kind of guy Edgar Hoffmann Price was. A unique character. And a real writer.

~ ~ ~ ~ ~

In his posthumously published memoir, *Book of the Dead* (2001), Price describes his first meeting with Otis Adelbert Kline. It was summer of 1926. Price was visiting the offices of *Weird Tales* in Chicago. The editor of that magazine, Farnsworth Wright, summoned Kline from an adjacent room.

The two writers were already familiar with each other's work. Kline had been a *Weird Tales* regular since its first issue, which published his novelette "The Thing of a Thousand Shapes." Kline was a sometime unofficial staff member at *Weird Tales*, while holding down a day job at a food and spice importing company.

Both Kline and Price had been prolific pulp writers, working in a variety of genres. Both had an interest in Middle Eastern and Arabic culture. Both had rejected traditional Christianity, Price becoming a lifelong Buddhist and Kline a Muslim of sorts. He could certainly not have practiced any orthodox variety of Islam, as Price was shortly to discover.

That very night Kline invited Price, Wright, and *Weird Tales*' business manager, William Springer, to his apartment to meet Mrs. Kline and their children, and to share a generous meal and a variety of tasty concoctions. Obviously the then-official Prohibition Amendment was widely and thoroughly ignored.

Price had been a member of an intercollegiate fencing team; Kline, also, was an amateur swordsman. Late that night, having consumed copious and varied alcoholic concoctions and after Wright and Springer had taken their leave and the rest of the Kline family had retired, Kline and Price engaged in an impromptu duel. They used sabers rather than *epées* and dispensed with such protective paraphernalia as masks and pads. How both emerged unscathed from this contest remains a mystery. The encounter, however, led to a friendship which lasted until Kline's untimely death in 1946 at the age of fifty-five.

The initial collaboration between the two men also grew from this first meeting. It was a novelette, "Thirsty Blades," which they sold to *Weird Tales*.

Illustration by **Allen Koszowski**

The novel is Satans on Saturn; *the omnibus is* Satans of Saturn — *first book edition, after three-quarters of a century*

Kline was a busy and versatile writer. His best known works were a series of fantastic novels serialized in *Argosy* magazine, one of the most prestigious and lucrative of pulp markets. Between 1929 and 1935 he placed eight such works with *Argosy*. They closely paralleled the interplanetary romances and jungle adventure tales written by Edgar Rice Burroughs. Kline even wrote a novel called *Maza of the Moon,* paralleling Burroughs' *The Moon Maid.*

A lengthy dispute eventually arose in the fan press, as to whether Kline was attempting to capitalize on Burroughs' popularity by imitating his *oeuvre*.

In the January, 1930 edition of *The Writer,* Kline published an essay, "Writing the Fantastic Story." In this piece he recounted the story of his father, an amateur astronomer, instructing him in the wonders of the night sky.

> *"He told me of the vast distances which, according to the computations of scientists, lay between our world and these twinkling celestial bodies—that the stars were suns, some smaller than our own, and others so large that if they were hollow, our entire Solar System could operate inside them without danger of the planet farthest from the sun striking the shell. He told me of the nebulae, which might be giant universes in the making, and that beyond the known limits of our universe it was possible that there were countless others, stretching on into infinity."*

~ ~ ~ ~ ~

Such, Kline averred, was the long-remembered inspiration of his interplanetary romances. He made no mention of Burroughs' immensely successful stories of John Carter, the Warlord of Barsoom. It is hard to believe that he was totally unaware of them, and yet . . .

Decades later, during the massive Burroughs revival of the 1960s and long after the demise of both authors, Robert A. W. Lowndes of Avalon Books and Donald Wollheim of Ace Books resurrected Kline's interplanetary romances and jungle adventures. Wollheim told me personally that he had tried to obtain publication rights to the Burroughs novels but been unable to get any response from the Burroughs interests, and published the Kline titles instead. In any case, once Kline's interplanetaries were available to a mass market the bonfire of controversy was reignited.

Throughout the 1930s Kline and Price maintained their friendship and collaborated from time to time on literary and even culinary projects. By this time Kline had established himself as a literary agent, and was one of his own more popular clients. In the same era, Price recalled,

> *"Otis sent me the synopsis and character sketches of several stories he had long hoped to write. There was ever less chance for him to get at these projects. One was a space opera serial*

Satans on Saturn, *widely damned as the worst of Kline and the worst of Price."*

~ ~ ~ ~ ~

In his memoir, Price goes on to relate Kline's unsuccessful attempts to market the serial. His prime market, *Argosy,* turned it down. Working his way through more conventional science fiction outlets, Kline finally reached *Thrilling Wonder Stories,* where he pleaded with editor Leo Margulies to take the novel for a token price of $250.

"Leo said, 'I'd not publish this God-damned mess if you paid me $250!' "

~ ~ ~ ~ ~

By this time, however, a new editor had arrived at *Argosy* so Kline gave that magazine another try and sold *Satans on Saturn* for $750! The story was serialized in five weekly installments starting with the issue of *Argosy* dated November 2, 1940.

Despite Price's own poor opinion of *Satans on Saturn,* it reads as a perfectly respectable and enjoyable example of its type. Space opera? Of course! On a par with the very best works of Jack Williamson, Edmond Hamilton, or Edward Elmer Smith? Perhaps not, but certainly far better than Price's own description and light-years superior to some of the inferior works produced in the US and UK during the "mushroom" years of out-of-hand publishing in the 1950s and '60s.

How much of the text is Price's work and how much is Kline's is subject to speculation. Price records that the original idea was Kline's. The rhythm and style of the prose seems to sway between the two, and one might speculate that since the narrative involves two major protagonists, each author penned the chapters narrated from the viewpoint of one.

Satans on Saturn takes place in the traditional version of the solar system, in which all the planets are pretty much like the Earth—only more so. In this model, Mars is cold and dry, rather like the Gobi desert. Venus is hot and moist, rather like the Amazon rain forest. Mercury is hot on one side, frigid on the other, with a livable, temperate, twilight zone separating the two. And so on.

In *Satans on Saturn* the planet Jupiter has a solid surface and a hot climate, while its moons are frigid but habitable. The Saturnians are giant, bat-winged, and horned. They bear a remarkable resemblance to the Overlords in Arthur C. Clarke's important novel *Childhood's End* (1953). The novel was developed from an earlier Clarke short story first published in 1946.

Could Clarke, an avid science fiction fan in his early twenties when *Satans on Saturn* was serialized in *Argosy*, have come across a run of issues and read the story in its serial form? It is entirely possible that he had read *Satans on Saturn* and developed his Overlords from Kline and Price's Saturnians. A caveat, however, must be expressed. This notion is purely speculative; should any evidence emerge to support it, the science fiction world will surely take note.

Another aspect of *Satans on Saturn* which causes the modern reader to shudder is the recurring theme of humans being sent "to the ovens" by the Saturnians, and the Saturnians using "privileged" humans—in effect, turncoats—as overseers of human slave laborers in exchange for being spared "the ovens."

By the time Kline and Price were working on *Satans on Saturn*, Adolf Hitler's "final solution" had not yet come into effect, and one may be sure that neither Kline nor Price would have wished to borrow this monstrous crime for use in a lightweight science fiction novel.

Otis Kline died long before the pulp magazine field withered and died. Ed Price enjoyed a long and productive life. He pursued a number of professions after his chosen literary markets had disappeared. Most notably he was highly regarded as a professional photographer. But he never lost his fondness for telling fantastic tales.

In 1967 a small collection of his short stories was issued by Arkham house under the title *Strange Gateways*. In 1975 a much larger collection, *Far Lands, Other Days,* was published by Carcosa. The stories in both of these books were gleaned from his contributions to the pulps.

Then in 1979, at the age of eighty one, he returned to writing and between 1979 and 1986 he produced six novels. Two of these are classified as fantasies: *The Devil Wives of Li Fong* and *The Jade Enchantress*. The others are a science fiction tetralogy: *Operation Misfit, Operation Longlife, Operation Exile,* and *Operation Isis*.

The day he departed this vale of tears, Edgar Hoffmann Price was found slumped over his typewriter, a partial manuscript on the platen.

The present Surinam Turtle Press edition is the first book edition of *Satans on Saturn,* and as far as we have been able to determine, the first republication, ever, of the 1940 serial. As such, it makes a valuable addition to the world library of science fiction.

As *lagniappe*, we have added two short stories by E. Hoffmann Price and a novelette by Otis Adelbert Kline.

"Web of Wizardry" is an example of the so-called Oriental Story of which Price was a master. Adventure tales set in the Middle East or in Asia, these stories are marked by their exotic settings and by a fascination with Eastern cultures, in this case those of the Arab-Muslim world. They are often, although not always, laced with elements of fantasy.

"Selene Slays by Night" is another fantasy by Price, but far different from "Web of Wizardry." A skillful blending of whimsy and horror, "Selene" has a realistic, contemporary setting, an unusual venue for a Price story.

Both of these stories appeared in 1942 issues of *Spicy Mystery Stories,* a pulp magazine that was ultimately suppressed because of its risqué contents. To the modern reader, a typical *Spicy* story would read like a tepid romance, but in its day attitudes were very different.

Otis Adelbert Kline's "The Man from the Moon" was first published in 1930 in *Amazing Stories,* Hugo Gernsback's pioneering science fiction magazine, although by 1930 Gernsback had lost control of *Amazing* and was publishing the *Wonder* group of magazines.

An odd story in its structure, "The Man from the Moon" is half earthbound exotic adventure, half space opera. The latter half is especially significant in that it describes an ancient solar system and the circumstances under which both Mars and Earth's moon were brought to the condition in which modern astronomers know them.

We have noted elsewhere that Edgar Rice Burroughs' version of Mars—Barsoom—is warmer, wetter, and more densely atmospheric than the present Mars. This has led to an exercise in Higher Criticism that suggests that Burroughs' heroic earthmen were transported not merely across space but through time as well, to find themselves on ancient Barsoom. While most of Kline's interplanetaries are set on Venus, he did transport an earthly adventurer to the red planet in *Outlaws of Mars* and his rationale for the differences between that planet's ancient condition and its modern state is convincingly presented in "The Man from the Moon."

BEASTS, SONGBIRDS AND WIZARDS
(*Washington Post* Bookworld)

Robert A. Heinlein's *The Number of the Beast* is a frustrating book. It's frustrating because it's a very bad book that could have been—well, certainly not a great book but surely a good one and possibly a very good one.

It opens with a quartet of typically Heinleinian characters: a brilliant, crotchety, middle-aged scientist; his tough, savvy, pragmatic, second wife; the statuesque, lusty daughter of the scientist's first marriage; and her brilliant but muscular husband.

While off for a double honeymoon at the underground country retreat of the elder scientist, the four discover that the earth is being invaded by a race of malevolent aliens aided and abetted by a secret network of human traitors and/or dupes. They escape an assassination attempt in the senior brilliant scientist's computerized dimension-hopping Ford, the *Gay Deceiver*. Discovering that *Gay* can pop into and out of any point along the six axes of space-time gives the adventurers access to a virtually limitless number of universes. And so, off they go . . .

It's a promising premise, although possibly too great for much suspense. E.g., suppose the bad guy gives you a terrible thrashing and leaves you all but dead. You need merely pop back through space-time and await his arrival with a Reggie Jackson model Louisville Slugger in your fist, then cream the bejesus out of him before he can lay a mitt on you.

Totally ignoring this logical glitch, Heinlein pops his foursome into an alternate universe where Victorian England and Tsarist Russia have established rival colonies on the planet Mars. Colonists travel between the worlds in wonderful dream-image spacecraft with huge flapping wings and survive on Mars in a chronic state of not-quite-war. Heinlein's travelers get involved in the conflict, avert a dreadful disaster, and become drawn into the mini-court politics of the English colony. It's all lovely stuff, with the makings of a fine piece of pseudo-Victorian science fiction of the sort done occasionally by Christopher Priest, Brian Aldiss, or Michael Moorcock.

Unfortunately, Heinlein wanders away from this setting, getting his characters mixed up with various other worlds and problems. Some are very intriguing, especially a sort of alternate present-day USA in which *laissez-faire* is carried to a degree that would send Ronald Reagan screaming into the arms of Teddy Kennedy. But as far as novelistic structure is concerned, if one may fling about such elementary notions as *challenge, response,* and *outcome,* things turn totally to porridge.

Robert A. Heinlein in 1929

Midshipman Robert A. Heinlein's graduation portrait, reproduced from the 1929 yearbook of the United States Naval Academy — wasn't he a handsome devil!

Eventually even the author gives up. He brings a whole army of characters onstage for a sort of super World Science Fiction Convention. His own fictional creations rub elbows with those of other authors and the authors themselves. Heinlein forestalls harping critics *ante hoc* by inviting them to a special lounge furnished with typewriters and tape recorders but no ribbons or tapes, a dining room but no kitchen, and a bar but no booze.

A couple of characters bring up the original incident that started this farrago and dismiss it out of hand.

Aside from its overwhelming structural flaws, the book suffers from a gastropodous pace and from some of the most intolerable coyness on record. Here's an example from Chapter IV. The narrator is Deety, the sexy young bride.

"I pulled on briefs, started to tie on a halter—stopped and looked in the mirror. I have a face-shaped face and a muscular body that I keep in top condition. I would never reach semifinals in a beauty contest but my teats are shapely, exceptionally firm, stand out without sagging and look larger than they are because my waist is small for my height, shoulders and hips. I've known this since I was twelve, from mirror and from comments by others."

Six paragraphs later she's still ruminating about her teats. It takes this simpering imbecile four more paragraphs before she finally decides to wear the halter. Now why, why for God's sake, didn't Heinlein's editor just draw a big blue diagonal through those paragraphs and knock the whole internalization out of the book? Easily 200 of the novel's 512 pages could similarly have been eliminated, leaving a reasonably tight manuscript. The structure might then have been repaired.

I think the reason is that Heinlein, along with about a half-dozen other writers in this field, has reached such a level of commercial success that he can sell anything he writes. Editors and publishers don't dare demand solid structure, tight copy, or polished prose of this crew for fear that they will simply pull their manuscripts and sell 'em elsewhere.

In the short run this places Heinlein and others similarly situated in an advantageous position. But ultimately it makes for inferior books, thus working to the detriment of the reader's pleasure and the writer's reputation. Such an unbridled talent may occasionally produce a *Citizen Kane;* more often the result is—well, name your most unfavorite of Jerry Lewis's self-indulgent messes.

~ ~ ~ ~ ~

Songmaster, by Orson Scott Card is the story of one Ansset, a "Songbird" in a galactic empire of the fairly remote future. Like many such empires, the one created by Card is a strange mixture of the super-advanced (namely, interstellar travel) and the regressive (emperors, courts, armies, peasants, castles).

It's a too-familiar picture, but Card adds a most striking feature, the Songhouse of Tew. Here singing is raised to the level of a philosophy, virtually of a religion. And the finest of the singers, the Songbirds, are sent to the most deserving throughout the galaxy. The Songbirds are apparently all sopranos, sent out in childhood, their sexual maturation delayed a few years by drugs. Even so, by their mid or late teens, Songbirds return to the Songhouse to serve the rest of their lives as teachers, administrators or the like.

Ansset is the galactic emperor's own Songbird, and provides a unique point of view for a novel of personal growth and exploration melded into a tale of interplanetary politics and court intrigue. Card strives for emotional intensity and often achieves it. On occasion he deals from a stacked deck, as when he withholds information regarding a side effect of the Songbird's drug—from Ansset and the reader alike—for the sake of a melodramatic moment. But most often he plays fairly and he plays well.

If the book has a major—or even semi-major—flaw, it is a certain sense of coldness and austerity. Card is too controlled a writer for this to be inadvertent; perhaps the calculated starkness of the background is intended to make the story's physical drama and emotional intensity stand out. If so, Card sells himself short—he would have succeeded anyway. *Songmaster* is a first-class job, far superior to Card's previous novel, *A Planet Called Treason,* which was miles better than the still earlier *Hot Sleep.*

~ ~ ~ ~ ~

While Orson Scott Card's first three novels show steady Improvement, John Varley's—alas!—show the opposite. Varley's first, *The Ophiuchi Hotline* (1977), was vastly ambitious and substantially successful. Varley's short fiction had already generated huge excitement among science fiction readers, and the novel was joyously received.

His second, *Titan* (1979), was both more successful and less rewarding. It dealt with the discovery and exploration of a giant alien-built spaceship/artifact/worldlet. It was essentially a travelogue. Varley wrote it very well, but it had already been written by Larry Niven *(Ringworld)* and Arthur C. Clarke *(Rendezvous with Rama).* It's true that the Niven and Clarke versions had been almost pure travelogue while Varley enriched the brew with some interesting characters. But still, he was essentially re-examining familiar ground.

His third novel, *Wizard* is still another rewrite of a book that is now growing awfully tired. Again Varley adds a couple of new and interesting characters—a man suffering from a peculiar intermittent psychic condition on Earth and a woman raised in an all-Lesbian space colony. But it's the same worldlet, Gaea, and the same plot, namely a lengthy trek ending in a confrontation with the being who in one sense rules and in another sense *is* the world.

A third volume of this stuff is promised by Varley's publisher, and I shudder at the prospect. Is this truly dazzling young talent played out already? Or can he put these derivative trivialities behind him and regain the form that he showed in *The Ophiuchi Hotline?* Read Varley's novel-after-next and find out.

WANDERING WITH THE DEROS

Science fiction has had its share of colorful and controversial editors, including several who tried to hijack the field for an array of purposes. This started with Hugo Gernsback himself who saw science fiction as a tool for stimulating the minds of bright but underachieving adolescents and tricking them into appreciating the wonders of chemistry, astronomy, and so forth.

Let's all get out there and build ourselves a Wheatstone Bridge, classmates!

There were attempts in the 1930s and '40s to use pulp adventure magazines or fandom itself to spread the doctrines of Technocracy, Michelism (a form of Communism), or Esperanto. John W. Campbell, Jr., used the pages of *Astounding Science Fiction* to promote one unconventional notion after another; he was a very early booster of D**n*t*cs before moving on to Psionics (read your neighbor's poker hand and take his money), the Dean Drive (let's sail a submarine to Jupiter, gang!), the Hieronymous machine (draw a picture of a helicopter, jump in and fly away), and the Interplanetary Exploration Society (let's all chip in, buy parts at the local hardware store, and build our own spaceship).

Yes, the sainted John W. Campbell, the MIT drop-out who always paraded himself as a hardheaded engineer, was in fact as whack-o a cultist as the best of them.

What happened, time after time, was that the readers weren't as interested in riding the editor's latest hobbyhorse as they were in reading exciting, entertaining *stories*.

And then there was Raymond A. Palmer. His career paralleled Campbell's to a remarkable degree, but Campbell somehow managed to maintain a façade of respectability while Palmer was pilloried in the fan press and eventually driven out of the world of science fiction to wander in the wilderness of occultism and cults—okay, let's be honest, *nut-cults*—for the rest of his days.

Fred Nadis is a sometime academic, scholar and chronicler of popular culture. He's written in the past about "wonder shows," science, magic, and religion in America. He has now produced the first full-scale biography of Ray Palmer (aka "RAP"), who lived as strange a life as an *Amazing Stories* hero. The book is called *The Man from Mars: Ray Palmer's Amazinig Pulp Journey.*

Born August 1, 1910, Palmer led a normal, even idyllic early childhood. He was a beautiful toddler and actually appeared in advertisements for a local milk company. Nadis furnishes a photograph of Palmer as a glowing, golden-haired child. But at the age of seven he ran into the street and got tangled in the spokes of a wheel of a passing beer truck. He suffered a severe spinal injury and while surgery made it possible for him to walk he never grew taller than four feet. He overcame this handicap, which was exacerbated by later illnesses and injuries, and eventually found employment as a roofer and construction worker. He made a successful career as writer, editor, and publisher. His determination to live a normal existence must have been incredible. He learned to drive a car, eventually married and fathered several offspring. According to Nadis, when children expressed curiosity about Palmer's diminutive stature, he told them that he was from Mars.

Palmer discovered the first issue of *Amazing Stories* (April, 1926) on a newsstand and was immediately captivated by the Frank R. Paul cover painting. He became one of the earliest science fiction fans, editing and publishing the pioneering fanzine *The Comet,* in 1930. That same year he sold his first science fiction story to Gernsback's *Science Wonder Stories* and he was on his way.

In 1939 Palmer became the editor of *Amazing Stories.* The magazine had been part of a package deal and the new publisher, Ziff-Davis, wasn't really very interested in publishing pulp magazines. But they were willing to give it a shot if a new editor and a fresh package could make *Amazing Stories* profitable.

The former editor, the aged T. O'Conor Sloane, had produced a stodgy periodical that was steadily declining in popularity. Under Palmer's tutelage and with Ziff-Davis's support, *Amazing Stories* enjoyed a thorough revamping into a colorful, even garish format. Palmer replaced the magazine's dull formality with a chatty, friendly atmosphere. Palmer replaced the slow-moving, science-heavy stories that Sloane had favored with exciting, action-based adventure fiction. Readers responded to Palmer's innovations immediately. Circulation soared

Palmer was criticized for the juvenile appeal of his magazine (and a soon-introduced companion, *Fantastic Adventures)* but the publisher was more interested in sales figures than the complaints of serious-minded fans. And Palmer, whose compensation was pegged to circulation rather than to a fixed pay rate, prospered. Eventually, Ziff-Davis switched him to a steady salary.

Everything went swimmingly until Palmer's assistant, Howard Browne, conscientiously sorting through readers' letters, came across a semi-incoherent multi-page missive from one Richard S. Shaver. Shaver claimed that Earth had once been populated by a race of long-lived golden giants whose Edenic existence had been imperiled by harmful solar radiation. Most of these giants then built spaceships and rocketed away to safer worlds, but some were left behind on Earth.

Shades of the Pied Piper of Hamelin! Or for that matter, the Rapture!

Some of the left-behind had remained on the surface of the planet and became the ancestors of modern humans. Others had retreated to caves where they continued to degenerate, eventually becoming a race of malicious dwarfs who amused themselves by shooting ray-cannons up through the ground and causing mischief among humankind.

Browne tossed Shaver's letter into the wastebasket but Palmer retrieved it. He rewrote and expanded it into a 35,000 word novella and published it in *Amazing Stories*. As fiction, the story was relatively trivial, and even with Palmer's revisions (or outright ghost-writing) Shaver's story was pedestrian fare by *Amazing Stories*' standards. But Palmer retained Shaver's claim that the material came from ancient "thought records" that he had discovered in secret caves and was actually true.

In the mid- and late- 1940s the so-called Shaver Mystery came to dominate the pages of *Amazing Stories*. According to Nadis, Palmer's employers at Ziff-Davis were becoming increasingly uncomfortable with Palmer's activities while Palmer was becoming increasingly uncomfortable with the restrictions placed on him by the corporate hierarchy.

By 1950 Palmer left Ziff-Davis to start his own publishing company and create *Other Worlds Science Stories*. This digest-sized magazine was actually one of the unrecognized gems of the era. To "OW" Palmer brought the chatty, friendly atmosphere that he had established at *Amazing*. At the same time, his choice of stories was well above that of *Amazing*.

He also brought Richard Shaver with him as a contributor to the magazine, and he started *Fate*, a periodical devoted to occult topics. There were articles about Atlantis, Lemuria, ancient mystery religions, the secrets of the pyramids, spirit manifestations and—the favorite topic of the day—flying saucers. In issue after issue (under a bewildering array of pseudonyms) Palmer pounded away at the saucer sensation. If the Shaver Mystery had been the mainstay of Palmer's *Amazing,* UFO sightings and conspiracy theories played an equivalent role for *Fate.*

Piling wild claim upon wild claim, Palmer's magazines gave new exposure to the old hollow-earth theory, featured composite photographs "showing" the North Polar opening to the inner world, and suggested that the saucers emanated not from distant planets but from the hidden world inside the Earth itself.

With the passage of time, Palmer became ever more deeply enmeshed in the occult movement and increasingly alienated from the science fiction community. Nadis points out that Palmer was actually cautious about revealing his own beliefs. He was ever willing to publish the claims of occultist and esoteric theorists—but did he even take them seriously, or were they merely fodder to feed to a credulous audience? Palmer even published a New Age / esoteric "Bible," *Oahspe.*

But did he really believe in an ancient race of giants who had fled the sun's malignant radiation, leaving behind a gaggle of evil dwarfs who zapped innocent humans with ray cannons when they weren't busy torturing captives or cooking them for dinner?

For that matter, did Shaver believe his own claims?

In later years, this reviewer was told the following story by Stuart J. Byrne (1913-2011), a onetime writer for Palmer's *Amazing Stories* and *Other Worlds:*

> Shaver had invited Byrne to visit him at Shaver's cabin in rural Wisconsin. During this visit the two men went for a stroll in a nearby town. Byrne reported that he felt an uncomfortable tingling in his legs. Fearing that he was experiencing a medical emergency, Byrne described the sensation to Shaver.
>
> Laughing, Shaver told Byrne not to worry. "That's just a dero named Max. He has a crush on me," Shaver explained. "He lives in a cave under the sidewalk. He spies on me, and whenever he sees me with another man he gets jealous and shoots him with his ray cannon."

Scout's honor! Now—Was Shaver just pulling Byrne's leg? Or was Byrne just pulling Lupoff's leg? Or was the whole story absolutely true?

While Palmer burrowed ever deeper into the conspiracy-riddled world of paranoid UFO theorists and contactees, Shaver had also found a new interest. He decided that Mankind's ancient ancestors had left secret documents embedded in rocks. All you had to do was crack a rock open, exposing its interior, and you would find messages in the form of pictographs.

But they had to be the right rocks, of course. If you picked one up in your backyard and walloped it with a sledgehammer and found nothing inside but more rock, that didn't disprove Shaver's new claim. Clearly, you just weren't looking at it right. Or maybe you didn't have the right rock.

It appears that Palmer never totally broke with Shaver, but as Nadis describes events of the 1970s, the mutual enthusiasm of the two men cooled substantially. Maybe Max was at work.

At the same time, Palmer's always fragile health was deteriorating. He became involved in right-wing politics, supporting George Wallace in the Presidential election of 1972. But his marriage to Margery endured and his loyal following, although not large, continued to support his publications.

Richard Shaver died in November, 1975. Palmer survived him by two years. Palmer collapsed while he and Margery were visiting their daughter and infant grandchild. He rallied briefly, but succumbed on October 15, 1977.

He was surely one of the most distinctive characters to grace (some would say, *disgrace)* the science fiction field in the past century. Fred Nadis's book does him justice, and will provide invaluable insights into the science fiction world of the pulp era.

In the interests of full disclosure, I must tell you that I read Mr. Nadis's book in the form of an "ARC" or advance reader's copy kindly furnished by Tarcher, one of the many imprints of the international Penguin Group. While the substance of the book was fascinating, the text was riddled with just the kind of errors that one would expect from an author working in an unfamiliar field. For example—and this is just one of many, believe me—Nadis refers to at least one science fiction magazine that never existed. Something like *Science Wonder Tales.* I made note of as many of these errors as I could and emailed the publicity person who had sent me the book. She promised to get the corrections to the author in order to have them corrected before publication.

Amigos, I haven't seen a copy of the actual published book. Consequently, I don't know whether the corrections were made or not. Maybe the publicity rep took one look at my email and hit the delete button, the contemporary equivalent of Howard Browne's tossing Richard Shaver's famous letter into the waste basket. You'll have to check this out for yourself.

~ ~ ~ ~ ~

No sooner had I finished dealing with Fred Nadis's dual biography of Ray Palmer and Richard Shaver than there pops up in my mailbox a review copy of *War over Lemuria: Richard Shaver, Ray Palmer and the Strangest Chapter of 1940s Science Fiction,* by Richard Toronto, published by McFarland & Company.

Two dual biographies of Palmer and Shaver in rapid succession? I mean, neither of these fellers is exactly a household name any more. Kinda like reading two biographies in rapid succession of Thomas A. Hendricks and Levi P. Morton, two of the less memorable Vice Presidents of the United States. Makes you blink your eyes and go, "Huh?"

I won't repeat Palmer's and Shaver's vital statistics. Nadis did his homework and so did Toronto, and you can get the data from either of their books. Or, heck, just google their names and get it from Wikipedia or the ISFDB. (Internet Science Fiction Data Base, if anybody reading this is even less IT literate than I am, which is unlikely.)

If anything, Toronto gets extra credit for thoroughness and extensiveness of his research. As a serious biographer, he goes back a couple of generations in the ancestry of his subjects. The Palmers, for instance, are descended from a family of Irish Protestants called Prickett. Driven out of Ireland by religious persecution, Grandpa Phineas Prickett brought his family to the United States and changed their name to Palmer because it sounded more English.

The Shavers were of German descent; the name Shaver was adapted from Schaeffer because it sounded more English.

Toronto gives a far more detailed account of Palmer's early life, his medical travails, his role in the creation of science fiction fandom and the publication of both the first fanzine, *The Comet,* and of Palmer's own first professional story, "The Time Ray of Jandra," in Gernsback's *Science Wonder Stories.*

Once Palmer became the editor of *Amazing Stories* he surrounded himself with a circle of sub-editors and regular authors whose names were familiar fare in the science fiction world of the 1940s and '50s. These included William Hamling, who eventually became the editor and publisher of *Imagination,* a second line science fiction magazine and *Rogue,* a mid-level *Playboy* clone; Howard Browne, he of the famous waste basket incident, as well as a successful pulp editor, hardboiled mystery novelist, and screenwriter; David Wright O'Brien, Chester Geier, Leroy Yerxa, Paul W. Fairman, and Frank M. Robinson.

O'Brien was killed when his bomber was shot down over Germany during World War Two. (Toronto has O'Brien in the wrong model airplane, by the way: one of the few factual errors in this book.) Yerxa fell dead while working on a pulp story. He was 30 years of age. Hamling then married Yerxa's widow, Frances.

Robinson, a teenager at the time, was office boy for Palmer and his associates. He was drafted into the navy, returned to civilian life, then was called back to duty during the Korean War. He went on to an outstanding career as a novelist, and contributed to progressive politics by serving as speech writer for the late Harvey Milk.

Toronto provides a remarkably rounded and sympathetic portrait of Palmer. The automobile that Nadis mentions in passing, Toronto identifies as a red Buick convertible. (Palmer later drove a Pontiac station wagon.) He describes Palmer's social life, his relationships with women, and his long and successful marriage.

Shaver also receives detailed treatment, including his lifelong mental problems. Toronto tells the story of Shaver's marriages, especially his marriage to Sophie Gurvitz, a successful Detroit commercial artist. Despite opposition from both families (Sophie was Jewish) and the chronic stress caused by Shaver's mental illness, it looked as if the marriage had at least a chance to succeed. Sophie, however, was electrocuted when she handled an ungrounded electrical appliance while in the bathtub.

A bonus for any reader interested in the in's and out's of the publishing world, is Toronto's remarkably detailed coverage of office politics at Ziff-Davis and its various spin-offs and the personalities involved including a young fellow named Hugh Heffner.

And so, Ray Palmer is now a half-forgotten figure from the past of science fiction, science fiction fandom, and pseudoscientific fringe cults. The Shaver Mystery has faded; I imagine there are still a few of Richard Shaver's followers out there somewhere, searching for the entrance to the caverns where Deros lurk, or maybe picking up rocks and cracking them open and to look for secret messages inside.

Two questions remain.

The first: Was Richard S. Shaver a charlatan, or did he really believe in Deros and Teros and the Mantong Alphabet and ancient ray machines hidden in caverns beneath the earth?

The second: Was Raymond A. Palmer a charlatan, or did he really believe in Shaver's hooey?

To the first question, I don't think there can be much doubt. Shaver was certifiably insane. He heard voices, he was accompanied by invisible people including his Dero stalker Max and the blind Tero girl Nydia, who emerged to him out of the pages of *The Last Days of Pompeii* by Edward Bulwer-Lytton. He was certified and institutionalized by his wife and members of her family, and he bounced repeatedly between mental hospitals and hoosegows.

To the second question, I will defer to my friend Frank Robinson, Palmer's onetime office boy. "Palmer was a con man," Robinson says, "it didn't matter whether he believed Shaver's stuff or not, he knew that Shaver would sell magazines for him, and he was right."

MILTON MAKES THE GRADE

Howard Browne (1908-1999) told me this story. I have no documentation for it, and you can believe it if you choose, or regard it simply as an amusing lie.

As for Howard Browne, he was born in Omaha, Nebraska. He was a baseball fan as a youngster, and hitchhiked from Omaha to Chicago to see Babe Ruth hit a home run. Unfortunately he wound up on the wrong side of Chicago, and had to walk the entire length of the city to watch the Yankees play the White Sox. He didn't let that stop him.

And he fell in love with the city of Chicago. He scraped a living at a variety of jobs including that of bill collector. Although his vision was always poor, his impressive bulk and powerful voice overcame reluctant debtors. However, he hoped to find a more rewarding profession, and eventually wound up as a magazine editor at Ziff-Davis Publications, where he edited the company's detective pulps, *Mammoth Mystery* and *Mammoth Detective,* and worked as an assistant to Ray Palmer on *Amazing Stories* and *Fantastic Adventures.*

Palmer left Ziff-Davis in 1950 to create his own publishing company. Browne had already moved to the West Coast to pursue a career in screenwriting. Now Browne was lured back to take over Palmer's position running Ziff-Davis's fiction group.

And, yes, this is the same Howard Browne who threw Richard Shaver's infamous 1943 letter to *Amazing Stories* in the wastebasket, from whence it was retrieved by Ray Palmer to become the founding document of the infamous Shaver Mystery.

One day in 1946 Browne was working his way through the slush pile of unsolicited manuscripts, performing the usual triage: *This story is terrific, let's buy it; This one is hopeless, return to author; This one just might make it, put it aside for a second look.*

Then came a fat envelope. Browne opened it and found the manuscript for a novel, *The Cuckoo Clock,* by one Milton K. Ozaki. The story was much too long to use in one issue of *Mammoth Mystery* or *Mammoth Detective* and Ziff-Davis's policy did not allow for serials. Ziff-Davis had a book division, however, including a line of mystery novels, so Browne slapped a buck-slip on the manuscript and sent it over to the book division.

Several months passed. Browne heard nothing and forgot about the incident. Then one day he found a finished copy of *The Cuckoo Clock* on his desk, with a note from the mystery book editor thanking him for the manuscript.

Browne trotted over to the book department and sought out the mystery editor. "Glad this book worked out for you. Obviously you liked it."

"Liked it," the book editor exclaimed, "I never read it!"

"Then why did you publish it?"

"Well, you recommended it, Howard, and I trust your judgment."

Browne shook his head. "I never read it either. I just sent it to you because I couldn't use it and I thought you might be interested."

And thus an aspiring mystery novelist sold his first novel—without an editor ever reading his manuscript.

Fortunately *The Cuckoo Clock* was well received, and Ozaki followed it with another mystery novel published by Ziff-Davis, *A Fiend in Need*. He was on a roll, and soon was turning out mysteries in such volume that he needed a second by-line to avoid overcrowding the market. In 1949 he became Robert O. Saber and sold *The Black Dark Murders* to Handi-Books. He had entered the paperback original market.

Over the years he worked his way up through the second- and third-rank paperback houses until he reached Fawcett Gold Medal Books, generally regarded as the top market in the paperback original field. In the meanwhile Ozaki juggled a profession as a beauty parlor operator—this provided a distinctive background for his first book!—and a journalist. But he was most notable as a writer of detective novels. His style was fairly hardboiled, but he didn't go in for the brutality of the extreme tough-guy school.

Milton Kiyoshi Ozaki was born in Racine, Wisconsin, in 1913. He lived for many years in Chicago, before retiring to Sparks, Nevada, a suburb of Reno.

He was the author of more than two dozen novels as Milton K. Ozaki or Robert O. Saber. He died in 1989. Along with far too many meritorious novels published in the past half century, most of Ozaki's work was long out of print, although Ramble House reissued *The Black Dark Murders* in 2004.

Then the long arm of coincidence reached into the muddle that we call life. I was chatting with my friend Trina Robbins, cartoonist, author, and scholar. She mentioned a friend of hers named Frank Ozaki. Not exactly an everyday name. I asked her if Frank Ozaki was related to the mystery writer Milton Ozaki, and it turned out that he was Milton's son.

My daughter, Kathy, was operating a restaurant in Tahoe City, California at the time, not far from Reno. And Frank Ozaki lived in Reno. One thing led to another, and eventually my wife and I were sitting down to lunch with Frank and his partner, Craig Chapman. In the course of conversation Frank mentioned that a mystery novel had remained unpublished at the time of Milton's death.

You can imagine the look of lust in an editor's eyes when I heard about that novel! It wasn't easy to pry the manuscript out of the hands of the Ozaki family. Frank has several sisters, and they had long hoped to see the book published.

This leads to the question, Why wasn't *Win, Place and Die!* published during its author's lifetime? One of Milton Ozaki's daughters, Vara, recalls her father's addressing the subject. "After things like the Sharon Tate killings (August, 1969), the public was not intrigued by a murder case involving one murder, so he didn't think there was a market for his kind of murder mystery. He said, in his day one murder would shock and appall people, but now they were desensitized."

Frank Ozaki adds, "I don't know if that means that he chose to set it aside, intending to work on it again later, or that some publishers wanted to increase the body count and he didn't want to, but it seems that he was discouraged that it would take so much bloodshed to get a reader's attention. His love was the 'whodunnit' part, the how and why, not the body count."

Indeed, it's hard to deny that some modern mystery novels actually border on the horror story rather than involving any real detective work. To say that *Win, Place and Die!* harks back to a kinder, gentler era in detective fiction would be an exaggeration, but possibly not an entirely inapt one. Ozaki's books, even when they earned the hardboiled rubric, dealt more with the nature of their characters, their relationships with one another, and the intriguing process of solving a crime.

Yes, the world of detective fiction had moved on, leaving behind such talented writers as Harry Whittington, Day Keene, William Ard, Ennis Willie, Joel Townsley Rogers, Fletcher Flora,

Richard S. Prather, Leigh Brackett (one of the few female hardboiled writers), C. Daly King, the great John Dickson Carr and that enigmatic genius who hid behind the pseudonym N. R. de Mexico.

Cover design by **Frank Ozaki**

A novel of gamblers in Reno, courtesy of the author's son, Frank Ozaki

Publishing the last Ozaki mystery looked liked a match made in hardboiled heaven. Ramble House, the parent company of Surinam Turtle Press, had already reissued one of Milton Ozaki's pseudonymous Robert O. Saber novels, but here was a chance to publish a brand new Ozaki mystery, a quarter century after the author's death!

For what it's worth, this time the editor *did* read the book before it was published. *Win, Place and Die!* is a marvelous story set in Reno in the 1970s. The self-styled Biggest Little City in the World was a lot littler then than it is today, but Ozaki's writing is smooth and the world of Reno that he describes, complete with casinos, sports books, and nightclubs, rings true to the last detail.

If you're an Ozaki fan from way back, *Win, Place and Die!* will be a treat you might never have expected to experience. If you're unfamiliar with Ozaki's work, be prepared to be hooked and start looking for those two-dozen-plus novels you've been missing for all these years!

FORRY

In all the years that science fiction fandom has been around—since 1930 or so—I can think of just three fans who have actually made a career of the hobby. I don't mean fans-turned-pro. There are lots and lots of those, from Ray Palmer to Bill Hamling to Marion Zimmer Bradley to Donald A. Wollheim to Terry Carr to Robert Silverberg to Harlan Ellison to . . . the list is very long.

But to stay a fan, to make a profession out of being a fan—now that's another matter. There was Sam Moskowitz, the self-styled historian of science fiction. And he did a good job of it, too! There was Charles N. Brown, who started publishing a little mimeographed newsletter called *Locus* and built it into a publishing mini-empire. And there was Forrest J Ackerman. No period after the "J," thank you very much.

Oh, was there ever Forrest J Ackerman. Uncle Forry. The Ackermonster. Dr. Acula. A few people despised him. Thousands loved him. He's been gone for three years now—born 1916, died 2008—and Deborah Painter, a longtime friend of Forry's and sometime contributor to his magazines, has written a full-scale biography of the most Famous Monster of them all.

Considering the long-term affectionate relationship between Ackerman and Painter, one would hardly expect this book to present an objective view of its subject. Nor does it. And that's all right. We know what to expect going in. We should not be surprised when we get it.

Painter starts her biography with a quick background sketch of Ackerman's family history, but she quickly gets into the substance of her subject. She introduces us to Ackerman as a boy and moves into a lengthy description of the cultuRal milieu which formed him, and in which he immersed himself for the rest of his life. There were two major elements in this compound: pulp magazines and motion pictures.

While colorful and evocative, this section of the book is regrettably riddled with errors. I counted several dozen in the first half of the book alone. I will not regale you with a long list of these, but I will cite a few of the more egregious:

~ Dorothy McIlwraith is credited with editing *Weird Tales* in the 1920s. But she did not become editor of that magazine until 1940. Major editors in the 1920s were Edwin Baird and Farnsworth Wright.

~ Ackerman allegedly read *Spicy Mystery Stories* during this era (the 1920s), but *Spicy Mystery Stories'* first issue did not appear until 1934.

~ The female lead in the film *Metropolis* is described as wearing a green dress—but *Metropolis* was filmed in black-and-white.

~ Ackerman allegedly read comic books in the 1920s, but the first issue of the first (modern) comic book, *Famous Funnies,* was not published until 1933.

~ The author describes Ackerman as reading *Thrilling Wonder Stories* in the 1920s, but that magazine didn't even exist in the 1920s. It was a descendant of several earlier magazines—*Science Wonder Stories, Air Wonder Stories,* and finally, simply *Wonder Stories*—but "TWS," as it was affectionately referred to, made its debut with a cover date of August, 1936.

~ Bela Lugosi is credited with a starring role in the film *Ninotchka.* In fact he appeared in little more than a bit part—one scene—as a petty Soviet bureaucrat.

~ Amelia Reynolds Long is credited with writing "only ten" stories during her lifetime. Her obituary in the Harrisburg (PA) *Patriot-News* for March 31, 1978, credits her with thirty-four novels and "about 100" short stories. I have been able to locate only thirty-one of those novels and twenty-nine short stories. I cannot vouch for the others, but this output is far beyond that credited by Ms. Painter.

~ ~ ~ ~ ~

I guess there's a lesson here, and it's a familiar one that is drummed into would-be writers from junior high school onward. *Write about what you know about!* This maxim is subject to debate when it comes to writing fiction. After all, H. G. Wells never traveled to the year 802,701; Jules Verne never rode a hollow projectile to the moon; and Edgar Rice Burroughs never visited Pellucidar. In fact, there is no such place. And as the late Robert Bloch was fond of saying, Agatha Christie made a career out of murder and mayhem but she never shot, stabbed, or poisoned a soul in her life.

Even in a work of fiction you can't move Beijing to Brazil or make hydrogen heavier than iron unless you back it up with some convincing rationale. There's artistic license but then there's sheer absurdity.

And nonfiction writing, whether journalism, science, or biography, must meet a higher standard of accuracy. In the present book Ms. Painter is a biographer, a reporter of sorts, and it behooves her to get her facts straight.

Here's another howler. Pardon me, they just keep on coming. Speaking of the death of Boris Karloff, the author says, "Karloff passed in the summer of 1969."

That one stopped me cold. I remember the day I learned of Karloff's death. I was visiting Kansas City on a business trip and met my boss in the hallway of our hotel. He'd been listening to the morning news and he greeted me with the news that Karloff had died.

I remembered the encounter as occurring on a cold, wintry day. That just didn't jibe with Painter's report that, "Karloff passed in the summer of 1969." It was easy enough to pull up the great actor's date of death. It was February 2, 1969. Summer, I suppose, in Australia. But in North America it was midwinter.

All of these errors—and believe me, there are plenty more!—don't change Ms. Painter's affection for Forrest J Ackerman or alter her touching portrait of him. What they do, however, is undermine her credibility as a biographer. If she got so much wrong, how can the reader trust her about anything?

The fact is that Ackerman was a controversial character during his lifetime and he remains controversial to this day. His chief claim to fame is of course the magazine *Famous Monsters of Filmland.* This was ballyhooed in the fan press prior to its debut in February, 1958, as a serious magazine with carefully researched articles and archival photographs. It was to be the definitive journal of science fiction, fantasy, and horror films.

When the magazine actually appeared its very title suggested otherwise. The cover graphic was a photograph of a man in a rubber mask (actually, publisher James Warren) menacing a nubile young woman. There were indeed plenty of archival photos in the magazine, but the text was a mélange of corny gags, silly puns, and self-glorification by Ackerman, who not only edited the magazine but wrote most or all of its editorial content.

Ms. Painter asserts that Ackerman's original intention was indeed to publish a serious magazine. The planned title was *Wonderama*. It was at the distributor's insistence that the title was changed and the entire direction of the magazine was revised downward. The target audience, Painter states, was eleven-year-old children.

Serious science fiction fans were variously outraged or disappointed, but from a commercial viewpoint the distributor's decision was clearly right. The eleven-year-olds flocked to *Famous Monsters* by the hundreds of thousands, eventually by the millions. The magazine was a huge success. It ran for decades, spawned an array of spin-offs and imitators, and after ending its initial run was revived several times.

Was Ackerman a silly, shallow, ego-driven clown, or was he a noble, generous, warm-hearted—almost saintly!—individual? I suppose he was both. I know that my older son when he was a little boy met Forry at a convention and Forry took down Ken's name and address. A few days later Ken received a heavy package in the mail. When he opened it he found a silver-painted plaster bust of the Frankenstein monster. I don't know what eventually became of that keepsake but I do know that Ken loved it and treasured it for many years.

Sending that gift was the kind of thing that Forry did.

THE LAST HIEROGLYPH

The Last Hieroglyph, by Clark Ashton Smith, completes a monumental project, a major contribution to fantasy literature and a tribute to the dedicated scholarship of its two editors, Scott Connors and Ron Hilger. Publication of *The Collected Fantasies of Clark Ashton Smith* commenced, paradoxically, with *The End of the Story* in 2006. Succeeding volumes were *The Door to Saturn* (2007), *A Vintage from Atlantis* (2007), and *The Maze of the Enchanter* (2009).

The stories are presented in the sequence of composition rather than sorted by theme or setting. Thus, "The City of the Singing Flame" appears in Volume Two and its sequel, "Beyond the Singing Flame," in Volume Three. This might make for a slight inconvenience to the reader, but it is a rational and certainly defensible system established by the editors. In addition to extensive notes by the editors, each volume has included an introduction, variously scholarly, critical, and adulatory, by Ramsey Campbell, Tim Powers, Michael Dirda, Gahan Wilson, or (in the interest of full disclosure) Richard A. Lupoff.

The editors have shown themselves to be eminently qualified to undertake this remarkable project. Ron Hilger is a longtime admirer of Smith's, a researcher whose efforts have resulted in the recovery of at least one Smith manuscript previously believed lost, and the editor of *The Averoigne Chronicles,* forthcoming from Donald M. Grant Publishers. He is also the co-editor of *Lost Worlds,* a journal devoted to Smith and his works.

Scott Connors is the editor of *The Freedom of Fantastic Things,* a collection of Smith criticism. He is also the co-editor (with David E. Schultz) of the invaluable *Selected Letters of Clark Ashton Smith.*

In preparing the present five-volume collection, the obvious course would have been to comb earlier Smith collections, of which there have been a good many, most notably from Arkham House, and re-select and re-sequence the contents of these books. True dedication would have led the editors to seek out the pulp magazines, most often *Weird Tales* or *Wonder Stories,* but also such other periodicals as the legendary *Black Cat, Astounding Stories, The Magazine of Fantasy and Science Fiction,* and lesser known sources like *Oriental Stories* and *Saturn Science Fiction,* in which Smith's works originally appeared. Instead, Connors and Hilger sought out Smith's manuscripts in university libraries from Rhode Island to California, as well as obtaining the use of materials from private collections.

Clark Ashton Smith in 1912

Early photo of a very young, rather fey Clark Ashton Smith, author of many glittering fantasies and poems

From these source documents they reconstructed texts of story after story, including at least two that received magazine publication only through Connors' and Hilger's efforts, and are collected for the first time in the Night Shade volumes.

As for Clark Ashton Smith himself, he is best known today as the third member of the great *Weird Tales* triumvirate of which the other members were Howard Phillips Lovecraft and Robert Ervin Howard. The other two, Lovecraft and Howard, have achieved considerable fame and, at least in Lovecraft's case, growing critical acceptance as a significant figure in Twentieth Century American culture. Such is not the case with Smith, and critics have offered a variety of theories as to the reason.

One notion, which the present reviewer finds persuasive, points to the fact that both Lovecraft and Howard had champions. In Lovecraft's case, it was August W. Derleth. In partnership with

Donald Wandrei, Derleth co-founded Arkham House two years after Lovecraft's death. In the decades that followed, Derleth kept Lovecraft's work in print and kept it in the public eye, pounding away relentlessly until other publishers at last paid attention. Lovecraft's fame spread, and today his concepts and attitudes pervade every corner of popular culture.

In Howard's case, it was L. Sprague de Camp who persuaded Martin Goodman's Gnome Press to issue a uniform set of Howard's Conan tales more than half a century ago. Again, other publishers eventually climbed on the bandwagon. The first Lancer Conan volume published under the tutelage of editor Larry Shaw, featuring the classic Frazetta portrait of the muscular barbarian, may have represented the breakthrough event, followed in due course by the motion pictures starring Arnold Schwarzenegger as the barbarian.

Interestingly, Derleth also edited volumes of Howard's and Smith's stories for Arkham House. In later years, long after Lovecraft's and Howard's decease, he also solicited original stories from Smith for use in Arkham House anthologies. Still, Lovecraft was clearly Derleth's chief passion and Lovecraft's posthumous success is unarguably attributable to Derleth's persistent efforts.

Is it time for a similar emergence of Clark Ashton Smith onto the American (and international!) literary scene? Perhaps such a development may occur, but this reviewer is convinced that it would take a major shift in world cultural attitudes, away from the pessimistic, realistic orientation of our day, and toward the romantic, fantastic idealism of the late Nineteenth and early Twentieth Centuries for this to happen.

Clark Ashton Smith (1893-1961) spent most of his life on a hardscrabble hillside on the edge of Auburn, California, a onetime gold rush town not far from the state capitol of Sacramento. Smith's parents were both in their forties when he was born, their only offspring. For much of his life he was their main financial support and caregiver, earning a meager living as a fruit picker, wood-cutter, gardener or well-digger.

At one point he persuaded the publisher of the local newspaper to produce a collection of his works and then served as an unpaid columnist to work off the printer's bills.

Smith found little of interest in the local schools. He dropped out after a few years and became self-educated through study of the dictionary, encyclopedia, and assorted books from the public library. He developed an extensive vocabulary and a love of exotic words which he would utilize in an almost incantatory, hypnotic style in later years.

In adolescence he wrote two novels in the style of the Arabian Nights: *The Black Diamonds* and *The Sword of Zagan*. He became more involved with poetry, however, coming to the attention of George Sterling (1869-1926), himself a protégé of the famous Ambrose Bierce. Smith was also captured by the spell of the French poet Charles Baudelaire (1821-1867), translating Baudelaire's poetry into English. Baudelaire, in turn, was a devoted acolyte of Edgar Allan Poe.

Smith's early poetic works were cast in the glittering, romantic-decadent mode of Poe, Baudelaire, and Sterling. He was briefly acclaimed as a poetic Boy Wonder, "The Keats of the Sierras."

His timing could hardly have been worse. With the end of widespread optimism presaged by the first World War and the rise of the terse, earthy prose style popularized by Ernest Hemingway and Dashiell Hammett and plainspoken modernist poetry by the likes of Ezra Pound and T.S. Eliot, Smith found himself a young man born twenty years after his time. George Sterling's suicide in 1926 can only have deepened Smith's despair.

In part at the urging of a female friend, Smith returned to his boyhood pursuit of fantasy, and soon made himself a fixture of Farnsworth Wright's *Weird Tales* and David Lasser's *Wonder Stories*. In time he became one of the three luminaries of *Weird Tales*. His stories ranged widely through time and space, from the ancient realms of Hyperborea to palaces of lost Atlantis (which he called Poseidonis) to the medieval France of Averoigne to the alien planet Xiccarph to the last continent of a dying earth, Zothique.

The tracking down of literary sources and influences is an endless and fascinating exercise but one not to be indulged in at length in this review. Still, the comparison of Smith's Averoigne to the medieval tales set in James Branch Cabell's Poictisme is unavoidable. There is no doubt that Smith was familiar with Cabell's work, referring to it repeatedly in his *Selected Letters*.

The structural similarity between Smith's "The Last Hieroglyph" and Charles Dickens' "A Christmas Carol" may be an amusing coincidence and this reviewer will make nothing more of it than that.

While there is surprising variety in Smith's fiction, several qualities mark most of his work. Characterization is minimal, and what plot is present is often used only as a vehicle for glittering imagery and Smith's distinctive prose. When Smith is at his most "Klarkash-tonic," the modern reader may find himself initially put off by this stylized, mannered narrative. But persistence leads to acceptance, then enjoyment, and finally addiction.

The twenty-nine stories selected for *The Last Hieroglyph* cover a range of Smith's worlds and themes, some of them quite surprising.

Although known primarily for his fantasies—hence the title of this series of books—Smith produced a series of interplanetary or interstellar tales for *Wonder Stories*, featuring Captain Volmar and his crew on the exploration ship *Alcyone*. Ron Hilger recovered a lost story from this series, "The Red World of Polaris," included in an earlier volume of the present collection as well as in a self-contained collection of which it is the title story.

The plot is not unfamiliar. Volmar and crew land on a planet whose inhabitants have achieved immortality of a sort by transferring their brains to metallic robot bodies. They offer this treatment to their visitors, who decline the honor. Shades of Neil R. Jones's Zoromes and the sainted H.P. Lovecraft's "Whisperer in Darkness" among many others. Smith's writing here is crisper than usual. One can almost imagine Edmond Hamilton creating Captain Volmar and the *Alcyone* as prototypes for Curtis Newton and the *Comet*.

Even in his science fiction, Smith was never one to be hindered by mere scientific fact. Some fans wrote to his publishers complaining that he was playing fast and loose with the findings of modern science. He even had a good-natured postal debate with H.P. Lovecraft over the issue. But Smith would not yield.

In his story "Seven Geases" (*Weird Tales*, 1934) he clearly stood back and thumbed his nose at such strict constructionists. The story is a hilarious send-up of hard science. Set in ancient Hyperborea, Smith mixes knights in armor equpped with swords and speaking like characters out of Sir Walter Scott, with Neanderthals (called *Voormis*), "gods" from alien planets, a wizard with a pet archaeopteryx, and dinosaurs. It's all great fun that leaves the reader gasping for breath.

Filmmaker George Lucas may never have read "Seven Geases" but somebody on his staff surely did. If you've ever seen the *Star Wars* character Jabba the Hutt—you've seen Clark Ashton Smith's dark god Tsathoggua!

Another surprising story is "The Face by the River." This is a tale of a successful businessman caught in a triangle between a trusting wife and an increasingly demanding mistress. It is a tale of murder, remorse, madness, and suicide. Connors and Hilger quote Smith regarding the story, explaining that it was an experiment in psychological fiction, something which he claimed normally to eschew.

It is a more than passably competent story of its type. It might well have sold to *Thrilling Mystery, Dime Detective, Ten-Story Detective,* or any other of the *Black Mask* school of pulp magazines. It is surprising that Smith apparently never submitted it to any periodical.

Another Smith tale, "Schizoid Creator," is an hilarious send-up of psychological fiction, a good sample of Smith's wry and often satirical sense of humor.

Obviously, not all of Smith's stories were equally successful, nor do all of them hold up equally well. The reader is certainly startled by "An Adventure in Futurity," a long story written at the urging of *Wonder Stories* editor David Lasser in 1930 and published in that magazine the following April.

Smith's narrator encounters a time traveler and accompanies him to America some 13,000 years in the future. In this world a decadent humanity lives in comfort, supported by a network of plantations worked by Venusian slaves. The Venusians are portrayed as the worst stereotyped African Americans in the post-bellum South. They are described as having black-brown skins, practicing cannibalism, and even, astonishingly, resenting their masters and plotting rebellion.

But any artist may be forgiven an occasional slip, and Smith more than atones for his occasional poor outings with any number of glittering gems. Consider the opening lines of "The Voyage of King Euvoran," written in 1933 but not published in *Weird Tales* until 1947, and even then in shortened form. Smith later restored the excised portions and Connors and Hilger, happily, use the full text.

> *The crown of the kings of Ustaim was fashioned only from the rarest materials that could be procured anywhere. The magically graven gold of its circlet had been mined from a huge meteor that fell in the southern isle of Cyntrom, shaking the isle from shore to shore with calamitous earthquake; and the gold was harder and brighter than any native gold of Earth,*

and was changeable in color from a flamelike red to the yellow of young moons.

Glorious! Glorious!

The reviewer could go on describing and analyzing the stories in these five lovingly-designed volumes, but Connors and Hilger have already done an admirable job of doing this. Each volume in the set includes notes on every story—well over a hundred all told!—detailing the circumstances under which each was written, Smith's travails in dealing with editors, and the publication history of the work.

Connors and Hilger provide partial alternate texts where they differ significantly from the final version of the story. They explain the source of each text. This last, in itself, is evidence of their dedication and scholarship. In preparing such a compilation, one might have expected them simply to mine the earlier volumes issued by Arkham House and other publishers, or at most to track down earlier magazine appearances of the works for variorum texts.

Instead, they retrieved manuscripts wherever possible, studying various versions of each story to produce as close to a definitive, authentic text as possible.

With lovingly crafted jacket art by Jason Van Hollander and design by Claudia Noble, these books make an impressive presentation on any shelf. The cloth bindings are a virtual throwback to an earlier and more committed age of book-making. The paper is smooth and promises to be durable. The type is clear and attractive.

At $39.95 per volume, the five volumes of *The Collected Fantasies* will take a hefty bite out of any bibliophile's budget, but in this reviewer's opinion the money would be very well spent. Anyone who cannot afford to purchase the books would do well to plead, beg, or threaten his or her librarian to make the books available.

And one further word regarding the cultural acceptance of Clark Ashton Smith, especially as contrasted with that of H.P. Lovecraft or Robert E. Howard, may be in order. While you are not very likely to hear references to the Emperor of Dreams on the national TV news tonight, nor to find a film set in Zothique or Xiccarph on your Netflix menu, the fact is that hardly a year has gone by in the last half century or longer without the appearance of a new Smith collection, the issuance of a freshly discovered work, or the publication of a volume in appreciation or criticism of the man from Auburn.

Smith may appeal to a rarified sensibility but appeal he does. His body has lain in the earth for fifty years but his works have outlived those of ninety per cent of his contemporaries. They will continue to live and to find an audience as long as there are readers who prefer the glitter of gems and the scent of rare herbs and perfumes to the roar of gunfire and the smell of perspiration and gin.

Believe it.

MEET JOHN THUNSTONE

Manly Wade Wellman (1903-1986) was a longtime, prolific North Carolinian who devoted himself largely to "low" fantasies based on regional folklore and settings. The term low fantasy, by the way, is not of my creation. I've come across it in academic writings, where it refers to works involving supernatural, magical, or other such "counter-realistic" themes set in the otherwise mundane world, in contrast to "high" fantasy set in imaginary realms. For examples, consider Thorne Smith "low" and J. R. Tolkien "high."

I don't know as much as I'd like to about Wellman's personal biography. I suspect that he was descended from old Southern aristocracy, was very well educated, and never had to worry much about where his next paycheck was coming from. In a long career he strayed from the fantasy realm into science fiction, historicals, books for young adults, and nonfiction. His stories were a staple in the pulps, most particularly in *Weird Tales,* where he appeared on a regular basis for many years.

In an introduction to this new collection, Ramsey Campbell reveals that the character of John Thunstone was created in a conference between Wellman and *Weird Tales* editor Dorothy McIlwraith, who had succeeded the legendary Farnsworth Wright upon Wright's retirement. The first Thunstone story appeared in *Weird Tales* for November, 1943. Fifteen Thunstone stories appeared in *Weird Tales,* the last of them in the issue dated May, 1951. One more short story appeared in another magazine in 1982, followed by two Thunstone novels, in 1983 and 1985.

Thunstone himself was a fairly standard pulp hero: tall, broad-shouldered and muscular, with dark hair and neatly trimmed moustache. He lived in a series of comfortable hotel suites, usually in Manhattan, and dined and drank extremely well. I suspect that Wellman was something of a gourmet, for he describes many a breakfast and dinner in loving detail. And if the Thunstone stories are a reliable indicator, he was more than passingly fond of womankind.

Wellman doesn't provide many details of Thunstone's background, although hints are dropped from time to time. For instance, we learn that Thunstone was a collegiate football player, that his nose was broken at least once and healed with a slight sidewise tilt, and that he performed military service—but in which war, branch of service, or campaign we are not told. He seems to have fallen seriously in love at least once. The object of his affection ran off and married a wealthy, elderly Count, who conveniently died, leaving her a well-to-do and beautiful widow who flits in and out of Thunstone's life.

One of the problems for creators of adventure heroes is, *How does this person earn a living?* Some of them, of course, are conveniently independently wealthy (Clark Savage, Curtis Newton, Kent Allard, and most notably Bruce Wayne). Others have to work for a living. John Thunstone is a researcher, largely in the realm of supernatural themes in world folklore. He seems to receive extremely generous fees from scholarly journals and the sponsors of academic symposia. *Hmm* ... might be nice to know his agent's name.

Throughout Thunstone's career he faces two recurring foes. One is an evil sorcerer named Rowley Thorne. The other is actually a collective menace, the Shonokins. These are an almost-human species, distinguishable from *homo sapiens* by the fact that their ring fingers rather than their middle fingers are the longest, and by the fact that the irises of their eyes are vertical rather than round.

They're a fascinating invention. They claim to have owned the Earth before humankind, and intend in due course to retake possession. They are all, apparently, adult males. They have no women or children, or so it appears. This leaves the reader wondering how they got here, and how long they're going to be around since there is no way they can breed. (One wonders if they could interbreed with *h. sapiens sapiente;* unfortunately, Wellman does not address this issue.)

I wish Wellman had told us more about these strange folk. I guess we'll just have to devise our own explanations, or else allow the mystery to stand.

Now this fellow Rowley Thorne. As described, he's a very big man, as big as John Thunstone. He's bald. He practices evil magic, and he bears a remarkable resemblance to Aleister Crowley (1875-1947) the self-proclaimed "wickedest man in the world" and alleged guru of L. Ron Hubbard. Largely forgotten today except for practicing occultists and historians of the peculiar, Crowley turns up in horror literature ranging from the works of M. R. James to those of Somerset Maugham. You may rest assured that the similarity of names—Rowley and Crowley—is by no means coincidental.

Thunstone claims no psychic or supernatural powers of his own, but he believes firmly in the existence of such things. He battles an array of sinister forces chiefly by using his knowledge of the occult. He also, fortunately, owns a sword cane which does possess magical abilities. It tingles when in contact with objects of black magic, it's a nonpareil lock-pick, and it also serves on occasion as a perfectly splendid enemy-killer.

All in all, Thunstone seems a fairly standard spook fighter. Think Carnaki, think Jules de Grandin, think Solange Fontaine, think Sax Rohmer's Moris Klaw. What sets Thunstone apart is Wellman's erudition and courtliness. There is something of the Wellmanesque Southern aristocrat in Thunstone, and in Wellman's own formal, restrained prose. It takes a little getting into to get the feel of the Thunstone stories. But after the first few, they become addictive. They are formal yet terse. They were published in a pulp magazine but they do not read like pulp fiction. Don't look for car chases, blazing gun battles, or lengthy descriptions of tentacled Lovecraftian monstrosities. The only descriptions that Wellman seems to dote on are of food, liquor, tobacco, and beautiful women. The tobacco, politically incorrect in this enlightened Twenty-first Century, should really be forgiven in the works of a North Carolinian writing in the 1940s.

The two Thunstone novels, *What Dreams May Come* and *The School of Darkness,* are obviously the product of Wellman's final years. *What Dreams May Come* borders on the English country house mystery, layered over with a marvelous bit of history, prehistory, and mystically induced time travel. The tale moves in a stately manner. One needs to shift gears from the compact narratives of the short stories to this leisurely, mannered storytelling, but again Wellman rewards the faithful reader with a fine, solid development and resolution. *The School of Darkness,* as Ramsey Campbell suggests in his affectionate introduction, was one of Wellman's final works. It has an academic setting and serves as both John Thunstone's valedictory, and Manly Wade Wellman's.

While there have been earlier Thunstone collections, the Haffner edition is the first complete compendium of all the Thunstone short stories and the two novels. The book is handsomely illustrated with drawings by the late George Evans, reproduced from an earlier Wellman collection. Splendid end papers and dust jacket painting by Raymond Swanland complete a beautifully packaged and produced volume.

This book is one that belongs in the personal library of every lover of psychic detective tales, or of Southern regional prose, or of literate, sophisticated, modern fantasy fiction.

A WORKING CLASS HERO

We sometimes look back at the late 1940s and 1950s as a golden age of science fiction. I suppose people have always looked back through time and seen—or thought they'd seen—golden ages. But that brief period, *circa* 1950, would be hard to match.

Most science fiction appeared in magazine form in that era, and by the 1950s the classic pulps were enjoying their last hurrah while the digest revolution burgeoned just beyond the horizon. *Astounding Science Fiction* had moved to the smaller format as early as 1943. In 1949 *The Magazine of Fantasy* made its debut, morphing into *The Magazine of Fantasy and Science Fiction* with its second issue. And *Galaxy Science Fiction* commenced publication in 1950.

This was an era when the very idea of a full-time science fiction writer was virtually unknown. Even the leading figures in the field were expected to have day jobs and to write science fiction in stolen moments, chiefly as a labor of love. Let me cite just a handful of examples:

Isaac Asimov was a chemistry professor at Boston College.
James Blish was a public relations man.
A. Bertram Chandler was a ship's captain.
Hal Clement was a high school teacher.
Joseph L. Hensley was a state assemblyman and circuit court judge.
Fox B. Holden was a newspaper reporter.
Malcolm Jameson was a Navy officer and ordnance expert.
Keith Laumer was an Air Force officer and later a member of the Diplomatic Corps.
S. P. Meek was a career Army officer.
Alan E. Nourse was a medical doctor.
Rog Phillips was a night watchman at a coffin factory.
H. Beam Piper was a trackwalker for the Pennsylvania Railroad.
Clifford Simak was a newspaper editor.

... and that's not counting successful practitioners of other professions who chose to dip their quills into the ink of science fiction on occasion, including scientists like Fred Hoyle or (in later years) politicians like Newt Gingrich.

This is a fascinating topic and I could go on, but it's about time I started talking about Basil Wells.

Illustration by Ditmar 'Dick' Jenssen

Omnibus cover of short story collections by Basil Wells, a true "working class hero" of the pulps (cover artwork by "Ditmar")

Born in 1912 to a family of modest means, Wells was never a major headliner. He made his debut as a professional writer in *Super Science Stories* with a short story, "Rebirth of Man," in the issue dated September, 1940. His last appearance in a recognized, commercial science fiction magazine came in *Venture Science Fiction* for August, 1970, with a story titled "Prosthete." But even the disappearance of his markets—every magazine that Wells wrote for eventually went out of business—didn't stop him. He switched to semi-professional magazines like *Weirdbook, Other Worlds* (not the Ray Palmer version but Gary Lovisi's admirable albeit short-lived attempt to revive that title), *Space & Time, Expanse,* and *Fantastic Collectibles.*

His last published story, as far as I have been able to determine, was "Starkol," in *Fantastic Collectibles Magazine* in 1998. Wells died in 2003.

Over a span of fifty-eight years Basil Wells published no fewer than 71 science fiction stories, but that wasn't all. Basil Wells fan Richard Simms has compiled an extensive Wells bibliography, listing stories published in non-science-fiction magazines including *Crack Detective Stories, Ten Detective Aces, Mike Shayne's Mystery Magazine, Double-Action Western, Thrilling Western,* and even one called *Blazing Armadillo Stories.* I have not seen these magazines, and I shudder to think of a publication called *Blazing Armadillo Stories.* The mind, as they say, boggles.

In an essay about Wells, Richard Simms states that Wells made his first sale during a period of unemployment. And here's where the "working class hero" reference comes in.

Basil Wells was a man of modest means and limited education. He completed high school but dropped out of college. He lived on a fifty-acre farm in western Pennsylvania with his wife, Margaret, and their two sons. For many years he worked for the Talon Zipper Company as a machine operator.

He was able somehow to work his farm, raise his family, hold a full-time, distinctly blue-collar job—and write and sell science fiction, fantasy, detective, and western pulp stories. I have an image of him—a photo on his 1949 collection shows him sporting a neatly-trimmed moustache and wearing a heavy plaid jacket—coming home from the zipper factory, tending to some farm chores, and sitting down to supper with his wife and children. Then, after dinner, at a time when his co-workers at the factory were perhaps playing poker or bowling or quaffing beverages at a local tavern, Basil Wells would have better things to do. His wife, Margaret, would clear the kitchen table of the dinner dishes. Basil would place his Underwood portable typewriter on the table and battle through the evening's quota of adventure prose.

He was a personally modest man. I had the pleasure of meeting him and his wife only once. The occasion was a miniature pulp convention in July, 1990, in Keystone Heights, Florida, where Mr. and Mrs. Wells were living in retirement. The other guests included pulp writer and naval historian Theodore Roscoe and scholar-bibliographer Audrey Parente. Roscoe was a cheerful, outgoing individual; Basil Wells was more retiring. He never claimed to be a great writer. As far as I know, he was never Guest of Honor at any science fiction convention and never won a Hugo or Nebula Award. He just cared for his family and wrote his stories.

Dozens of his stories were collected in two books published by William and Margaret Crawford's Fantasy Publishing Company Incorporated. FPCI was located in Los Angeles. In an era when mainline book publishers turned up their noses at science fiction, the Crawfords' company issued a series of books that are sought after and treasured by collectors today.

FPCI's authors included Raymond F. Jones, Stanley G. Weinbaum, Stanton A. Coblentz, Ralph Milne Farley, Murray Leinster, Ed Earl Repp, Olaf Stapledon, L. Ron Hubbard, John Taine, Austin Hall, A. Reynolds Morse, and A.E. van Vogt and E. Mayne Hull. Cover prices were either $2.50 or $3.00. Imagine a shelf of those books today—what a delight they would be, and what they would cost!

Wells' first FPCI collection, *Planets of Adventure*, was published in 1949 with a striking dust jacket designed by Jack Gaughan, who would go on to become one of the leading science fiction cover illustrators of the 1960s and '70s. The stories in the book had been previously published in *Planet Stories, Future Science Fiction,* and *Fantasy Book*, the latter another FPCI production.

Wells' second FPCI collection, *Doorways to Space*, published in 1951, comprises all original material. Its spectacular dust jacket is credited to William Benulis, a talented artist who abandoned a career in the comic book industry in order to earn a steady salary from the Post Office Department.

FPCI was very much a low-budget operation. I don't know how much Basil Wells or any other Crawford author was paid, but Jack Gaughan did tell me, in a reminiscent moment many years after the fact, that his alleged fee for a dust jacket was $25. That was the theory. Collecting the money was another matter.

"Crawford tried to pay me in books," Gaughan said. "But I was really poor then. I needed the money, so I insisted on cash. Crawford finally paid me in the form of a United States Savings Bond. Its face value was $25, but I had to wait ten years to cash it in. Crawford bought it from Uncle Sam for $18.75."

Wells continued to produce quirky, individualistic fiction for the rest of his life. While most of his work appears to be quite conventional, the reader will occasionally be brought up short by a startling image or device. Wells said that he was influenced by Edgar Rice Burroughs and H.P. Lovecraft. This is entirely believable. His images of Venus ("Rebellion on Venus") embody the then-standard version of a hot, swampy world populated by giant amphibians. This of course was the imagery employed by many writers of the era including Burroughs. And the bizarre plant life of "The Sudden Forest" is reminiscent of that in Lovecraft's "The Color out of Space."

But then what of his talking taxicab (in "Automar") decades before Philip K. Dick used that device? Or possibly Wells' most striking single image—it could have straight out of the film *Avatar* half a century before James Cameron made his film? That one is in "The Lurker of Burm."

In a brief memoir published in Gary Lovisi's *Other Worlds* in 1988, Wells lavished praise on editors who had encouraged and guided him throughout his career. He singled out Malcolm Reiss, Wilbur Scott Peacock, Chester Whitehorn, and Paul L. Payne of *Planet Stories,* as well as Leo Margulies of the Thrilling pulp group (and later of *Fantastic Universe* and *Mike Shayne's Mystery Magazine)* and Robert A. Lowndes of *Future Science Fiction* and *Famous Detective Stories.*

A number of Wells' stories were anthologized, most notably an appearance in *The Best of Planet Stories,* edited by Wells' friend and fellow contributor to *Planet,* Leigh Brackett.

Wells eventually self-published two further small collections, but *Planets of Adventure* and *Doorways to Space* remain the definitive Basil Wells collections.

A total of thirty stories filled the two FPCI books; they are all included in the present volume.

There remains, I am compelled to report, a major mystery concerning Basil Wells. In a series of letters to Gary Lovisi written in the 1980s, Wells made the following startling statement:

"I have written several novel lengths, among them a historical keelboat and two mysteries." He then goes on to describe neither a "historical keelboat" (whatever that odd phrase may mean) nor a mystery, but is more specific about a science fiction novel based on his Thrane stories, several of which are included in the present volume.

Where are those manuscripts? There are apparently at least four unpublished Basil Wells novels. Wells is deceased, his wife is deceased, and attempts to locate their two sons have proved unsuccessful. *Where,* I ask again, *are those manuscripts?*

One would hope that Basil Wells' remaining pulp stories, especially the westerns and mysteries, might yet be unearthed and collected. If some avid pulp collector would undertake this task, Surinam Turtle Press would be honored to publish the book. I'd love to read it myself! And if anyone can locate the Wells sons or other relatives or heirs, or those four (at least four!) novel length manuscripts, said literary detective is urged to get in touch with the undersigned. We will have a lot to talk about!

CREDITS AND ACKNOWLEDGMENTS

As was the case with *WRITER Volume One,* the present compilation, *WRITER Volume Two,* is a compendium of new and previously published works, memoirs, essays, interviews and reviews. The previous volume was primarily autobiographical; the present volume delves more into the works and personalities of others.

Once again I confess to being a careless record keeper and a poor administrator. Consequently, the following list of credits may be less than comprehensive and totally accurate. If I have failed to give credit below, I tender my apologies to the victim. Hit me up for a tasty beverage next time our paths cross, and I will try to assuage your feelings.

The introduction to this volume was contributed by scholar, editor, author, and my very good friend, John Pelan.

The interview with John D. MacDonald was originally published in *The Mystery Scene Reader,* edited by Ed Gorman.

The interview with Allen Ginsberg was originally published in *Changes* magazine.

The interview with Michael Chabon was originally published in *ERBzine,* edited by Bill and Sue-On Hillman.

The interview with Richard Prather was originally published in *Paperback Parade* magazine, edited by Gary Lovisi.

The interview with Richard A. Lupoff was conducted by J. Alec West and was originally published in *Murderous Intent* magazine, edited by Margo Power.

The essay "The Road to Barsoom" was originally published in *John Carter and the Gods of Hollywood* by Michael Sellers.

The essay "Not Exactly a Show Salesman" appears simultaneously in the present volume and in *Homicide House and Other Stories,* Volume 6 of the collected works of Day Keene in the Detective Pulps, edited by John Pelan.

The interviews and essays devoted to Marion Zimmer Bradley and Philip K. Dick were originally published as introductions to books by those authors, published by Gregg Press and edited by David G. Hartwell.

Essays devoted to Fredric Brown, Jim Harmon, Otis Adelbert Kline and E. Hoffman Price, Malcolm Jameson, Basil Wells, and Clark Ashton Smith, were originally published as introductions to books by those authors, published by Ramble House, Surinam Turtle Press, Wildside Press, or Night Shade Books.

The speech "Very Near to my Heart" was delivered at the West Coast Science Fiction Convention in San Francisco, in 1979, and published in *Algol* magazine, edited by Andrew Porter. The speech "A Story and a Message" was delivered at the Left Coast Crime Convention in Monterey, California, in 2004, and is published here for the first time.

The essays "Shameless Self-Promotion," "Cut to the Flag," and "Hand me Down my Cape and Tights" were originally published in *Vegas Fandom Weekly* or *fanstuff*, both edited by Arnie Katz.

All other reviews appeared in *Locus* magazine, founded by Charles N. Brown.

Finally, the author wishes to thank his editors, designers, and publishers at Surinam Turtle Press and its parent company, Ramble House Publishers, Fender Tucker and Gavin O'Keefe, without whose ongoing support and assistance *WRITER* would never have come into being.

RAMBLE HOUSE'S
HARRY STEPHEN KEELER WEBWORK MYSTERIES
(RH) indicates the title is available ONLY in the RAMBLE HOUSE edition

The Ace of Spades Murder
The Affair of the Bottled Deuce (RH)
The Amazing Web
The Barking Clock
Behind That Mask
The Book with the Orange Leaves
The Bottle with the Green Wax Seal
The Box from Japan
The Case of the Canny Killer
The Case of the Crazy Corpse (RH)
The Case of the Flying Hands (RH)
The Case of the Ivory Arrow
The Case of the Jeweled Ragpicker
The Case of the Lavender Gripsack
The Case of the Mysterious Moll
The Case of the 16 Beans
The Case of the Transparent Nude (RH)
The Case of the Transposed Legs
The Case of the Two-Headed Idiot (RH)
The Case of the Two Strange Ladies
The Circus Stealers (RH)
Cleopatra's Tears
A Copy of Beowulf (RH)
The Crimson Cube (RH)
The Face of the Man From Saturn
Find the Clock
The Five Silver Buddhas
The 4th King
The Gallows Waits, My Lord! (RH)
The Green Jade Hand
Finger! Finger!
Hangman's Nights (RH)
I, Chameleon (RH)
I Killed Lincoln at 10:13! (RH)
The Iron Ring
The Man Who Changed His Skin (RH)
The Man with the Crimson Box
The Man with the Magic Eardrums
The Man with the Wooden Spectacles
The Marceau Case
The Matilda Hunter Murder
The Monocled Monster
The Murder of London Lew
The Murdered Mathematician
The Mysterious Card (RH)
The Mysterious Ivory Ball of Wong Shing Li (RH)
The Mystery of the Fiddling Cracksman
The Peacock Fan
The Photo of Lady X (RH)
The Portrait of Jirjohn Cobb
Report on Vanessa Hewstone (RH)
Riddle of the Travelling Skull
Riddle of the Wooden Parrakeet (RH)
The Scarlet Mummy (RH)
The Search for X-Y-Z
The Sharkskin Book
Sing Sing Nights
The Six From Nowhere (RH)
The Skull of the Waltzing Clown
The Spectacles of Mr. Cagliostro
Stand By—London Calling!
The Steeltown Strangler
The Stolen Gravestone (RH)
Strange Journey (RH)
The Strange Will
The Straw Hat Murders (RH)
The Street of 1000 Eyes (RH)
Thieves' Nights
Three Novellos (RH)
The Tiger Snake
The Trap (RH)
Vagabond Nights (Defrauded Yeggman)
Vagabond Nights 2 (10 Hours)
The Vanishing Gold Truck
The Voice of the Seven Sparrows
The Washington Square Enigma
When Thief Meets Thief
The White Circle (RH)
The Wonderful Scheme of Mr. Christopher Thorne
X. Jones—of Scotland Yard
Y. Cheung, Business Detective

Keeler Related Works

A To Izzard: A Harry Stephen Keeler Companion by Fender Tucker — Articles and stories about Harry, by Harry, and in his style. Included is a compleat bibliography.

Wild About Harry: Reviews of Keeler Novels — Edited by Richard Polt & Fender Tucker — 22 reviews of works by Harry Stephen Keeler from *Keeler News*. A perfect introduction to the author.

The Keeler Keyhole Collection: Annotated newsletter rants from Harry Stephen Keeler, edited by Francis M. Nevins. Over 400 pages of incredibly personal Keeleriana.

Fakealoo — Pastiches of the style of Harry Stephen Keeler by selected demented members of the HSK Society. Updated every year with the new winner.

Strands of the Web: Short Stories of Harry Stephen Keeler — 29 stories, just about all that Keeler wrote, are edited and introduced by Fred Cleaver.

RAMBLE HOUSE's LOON SANCTUARY

A Clear Path to Cross — Sharon Knowles short mystery stories by Ed Lynskey.
A Corpse Walks in Brooklyn and Other Stories — Volume 5 in the Day Keene in the Detective Pulps series.
A Jimmy Starr Omnibus — Three 40s novels by Jimmy Starr.
A Niche in Time and Other Stories — Classic SF by William F. Temple
A Roland Daniel Double: The Signal and The Return of Wu Fang — Classic thrillers from the 30s.
A Shot Rang Out — Three decades of reviews and articles by today's Anthony Boucher, Jon Breen. An essential book for any mystery lover's library.
A Smell of Smoke — A 1951 English countryside thriller by Miles Burton.
A Snark Selection — Lewis Carroll's *The Hunting of the Snark* with two Snarkian chapters by Harry Stephen Keeler — Illustrated by Gavin L. O'Keefe.
A Young Man's Heart — A forgotten early classic by Cornell Woolrich.
Alexander Laing Novels — *The Motives of Nicholas Holtz* and *Dr. Scarlett*, stories of medical mayhem and intrigue from the 30s.
An Angel in the Street — Modern hardboiled noir by Peter Genovese.
Automaton — Brilliant treatise on robotics: 1928-style! By H. Stafford Hatfield.
Away From the Here and Now — Clare Winger Harris stories, collected by Richard A. Lupoff
Beast or Man? — A 1930 novel of racism and horror by Sean M'Guire. Introduced by John Pelan.
Black Beadle — A 1939 thriller by E.C.R. Lorac.
Black Hogan Strikes Again — Australia's Peter Renwick pens a tale of the 30s outback.
Black River Falls — Suspense from the master, Ed Gorman.
Blondy's Boy Friend — A snappy 1930 story by Philip Wylie, writing as Leatrice Homesley.
Blood in a Snap — The *Finnegan's Wake* of the 21st century, by Jim Weiler.
Blood Moon — The first of the Robert Payne series by Ed Gorman.
Bogart '48 — Hollywood action with Bogie by John Stanley and Kenn Davis
Calling Lou Largo! — Two Lou Largo novels by William Ard.
Cornucopia of Crime — Francis M. Nevins assembled this huge collection of his writings about crime literature and the people who write it. Essential for any serious mystery library.
Corpse Without Flesh — Strange novel of forensics by George Bruce
Crimson Clown Novels — By Johnston McCulley, author of the Zorro novels, *The Crimson Clown* and *The Crimson Clown Again*.
Dago Red — 22 tales of dark suspense by Bill Pronzini.
Dark Sanctuary — Weird Menace story by H. B. Gregory
David Hume Novels — *Corpses Never Argue, Cemetery First Stop, Make Way for the Mourners, Eternity Here I Come*. 1930s British hardboiled fiction with an attitude.
Dead Man Talks Too Much — Hollywood boozer by Weed Dickenson.
Death Leaves No Card — One of the most unusual murdered-in-the-tub mysteries you'll ever read. By Miles Burton.
Death March of the Dancing Dolls and Other Stories — Volume Three in the Day Keene in the Detective Pulps series. Introduced by Bill Crider.
Deep Space and other Stories — A collection of SF gems by Richard A. Lupoff.
Detective Duff Unravels It — Episodic mysteries by Harvey O'Higgins.
Diabolic Candelabra — Classic 30s mystery by E.R. Punshon
Dictator's Way — Another D.S. Bobby Owen mystery from E.R. Punshon
Dime Novels: Ramble House's 10-Cent Books — *Knife in the Dark* by Robert Leslie Bellem, *Hot Lead* and *Song of Death* by Ed Earl Repp, *A Hashish House in New York* by H.H. Kane, and five more.
Doctor Arnoldi — Tiffany Thayer's story of the death of death.
Don Diablo: Book of a Lost Film — Two-volume treatment of a western by Paul Landres, with diagrams. Intro by Francis M. Nevins.
Dope and Swastikas — Two strange novels from 1922 by Edmund Snell
Dope Tales #1 — Two dope-riddled classics; *Dope Runners* by Gerald Grantham and *Death Takes the Joystick* by Phillip Condé.

Dope Tales #2 — Two more narco-classics; *The Invisible Hand* by Rex Dark and *The Smokers of Hashish* by Norman Berrow.
Dope Tales #3 — Two enchanting novels of opium by the master, Sax Rohmer. *Dope* and *The Yellow Claw*.
Double Hot — Two 60s softcore sex novels by Morris Hershman.
Double Sex — Yet two more panting thrillers from Morris Hershman.
Dr. Odin — Douglas Newton's 1933 racial potboiler comes back to life.
Evangelical Cockroach — Jack Woodford writes about writing.
Evidence in Blue — 1938 mystery by E. Charles Vivian.
Fatal Accident — Murder by automobile, a 1936 mystery by Cecil M. Wills.
Fighting Mad — Todd Robbins' 1922 novel about boxing and life
Finger-prints Never Lie — A 1939 classic detective novel by John G. Brandon.
Freaks and Fantasies — Eerie tales by Tod Robbins, collaborator of Tod Browning on the film FREAKS.
Gadsby — A lipogram (a novel without the letter E). Ernest Vincent Wright's last work, published in 1939 right before his death.
Gelett Burgess Novels — *The Master of Mysteries, The White Cat, Two O'Clock Courage, Ladies in Boxes, Find the Woman, The Heart Line, The Picaroons* and *Lady Mechante*. Recently added is *A Gelett Burgess Sampler*, edited by Alfred Jan. All are introduced by Richard A. Lupoff.
Geronimo — S. M. Barrett's 1905 autobiography of a noble American.
Hake Talbot Novels — *Rim of the Pit, The Hangman's Handyman*. Classic locked room mysteries, with mapback covers by Gavin O'Keefe.
Hands Out of Hell and Other Stories — John H. Knox's eerie hallucinations
Hell is a City — William Ard's masterpiece.
Hollywood Dreams — A novel of Tinsel Town and the Depression by Richard O'Brien.
Hostesses in Hell and Other Stories — Russell Gray's most graphic stories
House of the Restless Dead — Strange and ominous tales by Hugh B. Cave
I Stole $16,000,000 — A true story by cracksman Herbert E. Wilson.
Inclination to Murder — 1966 thriller by New Zealand's Harriet Hunter.
Invaders from the Dark — Classic werewolf tale from Greye La Spina.
J. Poindexter, Colored — Classic satirical black novel by Irvin S. Cobb.
Jack Mann Novels — Strange murder in the English countryside. *Gees' First Case, Nightmare Farm, Grey Shapes, The Ninth Life, The Glass Too Many, Her Ways Are Death, The Kleinert Case* and *Maker of Shadows*.
Jake Hardy — A lusty western tale from Wesley Tallant.
Jim Harmon Double Novels — *Vixen Hollow/Celluloid Scandal, The Man Who Made Maniacs/Silent Siren, Ape Rape/Wanton Witch, Sex Burns Like Fire/Twist Session, Sudden Lust/Passion Strip, Sin Unlimited/Harlot Master, Twilight Girls/Sex Institution*. Written in the early 60s and never reprinted until now.
Joel Townsley Rogers Novels and Short Stories — By the author of *The Red Right Hand: Once In a Red Moon, Lady With the Dice, The Stopped Clock, Never Leave My Bed*. Also two short story collections: *Night of Horror* and *Killing Time*.
John Carstairs, Space Detective — Arboreal Sci-fi by Frank Belknap Long
Joseph Shallit Novels — *The Case of the Billion Dollar Body, Lady Don't Die on My Doorstep, Kiss the Killer, Yell Bloody Murder, Take Your Last Look*. One of America's best 50's authors and a favorite of author Bill Pronzini.
Keller Memento — 45 short stories of the amazing and weird by Dr. David Keller.
Killer's Caress — Cary Moran's 1936 hardboiled thriller.
Lady of the Yellow Death and Other Stories — More stories by Wyatt Blassingame.
League of the Grateful Dead and Other Stories — Volume One in the Day Keene in the Detective Pulps series.
Library of Death — Ghastly tale by Ronald S. L. Harding, introduced by John Pelan
Malcolm Jameson Novels and Short Stories — *Astonishing! Astounding!, Tarnished Bomb, The Alien Envoy and Other Stories* and *The Chariots of San Fernando and Other Stories*. All introduced and edited by John Pelan or Richard A. Lupoff.
Man Out of Hell and Other Stories — Volume II of the John H. Knox weird pulps collection.
Marblehead: A Novel of H.P. Lovecraft — A long-lost masterpiece from Richard A. Lupoff. This is the "director's cut", the long version that has never been published before.

Mark of the Laughing Death and Other Stories — Shockers from the pulps by Francis James, introduced by John Pelan.

Master of Souls — Mark Hansom's 1937 shocker is introduced by weirdologist John Pelan.

Max Afford Novels — *Owl of Darkness, Death's Mannikins, Blood on His Hands, The Dead Are Blind, The Sheep and the Wolves, Sinners in Paradise* and *Two Locked Room Mysteries and a Ripping Yarn* by one of Australia's finest mystery novelists.

Money Brawl — Two books about the writing business by Jack Woodford and H. Bedford-Jones. Introduced by Richard A. Lupoff.

More Secret Adventures of Sherlock Holmes — Gary Lovisi's second collection of tales about the unknown sides of the great detective.

Muddled Mind: Complete Works of Ed Wood, Jr. — David Hayes and Hayden Davis deconstruct the life and works of the mad, but canny, genius.

Murder among the Nudists — A mystery from 1934 by Peter Hunt, featuring a naked Detective-Inspector going undercover in a nudist colony.

Murder in Black and White — 1931 classic tennis whodunit by Evelyn Elder.

Murder in Shawnee — Two novels of the Alleghenies by John Douglas: *Shawnee Alley Fire* and *Haunts*.

Murder in Silk — A 1937 Yellow Peril novel of the silk trade by Ralph Trevor.

My Deadly Angel — 1955 Cold War drama by John Chelton.

My First Time: The One Experience You Never Forget — Michael Birchwood — 64 true first-person narratives of how they lost it.

Mysterious Martin, the Master of Murder — Two versions of a strange 1912 novel by Tod Robbins about a man who writes books that can kill.

Norman Berrow Novels — *The Bishop's Sword, Ghost House, Don't Go Out After Dark, Claws of the Cougar, The Smokers of Hashish, The Secret Dancer, Don't Jump Mr. Boland!, The Footprints of Satan, Fingers for Ransom, The Three Tiers of Fantasy, The Spaniard's Thumb, The Eleventh Plague, Words Have Wings, One Thrilling Night, The Lady's in Danger, It Howls at Night, The Terror in the Fog, Oil Under the Window, Murder in the Melody, The Singing Room.* This is the complete Norman Berrow library of locked-room mysteries, several of which are masterpieces.

Old Faithful and Other Stories — SF classic tales by Raymond Z. Gallun.

Old Times' Sake — Short stories by James Reasoner from Mike Shayne Magazine.

One Dreadful Night — A classic mystery by Ronald S. L. Harding.

Pair O' Jacks — A mystery novel and a diatribe about publishing by Jack Woodford

Perfect .38 — Two early Timothy Dane novels by William Ard. More to come.

Prince Pax — Devilish intrigue by George Sylvester Viereck and Philip Eldridge

Prose Bowl — Futuristic satire of a world where hack writing has replaced football as our national obsession, by Bill Pronzini and Barry N. Malzberg.

Red Light — The history of legal prostitution in Shreveport Louisiana by Eric Brock. Includes wonderful photos of the houses and the ladies.

Researching American-Made Toy Soldiers — A 276-page collection of a lifetime of articles by toy soldier expert Richard O'Brien.

Reunion in Hell — Volume One of the John H. Knox series of weird stories from the pulps. Introduced by horror expert John Pelan.

Ripped from the Headlines! — The Jack the Ripper story as told in the newspaper articles in the *New York* and *London Times*.

Rough Cut & New, Improved Murder — Ed Gorman's first two novels.

R.R. Ryan Novels — Freak Museum and The Subjugated Beast, two horror classics.

Ruby of a Thousand Dreams — The villain Wu Fang returns in this Roland Daniel novel.

Ruled By Radio — 1925 futuristic novel by Robert L. Hadfield & Frank E. Farncombe.

Rupert Penny Novels — *Policeman's Holiday, Policeman's Evidence, Lucky Policeman, Policeman in Armour, Sealed Room Murder, Sweet Poison, The Talkative Policeman, She had to Have Gas* and *Cut and Run* (by Martin Tanner.) Rupert Penny is the pseudonym of Australian Charles Thornett, a master of the locked room, impossible crime plot.

Sacred Locomotive Flies — Richard A. Lupoff's psychedelic SF story.

Sam — Early gay novel by Lonnie Coleman.

Sand's Game — Spectacular hard-boiled noir from Ennis Willie, edited by Lynn Myers and Stephen Mertz, with contributions from Max Allan Collins, Bill Crider, Wayne

Dundee, Bill Pronzini, Gary Lovisi and James Reasoner.
Sand's War — More violent fiction from the typewriter of Ennis Willie
Satan's Den Exposed — True crime in Truth or Consequences New Mexico — Award-winning journalism by the *Desert Journal*.
Satans of Saturn — Novellas from the pulps by Otis Adelbert Kline and E. H. Price
Satan's Sin House and Other Stories — Horrific gore by Wayne Rogers
Secrets of a Teenage Superhero — Graphic lit by Jonathan Sweet
Sex Slave — Potboiler of lust in the days of Cleopatra by Dion Leclerq, 1966.
Sideslip — 1968 SF masterpiece by Ted White and Dave Van Arnam.
Slammer Days — Two full-length prison memoirs: *Men into Beasts* (1952) by George Sylvester Viereck and *Home Away From Home* (1962) by Jack Woodford.
Slippery Staircase — 1930s whodunit from E.C.R. Lorac
Sorcerer's Chessmen — John Pelan introduces this 1939 classic by Mark Hansom.
Star Griffin — Michael Kurland's 1987 masterpiece of SF drollery is back.
Stakeout on Millennium Drive — Award-winning Indianapolis Noir by Ian Woollen.
Strands of the Web: Short Stories of Harry Stephen Keeler — Edited and Introduced by Fred Cleaver.
Summer Camp for Corpses and Other Stories — Weird Menace tales from Arthur Leo Zagat; introduced by John Pelan.
Suzy — A collection of comic strips by Richard O'Brien and Bob Vojtko from 1970.
Tales of the Macabre and Ordinary — Modern twisted horror by Chris Mikul, author of the *Bizarrism* series.
Tales of Terror and Torment #1 — John Pelan selects and introduces this sampler of weird menace tales from the pulps.
Tenebrae — Ernest G. Henham's 1898 horror tale brought back.
The Amorous Intrigues & Adventures of Aaron Burr — by Anonymous. Hot historical action about the man who almost became Emperor of Mexico.
The Anthony Boucher Chronicles — edited by Francis M. Nevins. Book reviews by Anthony Boucher written for the *San Francisco Chronicle*, 1942 – 1947. Essential and fascinating reading by the best book reviewer there ever was.
The Barclay Catalogs — Two essential books about toy soldier collecting by Richard O'Brien
The Basil Wells Omnibus — A collection of Wells' stories by Richard A. Lupoff
The Beautiful Dead and Other Stories — Dreadful tales from Donald Dale
The Best of 10-Story Book — edited by Chris Mikul, over 35 stories from the literary magazine Harry Stephen Keeler edited.
The Black Dark Murders — Vintage 50s college murder yarn by Milt Ozaki, writing as Robert O. Saber.
The Book of Time — The classic novel by H.G. Wells is joined by sequels by Wells himself and three stories by Richard A. Lupoff. Illustrated by Gavin L. O'Keefe.
The Case in the Clinic — One of E.C.R. Lorac's finest.
The Strange Case of the Antlered Man — A mystery of superstition by Edwy Searles Brooks.
The Case of the Bearded Bride — #4 in the Day Keene in the Detective Pulps series
The Case of the Little Green Men — Mack Reynolds wrote this love song to sci-fi fans back in 1951 and it's now back in print.
The Case of the Withered Hand — 1936 potboiler by John G. Brandon.
The Charlie Chaplin Murder Mystery — A 2004 tribute by noted film scholar, Wes D. Gehring.
The Chinese Jar Mystery — Murder in the manor by John Stephen Strange, 1934.
The Cloudbuilders and Other Stories — SF tales from Colin Kapp.
The Compleat Calhoon — All of Fender Tucker's works: Includes *Totah Six-Pack, Weed, Women and Song* and *Tales from the Tower*, plus a CD of all of his songs.
The Compleat Ova Hamlet — Parodies of SF authors by Richard A. Lupoff. This is a brand new edition with more stories and more illustrations by Trina Robbins.

The Contested Earth and Other SF Stories — A never-before published space opera and seven short stories by Jim Harmon.
The Crimson Query — A 1929 thriller from Arlton Eadie. A perfect way to get introduced.
The Curse of Cantire — Classic 1939 novel of a family curse by Walter S. Masterman.

The Devil and the C.I.D. — Odd diabolic mystery by E.C.R. Lorac
The Devil Drives — An odd prison and lost treasure novel from 1932 by Virgil Markham.
The Devil of Pei-Ling — Herbert Asbury's 1929 tale of the occult.
The Devil's Mistress — A 1915 Scottish gothic tale by J. W. Brodie-Innes, a member of Aleister Crowley's Golden Dawn.
The Devil's Nightclub and Other Stories — John Pelan introduces some gruesome tales by Nat Schachner.
The Disentanglers — Episodic intrigue at the turn of last century by Andrew Lang
The Dog Poker Code — A spoof of *The Da Vinci Code* by D.B. Smithee.
The Dumpling — Political murder from 1907 by Coulson Kernahan.
The End of It All and Other Stories — Ed Gorman selected his favorite short stories for this huge collection.
The Fangs of Suet Pudding — A 1944 novel of the German invasion by Adams Farr
The Finger of Destiny and Other Stories — Edmund Snell's superb collection of weird stories of Borneo.
The Ghost of Gaston Revere — From 1935, a novel of life and beyond by Mark Hansom, introduced by John Pelan.
The Girl in the Dark — A thriller from Roland Daniel
The Gold Star Line — Seaboard adventure from L.T. Reade and Robert Eustace.
The Golden Dagger — 1951 Scotland Yard yarn by E. R. Punshon.
The Great Orme Terror — Horror stories by Garnett Radcliffe from the pulps
The Hairbreadth Escapes of Major Mendax — Francis Blake Crofton's 1889 boys' book.
The House That Time Forgot and Other Stories — Insane pulpitude by Robert F. Young
The House of the Vampire — 1907 poetic thriller by George S. Viereck.
The Illustrious Corpse — Murder hijinx from Tiffany Thayer
The Incredible Adventures of Rowland Hern — Intriguing 1928 impossible crimes by Nicholas Olde.
The Julius Caesar Murder Case — A classic 1935 re-telling of the assassination by Wallace Irwin that's much more fun than the Shakespeare version.
The Koky Comics — A collection of all of the 1978-1981 Sunday and daily comic strips by Richard O'Brien and Mort Gerberg, in two volumes.
The Lady of the Terraces — 1925 missing race adventure by E. Charles Vivian.
The Lord of Terror — 1925 mystery with master-criminal, Fantômas.
The Melamare Mystery — A classic 1929 Arsene Lupin mystery by Maurice Leblanc
The Man Who Was Secrett — Epic SF stories from John Brunner
The Man Without a Planet — Science fiction tales by Richard Wilson
The N. R. De Mexico Novels — Robert Bragg, the real N.R. de Mexico, presents *Marijuana Girl, Madman on a Drum, Private Chauffeur* in one volume.
The Night Remembers — A 1991 Jack Walsh mystery from Ed Gorman.
The One After Snelling — Kickass modern noir from Richard O'Brien.
The Organ Reader — A huge compilation of just about everything published in the 1971-1972 radical bay-area newspaper, *THE ORGAN*. A coffee table book that points out the shallowness of the coffee table mindset.
The Poker Club — Three in one! Ed Gorman's ground-breaking novel, the short story it was based upon, and the screenplay of the film made from it.
The Private Journal & Diary of John H. Surratt — The memoirs of the man who conspired to assassinate President Lincoln.
The Ramble House Mapbacks — Recently revised book by Gavin L. O'Keefe with color pictures of all the Ramble House books with mapbacks.
The Secret Adventures of Sherlock Holmes — Three Sherlockian pastiches by the Brooklyn author/publisher, Gary Lovisi.
The Shadow on the House — Mark Hansom's 1934 masterpiece of horror is introduced by John Pelan.
The Sign of the Scorpion — A 1935 Edmund Snell tale of oriental evil.
The Singular Problem of the Stygian House-Boat — Two classic tales by John Kendrick Bangs about the denizens of Hades.
The Smiling Corpse — Philip Wylie and Bernard Bergman's odd 1935 novel.
The Spider: Satan's Murder Machines — A thesis about Iron Man

The Stench of Death: An Odoriferous Omnibus by Jack Moskovitz — Two complete novels and two novellas from 60's sleaze author, Jack Moskovitz.
The Story Writer and Other Stories — Classic SF from Richard Wilson
The Strange Case of the Antlered Man — 1935 dementia from Edwy Searles Brooks
The Strange Thirteen — Richard B. Gamon's odd stories about Raj India.
The Technique of the Mystery Story — Carolyn Wells' tips about writing.
The Threat of Nostalgia — A collection of his most obscure stories by Jon Breen
The Time Armada — Fox B. Holden's 1953 SF gem.
The Tongueless Horror and Other Stories — Volume One of the series of short stories from the weird pulps by Wyatt Blassingame.
The Town from Planet Five — From Richard Wilson, two SF classics, *And Then the Town Took Off* and *The Girls from Planet 5*
The Tracer of Lost Persons — From 1906, an episodic novel that became a hit radio series in the 30s. Introduced by Richard A. Lupoff.
The Trail of the Cloven Hoof — Diabolical horror from 1935 by Arlton Eadie. Introduced by John Pelan.
The Triune Man — Mindscrambling science fiction from Richard A. Lupoff.
The Unholy Goddess and Other Stories — Wyatt Blassingame's first DTP compilation
The Universal Holmes — Richard A. Lupoff's 2007 collection of five Holmesian pastiches and a recipe for giant rat stew.
The Werewolf vs the Vampire Woman — Hard to believe ultraviolence by either Arthur M. Scarm or Arthur M. Scram.
The Whistling Ancestors — A 1936 classic of weirdness by Richard E. Goddard and introduced by John Pelan.
The White Owl — A vintage thriller from Edmund Snell
The White Peril in the Far East — Sidney Lewis Gulick's 1905 indictment of the West and assurance that Japan would never attack the U.S.
The Wizard of Berner's Abbey — A 1935 horror gem written by Mark Hansom and introduced by John Pelan.
The Wonderful Wizard of Oz — by L. Frank Baum and illustrated by Gavin L. O'Keefe
Through the Looking Glass — Lewis Carroll wrote it; Gavin L. O'Keefe illustrated it.
Time Line — Ramble House artist Gavin O'Keefe selects his most evocative art inspired by the twisted literature he reads and designs.
Tiresias — Psychotic modern horror novel by Jonathan M. Sweet.
Tortures and Towers — Two novellas of terror by Dexter Dayle.
Totah Six-Pack — Fender Tucker's six tales about Farmington in one sleek volume.
Tree of Life, Book of Death — Grania Davis' book of her life.
Triple Quest — An arty mystery from the 30s by E.R. Punshon.
Trail of the Spirit Warrior — Roger Haley's saga of life in the Indian Territories.
Two Kinds of Bad — Two 50s novels by William Ard about Danny Fontaine
Two Suns of Morcali and Other Stories — Evelyn E. Smith's SF tour-de-force
Ultra-Boiled — 23 gut-wrenching tales by our Man in Brooklyn, Gary Lovisi.
Up Front From Behind — A 2011 satire of Wall Street by James B. Kobak.
Victims & Villains — Intriguing Sherlockiana from Derham Groves.
Wade Wright Novels — *Echo of Fear*, *Death At Nostalgia Street*, *It Leads to Murder* and *Shadows' Edge*, a double book featuring *Shadows Don't Bleed* and *The Sharp Edge*.
Walter S. Masterman Novels — *The Green Toad, The Flying Beast, The Yellow Mistletoe, The Wrong Verdict, The Perjured Alibi, The Border Line, The Bloodhounds Bay, The Curse of Cantire* and *The Baddington Horror*. Masterman wrote horror and mystery, some introduced by John Pelan.
We Are the Dead and Other Stories — Volume Two in the Day Keene in the Detective Pulps series, introduced by Ed Gorman. When done, there may be 11 in the series.
Welsh Rarebit Tales — Charming stories from 1902 by Harle Oren Cummins
West Texas War and Other Western Stories — by Gary Lovisi.
What If? Volume 1, 2 and 3 — Richard A. Lupoff introduces three decades worth of SF short stories that should have won a Hugo, but didn't.
When the Batman Thirsts and Other Stories — Weird tales from Frederick C. Davis.
Whip Dodge: Man Hunter — Wesley Tallant's saga of a bounty hunter of the old West.
Win, Place and Die! — The first new mystery by Milt Ozaki in decades. The ultimate novel of 70s Reno.

Writer 1 and 2 — A magnus opus from Richard A. Lupoff summing up his life as writer.
You'll Die Laughing — Bruce Elliott's 1945 novel of murder at a practical joker's English countryside manor.

RAMBLE HOUSE
Fender Tucker, Prop.   Gavin L. O'Keefe, Graphics
www.ramblehouse.com   fender@ramblehouse.com
228-826-1783   10329 Sheephead Drive, Vancleave MS 39565

www.ingramcontent.com/pod-product-compliance
Lightning Source LLC
Chambersburg PA
CBHW031134160426
43193CB00008B/134